More praise for *No Vulgar Hotel* by Judith Martin

"Martin provides a guide for those hopelessly in love with Venice. She says there is no cure for this affliction, but this [book] will help you manage your condition." —*Publishing News*

"A fun-to-read paean. . . . Perfect for a swift, semi-intellectual overview of Venice that goes several steps deeper than the average tourist guide." —*Publishers Weekly*

"Interesting, frequently enlightening, and always amusing." —*Library Journal*

"Judith Martin is, of course, Miss Manners, America's queen of etiquette and writer of the syndicated column notable for its *cri de coeur* against gauche behavior and for its arch prose style, which Martin uses to generally amusing effect in her new book." —Robin Updike, *Seattle Times*

"An intimate tour from another confessed Venetophile—Miss Manners herself." —*Washington Post*

"In the spirit of Henry James. . . . Fans of Miss Manners' high comic style will find much to amuse them in this idiosyncratic slice of prosciutto on wry." —Amanda Heller, *Boston Sunday Globe*

"Reading her book, with its captivating mini-histories of Venetian literary salons, families of note and artists in residence, is like attending a gossipy Continental dinner party in which Martin not only plays the hostess but moonlights as various guests. . . . Not only does Martin know what she likes, she knows how to serve it." —Pamela Paul, *New York Times Book Review*

Also by Judith Martin

No Vulgar Hotel

The Desire and Pursuit of Venice

JUDITH MARTIN

ERIC DENKER, *cicerone*

W. W. Norton & Company   *New York London*

For information about permission to reproduce selections from
this book, write to Permissions, W. W. Norton & Company, Inc.,
500 Fifth Avenue, New York, NY 10110

Manufacturing by RR Donnelley, Bloomsburg
Book design by Amanda Morrison
Production manager: Anna Oler

Library of Congress Cataloging-in-Publication Data
Martin, Judith, 1938–
No vulgar hotel : the desire and pursuit of Venice /
Judith Martin ; Eric Denker, cicerone. — 1st ed.
p. cm.
Includes index.
ISBN-13: 978-0-393-05932-8 (hardcover)
ISBN-10: 0-393-05932-4 (hardcover)
1. Venice (Italy)—Description and travel. 2. Venice
(Italy)—Social life and customs. 3. Venice (Italy)—History.
I. Title.
DG674.2.M374 2007
945'.31—dc22   2006101496

ISBN 978-0-393-33060-1 pbk.

W. W. Norton & Company, Inc.
500 Fifth Avenue, New York, N.Y. 10110
www.wwnorton.com

W. W. Norton & Company Ltd.
Castle House, 75/76 Wells Street, W1T 3QT

2 3 4 5 6 7 8 9 0

For our Venetian friends,
whose warmth, hospitality, and knowledge bring Venice
alive for us—and with special thanks to those of them who have
the same romantic feelings about America as we do
about Venice

Contents

List of Illustrations

Acknowledgments

Warm thanks to Jeannie Luciano for suggesting this book, and to David Hendin for making all my books possible.

And to those whose work enhances it: Mark Leithauser, Jörg Schmeisser, Jack Boul, Lorene Emerson, Jeffrey Meizlik, Jacobina Martin, Bruna Caruso Cherubini, Angela von der Lippe, Kimberley Heatherington, Rhea Denker, Nicholas Martin, and Robert Martin.

No Vulgar Hotel

CHAPTER ONE

You're a Tourist and I'm Not

"'See Naples and die'?" Milly Theale must have wondered. "Why?" (She would have been too polite to ask "Of what?") Doctor Johnson's declaration that "when a man is tired of London he is tired of life" must have left her equally bewildered.

The heroine of Henry James's *The Wings of the Dove* was about to die, but she was not tired of life. She was just tired of London. So she did what any sensible person[*] with limited time and unlimited money would do: She picked herself up and went to Venice.

Her idea was not to see Venice so much as to be there, not to gaze at the wonders but to become a figure in the tableau. Here are her instructions to her Italian majordomo:

At Venice, please, if possible, no dreadful, no vulgar hotel; but, if it can be at all managed—you know what I mean— some fine old rooms, wholly independent, for a series of months. Plenty of them too, and the more interesting the better: part of a palace, historic and picturesque, but strictly inodorous, where we shall be to ourselves, with a cook, don't

---

[*]It has been brought to the author's attention that there are otherwise sensible people who prefer Tuscany. She has come to realize that there are Florence people and Venice people, just as there are Dostoyevsky people as opposed to Tolstoy people, Faulkner people as opposed to Hemingway people, and Oz people as opposed to Pooh people. She has not come to understand why.

you know?—with servants, frescoes, tapestries, antiquities, the thorough make-believe of a settlement.

"The thorough make-believe of a settlement": Such is the eternal lure of that miracle-from-the-swamp, Venice. Refugees from the mainland conjured it up from mud and reeds as they, too, tried to outrun death, in the very palpable form of Attila the Hun. And as if the city's mere existence is not preposterous enough, their prosperous descendents had it gilded.

They had made a magnet. Since the Middle Ages, Venice has been attracting dazed foreigners: pilgrims venerating holy relics, crusaders commissioning ships, Jews escaping persecution, artists looking for civic commissions, writers looking for dramatic settings, filmmakers looking for eerie urban scenery, royalty experiencing unpopularity at home, millionaires pursuing experiences that would have made them unpopular at home, and a millennium's worth of traveling tradesmen and tourists from whatever has constituted the known world at any given time. Together, we form an endless caravan of Marco Polos in reverse, journeying from around the globe to discover Venice.

Falling on the Canal

Among the visitors in each era and at any moment are many Milly Theales (typically in better health but worse financial shape) in whom the fantasy is burgeoning. You can observe its inception in newcomers on the Grand Canal waterbus. Amid the bustle of commuters, shoppers, and normal sightseers, these are the ones scanning the palaces for evidence of magical life inside. In the morning light, a lady or gentleman in a dressing gown may appear on a balcony, coffee cup in hand, to sample the weather. By night, the great chandeliers flicker and glint to reveal shadowy figures moving about their salons. High above the grand floors, there will be a plain window alight far into the night, as suggestive of lonely romantic and/or artistic yearning as the crystalline lights of their high-living neighbors below are of the assignations and intrigues of privileged society.

Perhaps there are observers who register all that as an animated touch to sightseeing and return to their modern lives undeterred from plans to spend their next vacation on a beach or in Angkor Wat. On a not-inconsiderable number of others, male and female, the Milly Theale fantasy will be taking permanent hold. From then on, they will be propelled by the determination to get inside those palaces, not only to look around, which is difficult enough for a tourist because many are privately owned, but to look out from within.

It is possible. The romantic figures who appear on balconies or cast mysterious shadows from gothic or plain square windows are often advanced tourists whose Venetophilia has led them to expensive lengths. First there is the splurge on a Grand Canal bed-and-breakfast or hotel room that supplies the view and an approximation of eighteenth-century-ish trappings (the formula being the more costly the quarters, the more rickety and threadbare the furnishings). From there, it is a remarkably short distance to more complex desires: No hotels, not even ones with astronomical prices and polished service. No matter what public accommodations may style themselves, they are no longer the palaces they once were. The fantasy demands a palace of one's own, for however short a time one can afford it.

Renting—not necessarily a palace, but no vulgar hotel—is also a requirement for savoring the living Venice. It makes it possible to avoid the great disadvantage of tourism, which is the inability to pursue friendships with local people by entertaining them. You can ask them to restaurants, but that is more apt to lead to

polite squabbling over who pays than to invitations to Venetian
homes and opportunities to know Venetian families.

Venetophiles always remember their first visits, when their individual versions of the fantasy were conceived. I was fourteen years
old, slowly taking the scenic/educational route home to
Washington with my parents and brother from my father's one-
year United Nations assignment in Greece. We stayed at the
Pensione Isak Dinesen, which is now named the Hotel American,
an unfortunate choice if the hope is to attract Americans. Decades
later, I pointed out the hotel to my brother as a humble detail of
the panoramic view we had rented along with the historic apartment where we and our spouses were briefly keeping house.

Satisfying as this adult sojourn was, it would not have served
to fulfill my adolescent fantasy. In that scenario, it is a wintry
night on the Grand Canal. Venice is enveloped in fog. I am
enveloped in furs. Behind me is my brightly lit, overly furnished
palace that I share with throngs of charming friends. Carefully
positioning a satin slipper on the slimy steps of my water
entrance, I step into a dark gondola to be rowed silently to
another brightly lit, etc., palace to attend a grand ball.

It took forty-one years, but, Gentle Reader, I did it.

All except for the gondola, that is. This having been a childish
concoction, it required adjustments to reality. For a nighttime
gondola, by the time of that ball, the meter started running at
$62, and it is half again as much now. Furthermore, the water
entrance at my palace was defunct, and later, when it was
repaired, it was in the exclusive use of the canal-level apartment
that had been sold off to people who prudently installed their
electric outlets closer to the ceiling than the floor. Oh, and incidentally, as it happens, it is not my palace. Those fine old rooms
on the piano nobile, with frescoes, tapestries, antiquities and
such, where I dwell among that throng of charming friends—we
pool resources and rent them, for two weeks at a time.

Everything else being pretty much as I had imagined (and as had Milly Theale before me, although I conceived the fantasy a decade before I had the pleasure of encountering her), I did not quibble about waddling to the ball wearing my rubber wellies. The host was in possession of a working water entrance, but no gondolas pulled up to discharge guests, only equally expensive motorboats. He had thoughtfully placed chairs in the back entranceway so that we thrifty pedestrian ladies, who were carrying our evening shoes in plastic bags, could tug off our boots before traipsing upstairs.

If this playing at being Venetian sounds like so much Cinderella-crazed girlish nonsense, consider some of the toughies who have thoroughly indulged their own fantasies: Lord Byron, Richard Wagner, Friedrich Nietzsche, Robert Browning, Ernest Hemingway, Ezra Pound. And if they all seem to be wild romantics, so as not to say disgracefully self-dramatizing show-offs, here is the confession of someone not exactly known for the expression of unfettered personal passions: "I adore it—have fallen deeply and desperately in love with it."

That is Henry James again, gushing to his friend Grace Norton, when Venice got the hold on him that he was to pass on to Milly. True, he had rhapsodized promiscuously over other European cities, even Florence, which he described as being in need of a lover, "and that lover *moi*." (Master, please. You are embarrassing us.) But that was a decade before he declared, Venice's "magic potion has entered my blood." Venice was the one that made him crave a permanent Continental relationship—as a residential mistress, to be kept as the object of his feverish attentions when he strayed from England, although he never did consummate his often-mentioned desire to keep a Venetian apartment of his own. Probably just as well, as we were to decide for ourselves. In Venice, one can easily go overboard.

Buying into Romance

The potion is commonly acknowledged to be potent enough to do subliminal sensual work even on those who have never visited or given Venice any particular thought. One can hardly open a catalogue or a magazine without finding a picture of Venice. We won't even count the cultural publications, which inevitably feature, per issue, one contemporary oil or watercolor rendering of a bridge, an artfully crooked streetlight, and a moored gondola. Television commercials use Venetian footage to evoke the passionate nature of international commerce. Luxury goods and settings in magazines are routinely pictured with a book on Venice or a Venetian scene painting discreetly in the background. Wherever picture frames are sold, at least one will be shown containing a photograph of Venice.

The products need not be connected with anything remotely Venetian. Maidenform brassieres featured several models dreaming in their underwear decades ago, and now Victoria's Secret models cavort in their underwear for Bob Dylan at the Doge's Palace for a television commercial. Fabio turns into a gondolier for Nationwide insurance. Absolut vodka, Jergens lotion, Seagram's whiskey, Kotex napkins, Gilbey's gin, and Coca-Cola have all run advertisements associating themselves with Venice. Even automobiles make a claim. How can disappointment not lie ahead when a customer is swept away by a sense of romance upon seeing a photograph of an Alfa Romeo or a Cadillac juxtaposed against the beauty of Venice? The disappointment might turn out to be the glamorous car's, when it finds itself deserted in one of the world's dingiest car parks at the edge of an auto-less city.

An advertisement for the iMac displays on its monitor a gray-haired couple snuggling in a gondola on the Grand Canal. It is labeled "Our 50th Honeymoon," and under the headline "Romeo

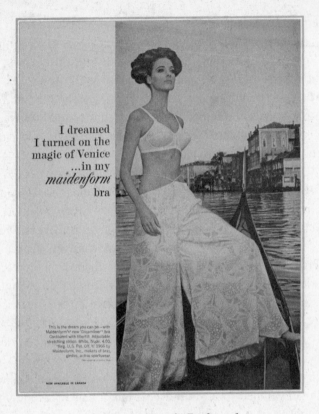

I dreamed
I turned on the
magic of Venice
...in my
maidenform
bra

This is the dream you can be—with
Maidenform's new 'Dreamliner' bra
Contoured with fiberfill. Adjustable
stretching straps. White, Nude. 4.00.
*Reg. U.S. Pat. Off. © 1966 by
Maidenform, Inc., makers of bras,
girdles, active sportswear

NOW AVAILABLE IN CANADA

*Venice Continues at the Forefront of
International Commerce.*

& Juliet, Part 2," the copy announces, "Star-crossed lovers,
rejoice. Now it's easy to turn the unforgettable moments of your
romance into an enthralling motion picture . . ."

Great. But Romeo and Juliet were a couple of kids from
Verona.

On the same stretch of the canal, with the church of Santa
Maria della Salute in the background, which has long been the
photographic angle of choice, another advertisement pictures a

different gray-haired couple snuggling in a gondola. One hopes the lovers all waved at one another as they passed, in recognition of their common enjoyment of lasting or late-onset love. The second gondola features Abraham Lincoln as the gondolier, and instead of the traditional striped shirt and beribboned hat, he is wearing his American native costume of frock coat and stovepipe hat. "Financial Freedom," it says; "It's a lot easier when Lincoln's [The Lincoln Financial Group] working with you."

DHL does have delivery service in Venice (as does UPS, for which the local pronunciation, Oops, is not necessarily spoken in irony), and its advertisement features its own boat on the Grand Canal instead of a gondola, with the claim, "We deliver to more countries than any other air express company. Come hell or high water." Never mind that during high water in Venice, deliveries would be problematic, as boats must avoid many side canals because these swell to limit clearance under the bridges. The headline is "Try Us to New Orleans." This ran in 2003, with the jokey presumption that high water was a quaint Venetian phenomenon that could never trouble, for example, New Orleans. Perhaps the idea was to target visiting Louisianans who, having succumbed to an impulse to buy a pair of antique, life-size Moorish statues with candelabra planted on their heads, were desperately in need of advice on how to get them home.

Two more recent advertisements tie for Most Nerve Shown in this genre. One was a full-page newspaper advertisement that the Starbucks chain ran during a promotional campaign about Italy. Half the page was occupied by a color photograph of Venice's island of San Giorgio Maggiore at dusk, as seen from the top of the Customs House. Superimposed on it were the words, "A great cup of coffee should transport you. Ours could take you to ITALY." The lower half of the page explained a contest whose main prize was "a Vespa tour of Tuscany." The other contender was a glossy advertising magazine called *The Cunarder*, whose cover had a golden-to-sepia photograph of that same stretch of the Grand Canal by the Salute and a banner enticing customers to "sail the world's most romantic sea." Inside were given the ports in Italy and elsewhere to be visited on these Mediterranean cruises. Florence was among them. Venice was not.

So Venice is used to sell not only computers, cars, drinks, brassieres, hand lotion, sanitary napkins, picture frames, and portfolios (both financial and leather) but—Florence! In the advertisers' book of wisdom, under the section on associating a product with enticing irrelevancies, Venice must be the example given right after scantily dressed women. Venice, world symbol of romance. Show them Venice, and they'll be unable to resist anything. True enough, in my and many cases.

What Do We See in Her?

Why? What is all this about?

Venice is a village, three miles across at its widest, which has not been a serious factor in world politics or trade for several hundred years. Its last burst of triumph was the Battle of Lepanto in 1571, and that was under a Spanish allied commander. Its historical reputation comprises the worst of opposites: as being both draconian and debauched, ruthless and frivolous.

Faced with a high cost of living and severely limited occupational opportunity, the sparse native population keeps drifting off to the mainland. Even the rich rapidly become house-poor, thanks to the eternal struggle between their ancient properties and the daily elements. Many family residences have been sold to hotel chains or other corporations, or to mostly absentee Venetophiles from a species formerly known as American Millionaires, but now called Industrialists from Milan. In others, the owners may seal off dozens of rooms to live in the few that they can afford to heat, or use their aristocratic titles and heir-looms to peddle themselves as "hosts" to the tourist trade.

Venice is remarkably inconvenient for even the most leisurely of vacationers. The topography and system of assigning addresses is so confusing that pedestrians depend on one stranger after another to pass them along to their destinations, and hosts talk their guests in by mobile telephone like Air Traffic Control. The concept that motorized transportation takes longer than walking is so counterintuitive that no visitor can get hold of it. "I'm late—I'll jump on a waterbus," one can't help thinking, only to make oneself significantly later as it bumps clumsily along from one floating stop to another.

High water floods the city more and more often. Teetering along on raised planks and watching Venetians wading to work wearing green rubber bibbed-and-booted overalls that were designed for standing in the same amount of water on purpose in order to fish are only amusing until you understand the damage that is being done. Or until you catch cold.

Venice's own director of Culture and Tourism declared publicly that the city has the worst pizza in Italy. (But then, pizza is a Neapolitan dish that Venice might be excused for not having mastered. Nor would proper, wood-burning pizza ovens be a good idea for a city constructed chiefly of wood and velvet, which has some old and recent experience of fire.) The official did not address the question of why Venetian polenta is so awful.

Venetophobes keep pointing out its obviously practical and allegedly psychological faults. Furthermore, they claim, Venice smells bad. This makes no impression on Venetophiles. Nor on perfume manufacturers who bottle and sell Venice, Venezia, Art of Venice, and Ballade of Venice, presumably not with the hope of evoking foul canals. Furthermore, we don't care what they say. When did high maintenance ever dissuade a lover from falling for a beauty?

Being such an obvious beauty, Venice attracts the inevitable presumption of superficiality. Its beauty is innocent of under-statement, a triumph of the conviction that there is no such thing as too much gold, brocade, and curlicued marble. Thus it is an outrage to no-nonsense functionalists. Before our own landmark-conscious era, Venice even had internal enemies, Venetian "futurists" with plans to demolish its vanity-ridden arti-ficiality. Had they succeeded, Venice might have become as visu-ally "honest" as Mestre, its ugly mainland sister.

Yet this beauty has conquered masses of people from different periods and sensibilities. Although its last stylistic infusions of note were Renaissance and late Baroque, infuriating that aes-thetic and historic prude Mr. John Ruskin, it does not appear to be impervious to fashion. Every three hundred years or so, it flaunts a different allure.

Imagination fails at what leap of imagination the first settlers made to convince themselves that desolate marshes, such as can still be seen in their unpromising natural state on the route from the airport, could be made homey, never mind palatial. Even the seabirds, individually perching on the bunched stakes Venetians plant to mark the safe route through the lagoon, know enough to be grateful for outposts of civilization. Yet those first budding huts with convenient front-door fishing and salt-harvesting became so dear in their builders' eyes that their refugee dreams of returning to their prior homes once the Hun Alert passed were forgotten.

In its pride of empire, Venice put the highest priority on deco-rating its home base, creating a showcase of art and architecture and a city-wide mall of luxury goods. When Doge Enrico Dandolo, aged ninety-seven and blind, hijacked the Fourth Crusade and sacked Constantinople instead of going to the Holy Land, he brought a shopping list. During the chaos of war, vic-tory, and shifting dynasties, he duly checked off choice art trea-

*"Come on, guys, we'll start with those
bronze horses and the Pala d'oro in aisle 3."*

sures and shipped them home. That these included the four high-stepping bronze horses that were to preside over the Piazza San Marco from its basilica did not prevent Venetians from denouncing Napoleon as a barbarian for exercising the next opportunity, six centuries later, to swipe the same horses as victory trophies on *his* shopping list. Crusaders whose tastes were less refined, and whose pillaging was therefore less focused, must have hoped that their wives had not heard about the Venetian take when they returned to their drafty old stone castles and faced the question, "What did you bring me?"

In the Romantic Era, as in our own age, a weakened and consequently benign Venice presents itself as picturesque. No amount of elective or emergency architectural surgery can conceal the ravages of age and the lack of an imperial budget. But since longing for the past is laced with poignancy, its present appeal would probably be blasted away by dazzle if we saw Venice as it was in its heyday. Decayed beauty suited the Romantics, with their gracefully consumptive stage heroines, and it suits the starker modern taste for irony and pathos. That Venice seems all the more lovely for being fragile is exasperating to its active caregivers, but they well know that pity and alarm are the basic fund-raising tools.

The Urban Virtues

This tendency to blather about Venice's beauty, using any excuse to pronounce the beloved name, is a hazard of being a Venetophile. A greater hazard is holding conversation with a Venetophile. But what lover ever failed to argue that beauty alone would not have been sufficient to ignite the noble fever? Venice also has its domestic virtues. Really.

It is quiet. Even a relentless noisemaker like Richard Wagner appreciated that. It was the absence of (perhaps competitive) noise that made him move there, he wrote his father-in-law, Franz Liszt, as if the place were some bucolic retreat, and he had failed to notice that Victorian Venice was also throbbing with foreigner-engorged sexuality.

That quietude was in peril, it was feared at the time. Technology was intruding, in the form of the railway, connected by land in 1846, and the steamboat, which began its in-town public transport service in 1881. But since industrial progress was bellowing with noisy growth elsewhere, such whistles and putts came to acquire a birdsong charm. The chief sounds of Venice today are church bells, footsteps, the slapping of water in the wake of motorboats, the folkloric cries of boatmen, and the animated shouts made by them, along with everyone else, into mobile telephones.

Venice is a healthy place to live, according to Venetians. We have heard this claim before, memorably in *Death in Venice,* where the tourists are told that everything is fine and not to concern themselves about any putridness they may happen to detect or the sudden disappearances of people who were beginning to look peaked. Earlier, there was that matter of ships carelessly bringing the plagues home and to all of Europe. A city where one of the churches is commonly known by the word "health" (the Salute) can be said to have known medical problems.

What is meant now is that it is healthy in the life-style sense. It is a mystery why the jogging and gymnasium crazes have any adherents in Venice, because treadmills and stair machines are provided by the municipality. With the necessity of walking everywhere, every few yards being up and down the steps of bridges, Venice's old people are said to be remarkably free of strokes and varicose veins. The greater peril would seem to be at the earliest stages of life, when they are taken up and down bridges in their baby carriages and strollers. The favored technique is to drag these vehicles up and push them down, with a resounding bump at each step. Whatever brain-rattling effect this may have on the hapless passengers, Venetian infants accept without protest.

For a proudly commercial power during its entire independent existence, Venice is, of all cities, the least disfigured by advertising. Graffiti, yes, but that is political, not commercial. There are no billboards, other than at the car park, waterbus stops, and on temporary scrims covering buildings in restoration, only artistic posters in the way of street advertising, and discreet names on ancient buildings to announce the shops within.

For all its grandeur, it is built to the human scale. While the tangle of streets, alleys, and canals forms a maze that can confuse even old-timers, the city is small enough to be comprehensible. You will continue to get lost, but it will be in places that are familiar and welcoming. It is a truism among Venetophiles that although you will never be able to find the particular attraction you have set out to see, you will find something just as interesting that you did not know existed, and the one you originally sought will pop up unexpectedly on a later, equally misdirected, expedition.

Venice is startlingly crime-free. Real life elsewhere has accustomed Americans to thinking of ourselves as constant targets at home and—with fears exacerbated by films and mysteries set in Venice—even more vulnerable ones when we travel. The experience of taking an urban walk at night, finding oneself in a dark passage, and suddenly hearing the echoes of a stranger's footsteps approaching from behind is disorienting in Venice, because all it heralds is the arrival of a matron carrying home a pastry box by its ribbons, and pleasantly open to being of help if you have lost your way. Internal alarms kick in when a shopkeeper says you don't need a receipt for the item you left for repair, but they must be silenced when the shopkeeper recognizes you on your return and produces your belonging without being asked. If you get the wrong change, it is likely to be in your favor, as there is disdain for accepting small coins.

I remember the citizenry being scandalized, only a few years ago, by the news that someone living in a ground-floor apartment had left the windows open on a warm night, and that a purse parked in plain sight was—stolen! It was embarrassing to listen to Venetians citing this travesty to ask one another what the world was coming to. Anywhere else, returning a wallet found on the street would involve hours of sifting through police records. When this happened to us in Venice, the policeman knew, without being told, the name and hotel of the victim, as it was the only pickpocketing reported.

Art heists have been known to happen. Our elderly landlady once told an elaborate tale of how she had heroically held the door against what she was sure was an attempt to break in and steal her ceiling frescoes. Two young men whom she had espied crossing the courtyard were on her steps, not ramming the massive door, just knocking politely, but her suspicions allowed no argument and she was proud of having delayed them until they got discouraged and went away.

"Venetians?" I asked incredulously.

"Oh, no," she reassured me. "Certainly not! No, no, no! Italians!"

This is not to claim that Venice eschews the machinations of modern Italian, and indeed global, corruption. On the contrary, historic Venetian mercenary cunning is yet supposed to contribute a special twist to the perils of encountering its legal system. It is only low-level chiseling, which is such an irritating ingredient of world travel, that is beneath them. Your tales of being stiffed by waiters refer to Italians—not Venetians—who are in Venice to pick up seasonal work.

Petty honesty may be less of a virtue than a necessity in a small town where it is physically impossible to make anything like a quick getaway. The criminally inclined have to make do with light pickpocketing or shell games in the two or three most crowded areas, rather than slipping bodies into dark canals, as they get to do in books and films.

However, rudeness is a crime in Venice. One rarely encounters it, possibly because of the soothing effect of the slow pace, which is the result of universal pedestrianism, and of the comforting midday shutdown that is slipping away elsewhere in the Mediterranean. Or it may be that the knowledge that everyone knows who everyone else is acts as a check on temper. For a people who have the equivalent of water in the basement several times a year (one reason they don't have basements), they are remarkably cheerful. In Venice, unlike some cities one could name, irritability and suspicion of being taken advantage of are not considered to be the normal human state.

So it was—not a relief, certainly, but at least a surprise—to hear what we do consider a normal emotional state articulated by a Venetian family woman on a small bridge in a modest residential neighborhood. This was during the last weekend of Carnival, recognized in this part of town mostly by costumed children and babies out with their parents. But there are masses of spectators for the outrageous displays in the historic center, and those newly arrived by train were being ushered toward the action through this neighborhood and over this bridge. A policewoman held back people already on the bridge, headed for home, making it temporarily a one-way passage for the visitors.

This was too much for that Venetian housewife, who alone gave voice to exasperation that would have inspired a full citizen uprising anywhere else. "Let me through!" she shouted. "I have to get home! I live here! Those people are tourists! They can wait! Not me! This is my neighborhood!" and so on. The policewoman gently administered an occasional "Piano, piano, signora," the graceful way of saying, "Hey, take it easy, lady." But the declaration of Venetian rights did not stop, and when the tourists had passed, the policewoman held this lady back and began writing her a ticket.

"For what? I live here!" etc.

"For being badly brought up," was the reply. "Mal educata" is the Italian expression for rude.

Assorted Wiles

If Venetophilia cannot be explained by aesthetics alone, adding the comforts of peace and quiet are not likely to push a contented visitor over the edge to obsession. But surely adding an erotic element will do it?

Venice may have to import its tap water, but a natural resource that she is believed to provide is love, or at least its holiday approximation. In the Republic's lush heyday, a Venetian super-courtesan could enchant a visiting king with her talents, not the least of which was favoring him with her poetry. After the fall, Venice's corps of gondoliers was considered an equally great resource (transportation included) for visiting ladies and gentlemen alike. Even now, the legend has persisted of Venice's providing romantic co-stars, but as only the occasional befuddled American movie star fails to realize that it is no longer fashionable to keep a pet gondolier, people are more likely to bring their own partners. Venice has become a watery honeymoon destination for the just-married, the unmarried, and the married-but-not-to-each-other, a sort of horizontal Niagara Falls.

But such couples are supposed to concentrate on each other. Pleasure, for a romantically inclined Venetophile, would require a threesome, in which the third party is Venice. A lover who seemed exciting enough elsewhere to be brought along, but who fails to grasp the excitement of Venice—who treats the city as a mere background and might even have the bad taste to become tired of walking or bored by looking around—is a nuisance. Romances can wither there as well as sprout.

Venice has a more powerful allure than any enticement to a mere human fling, although, like all seduction ploys, this, too, is a lie. She seems to offer perpetual life by placing you in the center of the busy flow of never-ending human history. In Venice, you are not peering into the past; you are standing in it. You are not only conjuring the private lives of people you would have longed to know; you are living in their houses. And you don't have to feel insignificant in comparison with your heroes and their peers, because right now they are offstage, and you are on the very stage they used.

The city undergoes enough minor physical changes to keep old-timers supplied with dismay, but if a new bridge has appeared or the bakery has turned into an electronics store, a Renaissance Venetian would still find the place recognizable. This is more than an American who has been five, or perhaps two, years absent from his or her hometown can say.

The house we often lease appears on Jacopo de' Barbari's map, dated 1500, which we could still use as a practical guide to getting around the city. Indeed, there is a CD called *Timeless Venice* that uses the map to trace a route that we happened to have already been using when living in a different apartment near the north side. The wine bar near the Rialto market, where grocers and shoppers on break could first have heard of the discovery of the New World, is filled today with their counterparts, taking their wine break and shrugging over the latest news. The barefoot teenaged lute player in faded blue whom Giovanni Bellini paints sitting at the steps of the Virgin's throne is right outside the museum, at the foot of the Accademia bridge, in faded blue jeans, bent over a guitar, missing only his predecessor's wings.

In the midst of a partially deserted town that peddles its past and fears for its immediate future, there is evidence everywhere that life is not a series of ever-more unprecedented upheavals burying the middle-aged, not to mention the dead. Rather it seems a continuous pageant with an uncanny record of survival. This gives you the heady feeling that you, too, will remain vivid

far into the future. That romance will never leave you. It only
hurts when it is you who has to leave Venice.

The American Connection

Delving beyond physical appearance, historic Venice is even
more recognizable to Americans. If we find the territory fantastic,
we nevertheless relate easily to the people and their government—
perhaps more easily than to the mind-sets and political conditions
of our own particular pre-American ancestors.

It is not necessary to make those strenuous leaps that sober
historians must in order to understand cultures that seem
ascetic, servile, cruel, contemptuous of trade, antagonistic to foreigners, fearful of sex, hostile to art, indifferent to artisanship,
intellectually rigid, fanatically religious, or otherwise possessed of
traits we do not consider to be among our own failings. A
national war or plague emergency might bring on a burst of what
we would recognize as McCarthyism, homophobia, and xeno-
phobia, but it was not a normal part of the Venetian character.
The company you find when projecting yourself into Venetian
history may be self-indulgent, materialistic, proud, vain, curious
about the world, foolish about love, greedy for commerce, avari-
cious about art and crafts, open-minded and pragmatic to the
point of cynicism about politics, sex, and religion, but surely
these are traits we understand.

Like American pioneers, the first Venetians were desperate
immigrants who took over virgin territory, succeeding in settling
it against formidable odds. Once their future seemed secure,
they, too, noticed that what they were lacking was a high-class
past. So they fabricated an ancient civic lineage, and accorded
status within living society by ranking families by their year of
arrival. From destitute escapees to the First Families of Venice—
we are familiar with that path to pride.

Venice skipped feudalism, as it lacked the nonnegotiable pre-requisite of land, and therefore missed many of the longer-lasting attitudes that devolved from feudalism. The Venetian Republic had a class system, but it was not only based on immi-gration rather than ancient wealth, it was also sporadically porous. Thus it did not foster the contempt or subservience characteristic of systems whose origins are obscure enough to support the pretense of being God-given. Its rare political rebel-lions occurred within the upper class, not between classes. Aristocratic titles were forbidden, so while the contemporary proliferation of counts and countesses resembles that of the rest of Italy, fancily labeled Venetians do not have great cause for pro-claiming historic dignity. Their titles were granted, upon humili-ating application, by the despised Austrian occupiers of Venice during the nineteenth century. "A count from Torcello," referring to the original Venetian island settlement, is a local term for a fake. It is far more snazzy to have at least one ancestor, maybe several, who held the nonhereditary title of doge. "Two doges," you will hear said about someone by means of identification.

The doge, the one duke in the Venetian Republic, had some regal paraphernalia—conspicuously, the papal present of an overblown parasol—but a funny-shaped hat in place of a crown. If he behaved himself, he had job security, but not, after some early, often bloody, arrangements, the accompanying perk of being able to pass along the succession. The election of each succeeding doge became the opportunity to drain ever more power from the position as the legislative branch of government became, from experience, ever more wary. The power of the tri-bunals, the Council of Ten and the Council of Three, was fear-some and fierce, but membership rotated rapidly. There was not much time to develop a stranglehold, as it were, and abuse of power could backfire on those who would soon be at the mercy of their replacements.

It is no coincidence that Americans find all this familiar. When our Founding Fathers were designing a new government, they were informed by the anti-monarchist writings of the eighteenth-century Commonwealthmen and James Harrington's seventeenth-century work *The Commonwealth of Oceana,* which extols Venetian statecraft as a model of just and workable governance. So although they were scornful of a faltering old oligarchy claiming the name of republic, the framers nevertheless helped themselves to Venetian ideas. Such old Venetian practices as checks and balances, minimum age requirements for office, and limited terms found their way into the American Constitution. The process of electing a doge (the Great Council selects thirty balloters by lot from whom nine are picked by lot to elect forty from whom twelve are selected by lot by a boy plucked from the piazza; these twelve choose twenty-five, from whom nine are selected by lot to elect forty-five from whom eleven are selected by lot to choose the doge from forty-one candidates) is only slightly more complicated than our electoral college. However, the doge, unlike a presidential candidate, scattered money to the masses after his election, not before. The prudent way to do this is illustrated in a painting by Francesco Guardi that depicts the newly elected doge tossing out gold coins in the piazza while henchmen push back the eager crowd with poles.

Like America, Venice was untouched by the feudalistic snobbery against being "in trade" that fettered the most advantaged class in that other island-naval-power-mercantile society, England, well into the twentieth century. The richest Venetians were merchants who lived above their storerooms. Commodity storage and related offices occupied the water-level and mezzanine floors of those palaces where costly but precarious apartments now exist.

World trade provided an international outlook that tempered Venetian participation in some of the more unfortunate enterprises that swept Europe, notably the Crusades and the Inquisition. Other people's enemies and heretics were Venice's customers.

So, for that matter, were the zealots who were chasing them. Until Venice recognized the Crusades as an opportunity to knock out annoying pirate bases (thus annoying the pope, who tersely explained that the idea was to attack infidels, not Christians), to obtain favorable trading positions abroad, and to acquire a lot of free art, its chief contribution was providing matèriel. Or, as it might be called, war profiteering.

Venice also endorsed, and attempted to practice, the principle of equal justice for all. One of its seminal legends tells of a baker-boy who was executed for murdering a noble, only to have the real murderer confess many years later. Thereafter, the warning "Remember the poor baker-boy!" was intoned to the Council of Ten whenever it debated pronouncing a death sentence. Aristocrats were well represented among those receiving such sentences, and a brokenhearted doge, Francesco Foscari, famously refused to mitigate the punishments that his beloved son had earned. The infamous Bocche dei Leone, the wall mailboxes of carved lions' heads, whose mouths were open for depositing anonymous denunciations of one's fellow citizens (most often for public-health violations), actually served as hotlines for giving tips to government agencies that then went in search of solid evidence. This is not to say that dramatic outrages of justice did not occur, merely that according to the system, they were not supposed to.

Another bond between historic Venice and modern America is the tendency to wallow in materialism and repeatedly fail at attempts to curb the national appetite for frivolous goods. Sumptuary laws elsewhere were designed to give the privileged exclusive rights to certain luxury goods or symbols. In Venice, sumptuary laws had the opposite intention: to prevent the privileged from wasteful and divisive showing off. Such measures, which included rations on party menus and pearls, were about as well respected as our Prohibition. The underlying objective

was only successful to the point that European nobles complained of disappointing simplicity—or what we would call good
taste—in their Venetian peers. The one rule that stuck was the
one against souping up personal vehicles with gaudy paint and
decorations. To this day, all gondolas, other than those that
compete in regattas, are black. But then, so are our rental limou-
sines, other than those used for proms and weddings, without
benefit of legal intervention.

Finally, Americans know what it is to be prosperous and
smug, only to find that your happy and open society has inadvertently attracted the hatred of the world. To believe your
country a civilizing and generous influence, and then to find
traditional enemies united by their eagerness to gang up on
you, as was the case with the sixteenth-century League of
Cambrai against Venice, is a shock we are beginning to appreciate. Especially when the shock is compounded by an unfavor-
able shift in the world economy, as was then happening with
the development of alternate trade routes that toppled Venetian
domination.

It is easy to point out the ways in which Venice, a supposedly
enlightened power, did not measure up to modern standards. No
country yet does. But the Republic was outstanding for her time,
lasted for an amazing thousand or so years, and was so much
beloved by her own citizens, even in her decline, that they—by
then Europe's most famous party animals—turned sullen during
the foreign occupations of the nineteenth century and voluntar-
ily gave up their nonstop partying. For decades after the demise,
society went dead, theaters went empty, and at the first oompah-
pah-pah from an Austrian band, Venetians stalked out of the
piazza that served as the center of their universe. Considering
that Venice had been primarily known, by that time, as a sort of
spring-break destination for the Western world, this was extraordinary evidence of their patriotism.

The Disneyland Connection

All of these points of identification have a paradoxical effect on the Venetophile. They do not exactly amount to a promise of immortality (laced with the more charming forms of immorality), but a hint is conveyed that the future will keep your memory, along with all that well-kept and still-present past. Venice, with its shortage of space, gives its dead a mere few years of burial on the funeral island of San Michele, and then tosses their bones into a heap for disposal on a nearby ossuary island, where survivors must know that those visible white shards may be the very people they still mourn. Yet she has the nerve to seduce her admirers with fraudulent visions of permanence.

Nobody admits to feeling this lure. It would be like confessing to some sort of hobbyist fantasy life, such as being a Civil War re-enactor or a Trekkie. On the contrary, Venetophiles, like Venetians, are always complaining that Venice is in imminent danger of turning into a theme park, if it has not already done so.

"Disneyland" has become the standard local threat, although preceding generations had to make do with comparisons to fairs, boardwalks, and circuses when bemoaning Venice's popularity with tourists, among whom they failed to count themselves. Now it is impossible to have a conversation about the city without Disneyland being invoked the way preachers once invoked Hell. For its part, Disney cheerfully welcomes the relationship. It has its own store near the Rialto bridge, reproducing under its stone nose a bridge on which Mickey and Minnie Mouse are batting eyelashes. And it is Venice that has inspired theme parks around the world, from Las Vegas to China (see chapter eight).

But what a theme park Venice is! You get to choose your own theme, and whatever it is, Venice will fall in with it. Death, adul-

Rush Hour at the Rialto.

tery, vengeance, and vanity are the top favorites, all of which have inspired centuries of both great and embarrassing poetry and novels (see chapter six), as well as much sighing and brooding fortunately not destined to see print.

You never have to stand in line. You easily can, if you pick popular attractions at popular times, but you needn't. There are off-times at museums, when respectable people go home for lunch, for example. But it is not necessary to go to museums to see paintings and other attractions of a quality that would be isolated and enshrined anywhere else. Through theft and commission, Venice accumulated so many valuables that, even after subtracting the enormous number that were lost, re-stolen, looted, sold to foreigners, or waterlogged, committed Venetophiles are still left with a lifetime of small discoveries along the streets and in the houses and churches. These cannot be real discoveries in such a pawed-over spot, but because Venice's wealth of treasures is strewn about in public spaces and tucked in every cranny, they seem thrillingly so. Besides, there are ice cream stands everywhere.

Venice's ravishing beauty is intimately knowable, because we camp in its midst. The entire city serves as a museum—a more refined way of putting it than "Disneyland," although this, too, is said in order to scorn those who fail to acknowledge that it is also a place where real people live real lives.

As the Sea Rat puts it in Kenneth Grahame's *The Wind in the Willows,* "O, Venice is a fine city, wherein a rat can wander at his ease and take his pleasure! Or, when weary of wandering, can sit at the edge of the Grand Canal at night, feasting with his friends, when the air is full of music and the sky full of stars, and the lights flash and shimmer on the polished steel prows of the swaying gondolas, packed so that you could walk across the canal on them from side to side! And then the food—do you like shellfish? Well, well, we won't linger over that now."

What Do They (and We) See in Us?

Indulging in this bizarre form of tourism, or, indeed, in any tourism at all, is exactly what our fellow Venetophiles deny about themselves and denounce in others. Typically, the most thorough item of make-believe on the part of Venetophiles is not their imaginary historical pageantry. It is the pretense that tourism is something that other people do—crass, ignorant people with no feel for Venice, which hardly explains why so many such types keep showing up. Their supposition is that tourists are people who are unaccountably eager to surrender their disposable time and money to endure blatant boredom, purely for the sake of bragging about their travels at home. Considering that we all know how even the most devoted friends flee from travel tales and vacation pictures, this does not sound like much of a bargain.

In contrast, what these critics think they themselves do is something else, something more significant, sensitive, and subtle. It is difficult to understand the distinction. We all travel to Venice to see the sights; we all talk about having done so. We should all know how foolish it is to claim to plumb the motives of passersby.

Yet practically everybody who has ever toured Venice has complained about the presence of tourists. A great many simultaneously make the opposite claim, of having discovered a "secret Venice" where "none of the tourists go," impervious to the logic that this would no longer be true once they trod there. Nor does it occur to them that if they believe there are too many tourists in Venice, there is something they could do about it. They could stay home.

To sustain this illusion, Venetophiles have to deny their own Venetian pasts, when they first stopped by on some sort of wider journey or tour and became enchanted. They have to identify so completely with Venetians that they forget that they meet the definition of visiting foreigners against whom Venetians are fond of delivering the polemics that they are so eager to second. To Venetians, the symbol of the blight tourists bring is the proliferation of mask and glass shops; many a Venetophile has taken up this lament without admitting to having one or two of those wittily handmade masks at home, or perhaps a liquidy chandelier, purchased on an early trip.

For Venetians, too, anti-tourism represents a peculiar form of denial. Venice has been in the tourist business almost throughout its history, and exclusively in that business for the last two hundred years. Her entire economy is based on tourism. And for

all her complaints, she is good at it. In each era, Venice inge-
niously went about providing whatever attractions drew the
tourists of the time.

The medieval tourist was a pilgrim. Typical European destinations were shrines built around the possession of some small relic
of a saint, perhaps a finger or a knuckle, and a major international
destination was Santiago de Compostela, Spain, which features
the translated body of not just a saint, but of an apostle, James.

Okay, but Venice went on saint-gathering missions that net-
ted not just the odd bone, including the skull of Saint John the
Baptist, a rib of Saint Stephen, an arm of Saint George, a part of
Saint Luke's arm, a finger of Mary Magdalene, an arm each of Saint
Andrew the Apostle and Saint Barnabas the Apostle and—take
this, Spain!—the arm of Saint James, but also entire dressed bodies of saints, many of them superstars. Not only did Venetians
bring home an evangelist, Mark, to be their patron saint, scoring
a decisive political-ecclesiastical advantage in the lagoon, but
they boast possession of the full bodies of Saint Zachary, father
of John the Baptist; Saint Rocco, the plague saint who exhibits
his running sores; Saint Lucy, whose Neapolitan praises are so
tirelessly and tiresomely sung by gondoliers on the Grand Canal
that if she hadn't already been a saint, she would be one now;
Saint Stephen the Proto-martyr, who finally rests in peace at San
Giorgio Maggiore;* Saint Nicholas, aka Santa Claus, who, off-
season, is also the patron saint of sailors and prisoners; and
Theodore, who was bumped from his position as Venice's patron
saint when Mark came to town and outranked him. It has so
many full bodies of less famous saints that they are sometimes
several to a church. These include, among many others, Saints
Albano, Anastatio, Aniano, Athanasius of the Creed, Bacco,

---

*The island's Web site confesses to having inadvertently mixed up the bones of Saints
Triphon and Demetrius so that it no longer knows which is which.

Cosima, Cosimo, Costantio, Damiano, Domenigo, Donato, Elio-
doro, Epimaeo, Eugenius, Felice, Floriano, Fortunato, Fosca,
Genesius, Gerardo, Gioria, Gondino, Grisogono, Hermacoro,
Hermoleo, Isadoro, Leo, Liberale, Ligerio, Magnus, Maximo,
Niceta, Niceto, Orso, Pancrazio, Sabina, Secondo, Sergio, Tabra
Tabrata, Teonisto, and Tharaso.

Many of these saints left other bodies and significant body
parts to be venerated in rival cities. John the Baptist left other
skulls in Damascus and Amiens. Saint Lucy has a head in
Bourges as well as the one she wears in Venice. Saint Rocco also
left his body in his native France under his birthname of Roch,
and the city of Bari has as dramatic a claim to having stolen Saint
Nicholas as Venice does to Saint Mark. Even less-disputed bodies came into question after Napoleon made havoc of Venice's
churches. So many saints' present addresses are in doubt that
the Venetian Curia is now undertaking an inventory of who is
left and where they and various valuables are stashed. Now that
tourists prefer their saints to be painted, this matters less, but
when it did, Venice, through selective body-snatching, had made
itself a four-star attraction.

Supplying the Crusades offered Venice, the great builder of
ships, with a new tourist opportunity. Ships are not made in a
day and the crusaders could spend a year or more there, waiting
for their orders to be filled. (Actually, a ship *could* be made in a
day in Venice's Arsenal, where assembly lines could start in the
morning with wooden planks and roll out a fully armed ship at
the end of the day, but this was done as a demonstration project
to impress visiting VIPs, especially ones suspected of having military designs on Venice.) It took more than saints' bodies to
amuse the crusaders while they were lolling around, and lest
they have too much messy fun, Venice cordoned them off on an
outlying island. Still, there was good business in feeding and
housing crusaders-in-waiting.

As a trade center, Venice was always full of foreign visitors, so many of whom were in residence as business agents that buildings and streets bear the names of the groups they once housed: Germans, Slavs, Albanians, Turks. Such segregation became infamous with the establishment of the original ghetto in 1516, an altogether different degree of zoning, among other reasons because while the others had sporadic curfews, Jews were locked into their neighborhood at night and, to top it off, charged for the guards. But the Jewish population had come there in the first place because Venice, with its cosmopolitan atmosphere and comparatively sophisticated appreciation of what is now called diversity, was a refuge from crucially less tolerant attitudes and laws elsewhere. Venice even practiced comparative tolerance toward Protestants at a time when this met the definition of religious extremism.

After Venice's dominance of international trade drained off, and even before its sovereignty collapsed in 1797, she lived off her tourists. This has not discouraged Venetians, even Venetian politicians—and, by extension, a great many visiting Venetophiles—from disparaging the tourist trade.

"We have fifteen million visitors a year," the director of Culture and Tourism said in a speech to a group of foreigners who put serious money and time into restoring Venetian buildings and art, "of whom four million are good." One could almost feel all those Venetophiliac hearts palpating from the restraint necessary to keep from shouting, "Me! Me! I'm good! You like me, don't you? I'm not like them!"

Indeed he did, as the criteria, not unnaturally, is whether the tourist spends money in Venice. "We like intelligent tourists," he said, tempering the hated word "tourist" with the placating adjective. "Cultured" is also used as a euphemism for people who stay in expensive hotels and eat in expensive restaurants. Yet to be any sort of tourist is considered so shameful that when the

Venetian police arrested some suspected art thieves from Milan and the men forcefully declared themselves to be innocent tourists, their guilt became obvious. No one in Venice would willingly declare himself a tourist unless as a cover. Still, by definition of their true profession, art thieves must be considered cultured.

Special derision is directed at day-trippers, the designation for the nine million or so yearly visitors who do not stay overnight, but return to their tour buses, campers, cruise ships, or cheaper mainland accommodations, thus burdening Venice's city services without contributing to the take. That the hordes who traipse through so briefly must surely contain the cultured, intelligent, money-spending, perhaps even money-donating Venetophiles of the future is not considered. Not every impressionable young person visiting for the first time sees Venice from his parents' suite at the Gritti Hotel. Or even from the humble Pensione ("Oil soup for lunch again?") Isak Dinesen.

Limiting entrance has long been a major topic. When Henry James described Venice as "a vast museum where the little wicket that admits you is perpetually turning and creaking," he was merely using a metaphor to make the usual touristic disparagement of other tourists. But Venetians discuss the idea seriously, as if one could legally wall off an entire modern city, or even its town center. Although "if we are too strict," the director warned, "it would become [watch out! here it comes] Disneyland."

Instead, the civic government has put great effort into identifying the sort of thing that drives tourists away, and then instituting it. Overcharging, for example. In other places, unscrupulous merchants may jack up their prices for the hapless tourist, but in Venice it is done officially. Public transportation for residents is a fraction of the cost that it is for tourists. When that policy had been in effect long enough to prove workable, the idea was launched of overcharging tourists to use public toilets. Residents would be issued cards, entitling them to pay a reasonable amount for facilities they probably didn't need, as they have homes, friends, and neighborhood bars, while tourists with no visible alternative would have to cough up, as it were, or else. One would think that a city with liquid streets would not want to tempt people it had already branded as being uncultured and crude.

The eventual result was the Venicecard, a limited-time pass for transportation, museums, and toilets, which a tourist can purchase in advance. Only so many are sold for any particular day, the hope being that those who are too late will be discouraged from visiting at all. Although they will be able to enter the city, they will have to pay more, stand in line, and control themselves, three things tourists hate to do. As who does not?

Venice also did what other municipalities with problems now do: brought in high-end public relations people to change its image. In 1999, at the instigation of Venice's then-and-again mayor, the edgy magazine *Colors,* a publication of Benetton, devoted an issue to the task. The style employed was the shock tactic associated with the Benetton clothing advertisements of the time, which showed dying AIDS patients and Mafia victims, rather than its later advertisements, which showed a diversity love-fest of colorfully well-dressed youths.

On the cover of the Venice issue was a child whose immobilized outstretched hand contained corn bought to feed the famous piazza pigeons. But the pigeons were not disposed to wait for his charity. A flock of them had knocked him to the ground—possibly murdering him, as he was not shown struggling—and were pecking at his face. Inside the magazine were full-page color pictures of floating trash, deserted and desecrated property, and a dead rat. A "Home Catalog" offered such souvenirs as toilet paper with the Lion of Saint Mark on each sheet, bottled water taken from the canals, and a flyswatter in the

Mrs. Claude Monet to Mr. Monet:
"Are you sure this is supposed
to be fun?"

shape of a gondola's oarlock. The text was devoted to suggestions that pickpockets are rampant, the cuisine is likely to contain salmonella, the pigeons drop worms on passersby, and vapors wafting in from neighboring Marghera cause cancer.

A credits box thanks those who helped make the issue possible, including the mayor, City Hall, the commissioner of culture, and officials from the transit system and press office. One can only be grateful that these Venetian city elders are not charged with coming up with a license plate slogan.

Tourism did slack off dramatically after this, but not because potential tourists considered that attack pigeons, food poisoning, and cancer might put a damper on their vacations. More realistic and immediate dangers had appeared: terrorism and a shrinking dollar.

Venice did not rejoice. Despite the claim that Venice loses money on short-term visitors, the economic consequences hurt. It seems that even cruise passengers in town for a few hours, with lunch waiting on their ships, had found their way into shops.

One began to hear wistful talk about those nice Americans, and some of it sounded suspiciously disinterested. The fact that Americans no longer had money to burn abroad, where post–World War II prosperity has increasingly lessened temptations of arrogance on the one side and envy on the other, apparently made us more likeable.

Stylistically, the American tourist is no longer generally considered to be the ridiculous figure with whom American tourists are so eager to disassociate themselves. The typical travel costume is not a polyester suit or dress now, but jeans and college sweatshirts, of which young Europeans wear inferior copies. American popular culture is admired and imitated in hilariously incongruous accents. The much deplored American informality is coming to be appreciated as perhaps an excess of warmth and spontaneity, rather than a deficit of sophistication. Venetians can be as chatty as Americans, and tourists endear themselves when they encourage Venetians to show off their pride in their city's history and art, or when they meet Venetian political criticism of America with their individual views, whatever these might be, rather than with national propaganda.

At another meeting of the foreign groups involved in restoration in Venice, the then-mayor was tactful enough to call the

Venetophiles "real Venetians. After all," he said, "I am Venetian because I happened to be born here. You chose to be Venetian."

A Touristic Honor Roll

Venice is actually proud of its previous generations of tourists. Mozart once dropped by for Carnival, and his fondest memory was of being attacked by seven women determined to spank him. This may explain why his father did not allow him to return. All the same, the city council and the tourist board put up a plaque to commemorate the two hundredth anniversary of his memorable visit. George Sand, who arrived with Alfred de Musset, is honored with a plaque on the house where she lived after she recovered from dysentery before he did and felt well enough to run off with their Venetian doctor. Cole Porter has no plaque (yet), but his name is remembered in connection with Ca' Rezzonico, the house he rented to give parties that featured a jazzy barge floating out front, to the annoyance of his neighbors. There is a plaque on Ca' Rezzonico, but it commemorates the death of another tourist, Robert Browning, whose son, Pen, once owned the building (see chapter four). For that matter, the Rezzonico family were not originally Venetians, either, only Genoese bankers who bought the house from the Bon family, who went broke. However, a Rezzonico became Pope Clement XIII, and the building, now the Museum of Eighteenth Century Venice, retains his family name.

Other tourists whose quickie visits are thought to add to the city's interest and prestige include Erasmus, Galileo, Albrecht Dürer, Johann Wolfgang von Goethe, Stendhal, Michel de Montaigne, Charles Dickens, Alfred, Lord Tennyson, Mark Twain, Honoré de Balzac, Herman Melville, Percy Bysshe Shelley, Friedrich Nietzsche, J.M.W. Turner, John Singer

Sargent, William Wordsworth, Henry Wadsworth Longfellow, James Fenimore Cooper, Pierre Auguste Renoir, Claude Monet, Marcel Proust, Edith Wharton, Rainer Maria Rilke, Pyotr Ilich Tchaikovsky, Thomas Mann, Max Beerbohm, and Evelyn Waugh, right on up to Dr. Seuss and Woody Allen. Full-fledged Venetophiles who honored Venice by long stays or frequent visits include—in addition to the aforementioned Byron, Wagner, James, Hemingway, and Pound—Petrarch, El Greco, Lady Mary Wortley Montagu, John and Euphemia Ruskin, William Dean Howells, James McNeill Whistler, Mariano Fortuny, Igor Stravinsky, and Serge Diaghilev, right on up to Elton John and Dame Edna.

Historically, Venice was a cosmopolitan city, fascinated by foreigners. True, the tourists mentioned above were all what might now be roughly classified as cultured. But Lord Byron and George Sand did not always behave in the spirit prescribed by the rules that Venice has issued for current tourists, even if they may not have disobeyed the specific ones that forbid wearing bikinis around town and picnicking inside churches.

It would appear that among Venetians, at least, the often-voiced anti-tourism is not deep. It is such a habit that Venetians do it freely in front of their non-Venetian friends, and are horrified if these people make a connection between such statements and the fact that they are also foreigners in town to see the sights, which is pretty much the definition of tourist. "Oh, not you, of course!" Venetians protest, in the time-honored tradition of some-of-my-best-friends-are.

Among Venetophiles, it is unfortunately often a deeper prejudice. Self-hatred coupled with denial has to be painful under any circumstances, although the holiday type is one of the less insidious forms. Still, it is not pretty to hear tourists condemning other tourists for being tourists, lapping up praise for being "not like them," the way a woman might once have been flattered to be told that she "thought like a man," and denigrating the experiences of others: "Oh, really, you went there/ate there/stayed there/bought that? But that's just for tourists! We prefer the authentic Venice. But of course you have to know how to avoid the tourist traps. So much has been spoiled since we started coming here. Why don't those people stay home or go to the beach or something? They're turning dear old Venice into Disneyland. But they can't be enjoying themselves. You have to know the real Venice to appreciate it . . . blah blah blah."

All this is nonsense. Venice attracts masses of tourists because it is dazzling and unique. From marshland refuge to city-state to world empire to world playground, it has both ensnared and enjoyed foreign company. There are infinite treasures, but no secret ones; Venice spreads its attractions for all to see. As in any crowd, some people behave better than others and some people are more appreciative than others. Nice and necessary as it may be to profit from all this, sorting people by the length of time they stay and the amount of money they spend is a dubious way of separating the sensitive from the insensitive.

The Proto-Venetophile

The danger of condemning tourists is that you never know who might make it into the Venetian pantheon. Here is the story of how Mark the Evangelist got to be patron saint of Venice:

He arrived as a day-tripper—a foreigner passing through quickly, as part of a longer voyage, seeing little and contributing nothing to the local economy. The weather was wretched. Yet he was instantly smitten. Although he had never been there before, he somehow knew that Venice was where he belonged. Circumstances forced him to hasten on to his business elsewhere, but he took with him a sacred promise to return, know-

How to Recruit a Patron Saint.

ing that he would never rest until he did. Centuries later, traveling under even more miserable conditions, he managed to get there, and there we find him today, quartered in the splendor of glittering decay and putting up with the inconveniences of encroaching water and visiting throngs.

This is not the version that conscientious tourists learn before peeping at the story's illustrations by such as Titian and Tintoretto. That one goes more like this:

Saint Mark was on a preaching tour from Alexandria to Venice's rival city, Aquileia, scheduled to continue on to Rome when he sought shelter from stormy seas on the islands of the unsettled Venetian lagoon. An angel appeared to him with a message: "Pax tibi, Marce, evangelista meus. Hic requiescet corpus tuum" (Peace be with you, Mark, my evangelist. Here your body will rest). And so it does, in the fabulous Basilica of Saint Mark, after some devout and patriotic ninth-century Venetian fishermen rescued the saint's body from his grave in Alexandria, distracting Muslim officials by covering the relic with pork. The repulsed inspectors hurried the mess through without asking if the fishermen had packed their own barrels or observed other security regulations.

It is endearing that Venetians make no attempt to hide aspects of the Story of How We Got Our Patron Saint that less-sophisticated civilizations might consider embarrassing. The triumph of the grave robbers smuggling their pig-smothered contraband past disgusted Muslims is proudly pictured in colorful mosaics smack on the front of the basilica, last mosaic on the right. That Venice already had a patron saint at the time and unapologetically dumped him from the post when someone more prestigious became available is also illustrated nearby, where a statue of the deposed Saint Theodore remains posted on one of the columns at the ceremonial entrance to the piazza, outranked by the Lion of Saint Mark, who occupies the other column. Nobody can tell you definitively why Saint Theodore happens to be precariously perched on a prone crocodile, or perhaps dragon, but everyone will tell you why nobody knows: The statue was stolen property, and probably wasn't intended to depict Saint Theodore, but someone who presumably had his own reasons for standing on a reptile. For that matter, the lion on the other column was also stolen, and may have started out life as an Asian chimera, to which the Venetians added wings. Even the columns were stolen, as is the case with the other ancient treasures of which Venice, which lacks an ancient history, is chock full. And with Saint Mark himself.

But for all that charming candor, Venetians and Venetophiles alike fail to see the connection between Saint Mark's story and that of the modern tourist.

CHAPTER TWO

Getting Your Feet Wet

A self-respecting tourist still craves local recognition and acceptance. We are not so foolhardy as to think we might really pass for Venetians, even if the men bought quilted coats the color of olives and we women dyed our hair bronze in the unfortunate modern rendering of Titian tresses. We only aspire to be mistaken for Americans who are continuing the grand nineteenth-century tradition of Anglo-American society in Venice (see chapter four).

We only wish to be addressed in Italian, asked for directions, and recognized by fishmongers. Our modest hope is to distinguish ourselves from promiscuous tourists, the kind who also freely give themselves to Paris and Rome and who-knows-where-else. Their pinnacle of worldly success is to be recognized by restaurateurs and concierges. Ours is to admit, when we are asked for restaurant and hotel recommendations, that we rarely frequent either, since we keep house. Hard to say who are the greater snobs.

This swaggering unpretentiousness is the correct demeanor for a Venetophile. Stylistically, you would be justified in suspecting the worst of people whose ambitions lead them to rent other people's palaces. But historic Venice siphons off the froth of our vainglorious imaginations, allowing us to appreciate the virtues of Venice as a modern, workaday village. Having usurped its

memories of glamorous youth and triumphant maturity, we lay
fond and fraudulent claim to the deeper devotion that comes
from shared longevity. Focusing on Tiepolo skies filled with
puffy clouds and puffier goddesses, we cope cheerfully with yet
another rainy day.

And so we do not ape the old Venetians, as our friends their
living descendents do not. We only feel fortified with illegiti-
mately acquired noblesse oblige when pondering the usual travel
matters: how to get around, what expressions to memorize, what
to wear, what to buy, what to eat and drink.

The touchstone rule is that Venetian good taste restricts use of
the very word "palace." I only strewed it around the previous
chapter to convey the fairy-tale improbability of these buildings, as
outsiders and Venetians contemplating inflated rent are wont to
do. This is not right. It is like calling your own house a mansion.
Henceforth, unless I slip, it is, please, to be interpreted as irony.

There is only one palace in Venice, no matter how much rent
Milly Theale can afford. The Doge's Palace, with its pink icing and
cockeyed fenestration, is a palace. Other buildings, no matter how
grand, bear the title of house, rendered in Venetian as "ca'," along
with the proper names by which they are known. The small canals
off the grand one are rivers, not canals. Not even Canalettos, of
which there was only one in Venice. (Canaletto's nephew, the not-
dissimilar painter Bernardo Bellotto, called himself Canaletto
when working abroad, but did not dare do so at home.) And there
is only one piazza in Venice, the Piazza San Marco, with its off-
shoot piazzettas. Other such spaces, even huge ones, such as San
Polo and Santa Margherita, go by the title "campo," and the littler
ones, "campiello." When speaking English, we try to call them
squares, although the Piazza San Marco is a trapezoid and the
others are ovals, rectangles, or lopsided.

This rapidly brings us to the danger of erring in the direction
of annoying disingenuousness. So as not to toss around Venetian

terms, as the novice Venetophile is tempted to do, I have been referring to waterbuses rather than using the name vaporetto, which dates from the first steam-powered fleet and is still in use today, although the system is computerized. I have been known to refer to the floating vaporetto docks as bus stops, and to use "down the block" or "across the street" in reference to the Grand Canal or, as we say, the GC. It is as well to stop this sort of thing before getting to the point of calling a gondola a canoe.

Getting Around (Feet)

Naturally, the more you learn about Venice, the more you will want to show off to newer tourists under the guise of helping them out. It is easy to find such victims, because they are all lost.

Giving street directions is simple. In the Venetian tradition, you point in the direction of the destination and urge anyone who asks to keep going straight ahead. "Sempre diritto" ("dritto" in the slurred Venetian version), "always straight ahead," is the only direction Venetians give. The accompanying gesture is an undulating forearm to indicate the number of bridges it will be necessary to cross.

Following this all-purpose direction is not as simple. Venice is a town where the physical possibility of going straight ahead for more than a few steps is nonexistent, other than across squares, along the banks of the lagoon, or on a couple of paved slashes that Napoleon thoughtlessly supposed would look like the Parisian boulevards of the future (of which he even more thoughtlessly supposed Venice was in need). As the city is a collection of small islands haphazardly strung together with bridges, dotted with dead ends, and sporadically decorated with whimsical street signs, straight ahead is not an option.

Yet Venetians are not the sort of people—said to exist

"Just keep going straight."

elsewhere—who give foreigners misleading directions for mali-
cious or nefarious reasons. They are kind and helpful to lost
strangers, which can be a serious commitment of time, as
strangers in Venice come in no other kind. "Sempre dritto" not
only makes sense to a subtle people who do not expect to be
taken literally, but is hallowed by its ancient use by one of
Venice's first heroines. Perhaps.*

This was an old lady who was left behind at Malamocco in the
year 810, as the terrifying fleet of King Pepin advanced on that
ancient Venetian settlement. Her compatriots had hastily moved
their families, seat of government, and portable goods to the
highest part of what is now Venice, the Rialto neighborhood,
where we find their descendents with lots of goods today.

"Where'd everybody go?" a puzzled Pepin asked the old lady
when he missed his welcome. He had, after all, been invited by
the Frank-loving doge to come shape things up, in disagreement
with that leader's departing constituency, who indicated their

---

*Everything having to do with Venetian history is a perhaps. The Venetophile is
advised to yield to popular belief, which is what has been done here.

displeasure by planting the ducal head on a pike at the beach.

A lesser heroine who had not been taken along on a lifesaving escape might have weighed the looming presence of Charlemagne's warrior son against the sudden absence of her neighbors and experienced no conflict. But the old lady remained a stalwart patriot.

Straight ahead, she said: Sempre dritto. What she knew and Pepin found out was that while the direction the Venetians had taken was indeed straight ahead, the route was not. Then, as now, the safe route was marked with wooden stakes, so that ships would not founder in shallow parts of the lagoon. The fleeing Venetians had pulled up the stakes as they sped ahead in their shallow-bottomed boats, and Pepin's thick ships got stuck. He was pelted not just with arrows but with loaves of bread (to show he couldn't starve them out); he gave up; Venice was saved.

Sempre dritto: Why use another set of directions when that one worked so well?

This legacy does little to save the bewildered tourist trying to wend his way as indicated. It is therefore fortunate that getting lost in Venice is a rewarding experience. Some things are closer than they would seem, some farther away, some are around unfathomable corners, and, quite possibly, the islands that comprise the city regroup themselves like a kaleidoscope when no one is looking. Being a seasoned Venetophile is no guarantee against failure to find your way, only an indication that you have learned not to mind.

Getting Around (Water)

Next to feet, the favored methods of public transportation are waterbuses and gondola ferries. Waterbuses are run on the honor system. Before boarding, you simply punch your own ticket. So it seems a touristic disgrace that spot checking is no longer enough regulation and that during high season, an official has to be posted at the most popular stops asking that all punched tickets be shown before boarding. Our dedication to assisting fellow tourists does not apply to those who are arrested on board, sputtering that they didn't know they needed tickets, as if they were accustomed to free public transportation at home. Many stops do not have ticket kiosks, so to avoid the embarrassment of having to buy on board—meaning the temptation not to do so—the Venetophile buys passes. The advanced Venetophile who has found partial employment or a claim to residence is entitled to get a photo identification card that is worth even more as a point of Venetophiliac pride than it is in reduced-price tickets, which is saying something.

Whenever possible, we use a traghetto to cross the Grand Canal, one of the handful of gondola ferries remaining from the centuries before the GC gained its present allotment of three bridges.* For a pittance, you get a ride in the old style, with two gondoliers instead of one and, as an added inducement, no accordion player. Most of the drill is obvious. You follow an "al traghetto" sign painted on a wall, wait in line until the boat approaches, stand to one side to let the passengers off, and get on (ladies steadying themselves, if necessary, by taking not the hand, but the bent forearm of the lead gondolier), paying either then or upon arrival, because in trustworthy Venice, good faith is not questioned.

The telltale, counterintuitive part is to walk down the middle of the craft as far as possible, and then turn around to face the sta-

---

*A fourth bridge linking the railway station and the car park is planned, and was even built. But when they took it down the GC to install it, it turned out to be too short. Knowing that Venetians were staying up all night to witness this historic installation, I asked one at what point the mismeasurement had been discovered. "When people started falling in the water," he said, deadpan.

tion you are leaving, rather than your destination. You must also steadfastly refrain from sitting down, although the thing wobbles, there are benches on either side and gondoliers who do not realize what a seasoned Venetophile you are may urge you to do so. Standing, with one knee slightly bent to absorb the movement, is simply the Venetian thing to do, and turning around is what the gondola traghetto does upon leaving its station, so that the passengers who reversed themselves are now smugly facing forward.

Sitting would be the sensible thing to do, as the canal, so glassy in old photographs, is constantly being churned up by motorized hot rods. Gondolas have the right of way over engine-powered transport, but the way is apt to be through someone else's wake. This provides the entertainment portion of the trip. You have a row of tightly packed standees, one of them is rocked backward or forward, and there goes the domino effect. If you weren't already intimate with anyone in Venice, this is a quick way of becoming acquainted.

It is a sign of failure as a Venetophile if a man in a striped shirt and straw hat (and in winter, perhaps a North Face jacket) asks "Gondola? Gondola?" as you cross a bridge. "Do I look as if I'm here for the first time and have nothing better to do than to take an overpriced, preprogrammed pleasure ride?" one thinks. "Isn't it enough that I have to listen to 'Volare' a hundred times a day as your flotillas pass my window?" (Not mentioned as a hazard of the high-rent district is that the mass tour gondola groups keep to a musical schedule, so that any given spot reverberates with the same song over and over. The occasional maverick rendition of "Hernando's Hideaway" becomes a relief.)

Yet we have the highest respect for the gondola industry, with its poignant persistence in the age of giant cruise ships. Gondolas are exquisitely crafted and the dignified and good-humored gondoliers speak movingly of fathers and grandfathers who rowed before them. When they strike, which is not infrequently, we cheer them on against the equally good-natured motorboat captains, although the latter are the ones we actually do hire to get our luggage to the airport.

One didn't used to have to choose between taking gondolas and feeling Venetian. In the heyday of the Republic, privately retained gondoliers were as common in large households as kitchen maids. In the nineteenth century, as fortunes declined, more and more gondolas were made available for hire by the hour, day, or week. American and English tourists, including Henry James and James Whistler, wrote lovingly of their experience in gondolas, and of their affection for their gondoliers, even if it happened to be perfectly respectable.

Even now, when there is a government-regulated rate for a fifty-minute ride along a set itinerary, most of it on the GC, it is possible to hire a gondola for a jaunt of your own fashioning. To say that you then witness Venice from an angle that was the expected view for most of the city's history is a truism, but what a stunning view it is. You glide effortlessly through a narrow, watery maze, propelled by the grace and adroitness of your gondolier, ancient buildings floating by on either side; you slide beneath bridges that you can reach up and touch; you become acquainted with a sizeable population of ancient stone faces who are unknown to the pedestrians passing above.

You also pick up some good gossip. As Venetians of many generations, gondoliers can draw on a sizeable inheritance of rumors to go with every house, a quality much prized by their earlier, private employers. But just when a gondolier is in danger of sounding like a mere aquatic tattler, he approaches a blind corner or an intersection and issues the primal cry "Oy-aa!" as a warning to other boatmen. All Venetians are enthralled with their past, but gondoliers continue to give it life.

Street Talk

It is all very well to resist using foreign terms when English ones will do, but some have no English equivalent. Venetian buildings have their peculiar structures and you can't admire anyone's house without knowing the terms.

Admire? You can't find anyone's house without knowing the terms. If your friends expect you to show up when they invite you for drinks on the altana and therefore give you real directions, these may involve going through a sestiere, past the scuola, down the fondamenta or the riva to the ramo, to the rio terà to the calle, ruga, rughetta, or salizzada and under the sottoportego. You begin to understand why "Sempre dritto" is a convenience.

To define a sestiere as one of Venice's six administrative districts is to miss its emotional hold. Beyond thinking of themselves as Venetians rather than Italians, locals identify themselves by their neighborhoods, perhaps not only the sestiere but also the parish. Each sestiere has a community center, some retain local archives, and the names of all six have to be memorized.

On one side of the GC are San Marco, where the main action is; Castello, which begins just beyond the Doge's Palace and goes on to contain a working-class area, the Arsenal, and the public gardens; and Cannaregio, which includes the whole northern part of the city from the railway station and the Ghetto to the canal in front of the church of Santi Giovanni e Paolo. On the other side are San Polo, with such major landmarks as the Frari church and the Rialto food market; Santa Croce, where the docks are; and Dorsoduro, which stretches from the Campo Santa Margherita to the Accademia art museum, the Salute church, and the Customs House. Jurisdictionally, Dorsoduro also includes the Giudecca, where the rich never used to live but

kept private retreats, and which has now supplemented its
Palladian churches and humble housing with ultra-luxury resort
hotels and increasing numbers of artist residents and movie star
absentee residents.

Although the term scuola is now used for school, a different
meaning survives from the days of the Republic: a lay confraternity, religious organization, neighborhood center, and charitable
institution likely to be chock-full of art. Before Napoleon did his
nasty work, there were six grand ones, of which San Rocco is the
only one that has remained in continuous use, and more than
four hundred smaller ones organized by professional or ethnic
affiliations or by devotional focus.

A fondamenta is a street along a waterway, beside the founda-
tions of buildings, and the largest of these are rivas. Caution is
advised around the slippery white marble that lines the edges of
the walkways along the canals. In the history of the Republic,
Istrian marble felled more Venetians than the Turks. A ramo is a
branch off a wide street; a rio terà is a street that used to be a
river before it was filled in, a salizzada is a long, paved street and
the rest are calles, callettos, rugas, and rughettas. The rare paluda
is a former swamp, as if the entire city were not.

A sottoportego is a passageway that goes under a building or
arcade, and is not to be confused with a portego, which is the
hallway and chief room that runs the entire length of an upper
floor inside one of those big houses we don't call palaces. The
altana is the rooftop patio.

All this is essential because nearly every house in Venice is
overstuffed with history, so real estate romance is rampant. You
will want to visit all who invite you, and if you stay in a particularly interesting house, you are bound to be popular. So no matter how warmhearted you are, you may find yourself prioritizing
invitations in terms of addresses.

Except there aren't any. Sensible addresses, that is. The streets

In the Republic's Tradition of Liberty,
Venetian Street Signs Offer a Choice
of Names and Directions.

and bridges and squares have names, sometimes a choice of them. If there is a solitary "o" in the middle of the sign—"Calle del Prete Zoto o Cortugola," "Ponte de l'Arsenal o del Paradiso," "Campo Bandiera e Moro o de la Bragora," "Campiello Giovanni Andrea della Croce o de la Malvasia"—it's your choice.

The names reflect the historic residents: old families (our corner is Barbarigo o Duodo), cultural heroes (Sanudo, from whose diaries much of Venetian history is gleaned, has an alley, while the largely forgotten nineteenth-century playwright Giacinto

Gallina has a wide street), ethnic groups (not only Slavs, Greeks, and Albanians but those strangers from the Venetian island of Burano), skilled laborers (the chic shopping street, the Frezzeria, is named for the arrowmakers, and other street names indicate where you can no longer buy hemp, swords, barrels, mirrors, soap, spindles, and shoe buckles whose gold and silver content was strictly regulated by the state), and grocery specialists (in such basics as fish, fruit, oil, salt, and wine).

Some names are actually helpful. The Calle Lunga San Barnaba is a long street leading to the church of San Barnaba, and the Salizzada San Lio leads to the church of San Lio. A newly rechristened alley is called the Calle of the Love of Friends, but we do not yet know what that will lead to.

In any case, the street name does not appear in the address of a house, which bears only a number with the name of its sestiere. Other than postmen, Venetians don't know, either, how any of this relates to finding a specific place. They use a gazetteer and word of mouth via mobile telephone.

However, the big houses have their own names. They are called after the families who built them, or one or more of the families who once lived there, or whoever lives there now, or an architectural feature of the house or, not uncommonly, any or all of these, with no discernable underlying principle about which one is used. It is often the name of the old Venetian family who built the house—or lived there long enough that people suppose so—and multiple houses bear the names of such doge-bearing families as Mocenigo, Barbarigo, Donà, Foscari, Loredan, Michiel, Giustinian, Dolfin, Grimani, Morosini, Moro, Dandolo, Venier, Gritti, and Pisani. Many have living descendents, but because of economic upheavals, inheritance complications, or restlessness they tend not to be living in those houses.

But if the house has an odd feature, forget the people. What is actually Ca' Corner-Contarini dei Cavalli has two such distinguished family names, Corner and Contarini, but it is the horses in their coats of arms by which the house is known: Ca' Cavalli. And when the Contarini flashily decorated another house, now an art museum, it became forever known as the Ca' d'Oro, for the long-since-worn-off golden exterior.

Even high drama doesn't trump that. Shakespeare is supposed to have mistaken the Venetian family of Moro for Moors when he wrote *Othello,* and anyone acquainted with Venice can point out Ca' Moro-Lin as well as the site of the Moro house in the Campo dei Carmini and the lacy little Desdemona's House, which is unaccountably farther up the Grand Canal and was built after Mrs. Moro's demise. All the same, Ca' Moro-Lin has extra-long rows of windows, so it is known as the House of the Thirteen Windows, and Desdemona's House is called locally Ca' Contarini-Fasan— Fasan not being a family but the pheasants that the Contarini family loved to shoot. (It is probably just as well. There were Moors in Venice, as well as Moros, and "The Moor of Venice," by Giambattista Giraldi, aka Cinthio, the story of a jealous Moor who murdered his wife, Disdemona, was published in Venice in 1566 in a collection that also contains the plot of *Measure for Measure*.)

A big enough celebrity did not need a house to get his or her name perpetuated on the property. The Ca' del Duca refers to Francesco Sforza, Duke of Milan, even though only a corner of the foundation was done before the government seized his property. His claim as a big shot remained unchallenged by the mere fact that Titian later had a studio on the grounds. The Ca' Corner della Regina is named for the Venetian superstar, Catherine Cornaro, erstwhile Queen of Cyprus and thus, in a determinedly republican state, the Grace Kelly of her day (see chapter three), although the house in which she was born was torn down to make way for it nearly three centuries afterward.

This is not a game at which Venetophiles have a chance. Buying a grand house will not prevent people from calling it after

Venetian tenants or features. Peggy Guggenheim's place was owned before her by another eccentric Venetophile, Luisa Casati, a Milanese aristocrat who did everything possible to attract attention, including taking near-naked walks through the piazza with her pet cheetahs. When the not-inconspicuous Miss Guggenheim left her house to a museum, it acquired her name on the facade in letters larger than the name of the fifteenth-century Venetian statesman, Giovanni Dario, on Ca' Dario, up the canal a piece. Yet the house, as opposed to the collection, is neither Ca' Casati nor Ca' Guggenheim. It is known as Ca' Venier dei Leoni because it was commissioned by the Venier family and one of its descendents kept lions in the garden (as did Marchesa Casati), or as Ca' Nonfinito, because only the first story of the house was built before the Veniers either ran out of money or succumbed to complaints from across the canal that the completed house would have blocked their view. And San Gregorio Abbey, next door to the Salute, is still the Abbey, although it really should be Ca' Cary: Some time after the monks left, Barbara Hutton fitted it up with closets to die for and gave it to Cary Grant as a wedding present.

Dress

Dress in Venice is not so much understated as under-Italianized. Edgy designs dominate the shop windows, and international fashion shoots can be as peskily underfoot as pigeons, but unleashed chic is out of place in Venice. The hussy look, with open-air belly buttons or other such privates made public is equally culpable whether on foreigners who don't know any better or Milanese who know more than anyone should. Elegance itself is suspect, as one wouldn't want to be taken for a Roman. Venetians render SPQR, the initials inscribed all over Rome, not as Senatus Populus que Romanus (the senate and people of Rome), but as Sono Porchi, Questi Romani (they're pigs, these Romans).

Remarkable clothes may be seen on the streets, but you can be sure they were packed abroad in anticipation of a landmark event. It is the wedding trip of a couple with a startling age difference. Or someone has rented a Grand Canal palace (the privilege of referring to it as a palace being implicitly included in the rental) to give a subscription party or an advanced-years birthday bash. Or an entire segment of foreign society has arrived to attend an international exhibition, art or cinema, and is wearing its peculiar native dress.

Venetians dress for outdoor urban life: sweaters, suits, raincoats, boxy furs for winter even on the lady who sells postcards near the Accademia Galleries and on the shrewdest old shoppers at the Rialto market. Most importantly, it means walking shoes and waterproof boots. A self-respecting Venetian shoe designer of international repute does not recognize the term "fashion boot"; footgear, no matter how beautiful and expensive, is supposed to remember its function.

Hats are taken just as seriously in a town of heavy sun, rain, wind, and dignity. The ratio of both ladies' and gentlemen's hat shops (as opposed to street stands selling funny hats) to population is surely greater than that of any American city. These are stocked with traditional styles—including the tradition of charmingly outrageous ladies' hats—and traditional knowledge about materials, suitability, and fit. You cannot expect to walk out with a choice unapproved by the milliner, or even with an approved choice if it is not worn at the approved angle. The wise customer does not attempt to argue with someone who knows more about his or her head than its owner.

Hat etiquette is strict. Some years ago, a group of mildly behaved American tourists was astounded to be set upon by angry Venetian youths in the basilica itself. The offense was showing disrespect for the church: The American men were wearing baseball caps.

As in all working cities that dislike being mistaken for resorts, athletic gear worn as streetwear meets with civic disapproval. Running shoes may be adult walk-to-work shoes elsewhere, but in Venice, where walking is neither a virtue nor a sport but the normal transportation system, people don't need to change shoes, because they wear sensible shoes or boots all the time. Here walking has been elevated into social theory. Venetians will tell you that the smoothness of society is related to the inevitability of encountering one another on the streets over and over again, rendering the popular American hit-and-run altercation impractical. Their rich are not whisked off in big cars, they point out (as if only our rich did that), but must take to the streets like everyone else. They claim it has a democratizing effect.

So then who would that be on the balcony of a private house on the Grand Canal, looking so eighteenth century in a tapestry-and-lace robe or so nineteenth century in a ruffled white tea gown, and lost in abstract poetic thought? Milly? Or Isabella Stewart Gardner, before she leaps radiantly back to her salon full of guests, as caught in her portrait by Anders Zorn?

No such luck. It is only one of their modern successors, mentioning no names, a veteran Venetophile seeking to gratify the beginners' class of Venetophiles in the canal traffic. To break the pose when summoned by stares and pointed fingers from a waterbus or gondola is to inspire delighted laughs and waves. (No fair waving first or otherwise trying to attract attention.) This is a most pleasant way to start the day. Royalty does not let on what an easy job it is to bestow smiles and waves, and how gratifying to see the happy effect this produces on upturned faces.

Glass slippers are out of the question, however. Palace floors are cold, as fairy-tale heroines presumably find out when the princes who carry them off finally set them down. Beneath those robes, we wear woolen booties, knitted in fetching colors by the group's den mother.

Such throwback shenanigans should be strictly confined to the privacy of one's balcony and whoever happens to be going up or down the city's main thoroughfare at the time. To dress for the real Venice is to acquire accessories that are more defining than any lapses into fancy-dress, and have rescuing powers more relevant than any prince might offer.

These are rubber boots, green for men and black for women, and snap-top canvas grocery shopping bags on wheels, in bright colors. Besides being badges of belonging, they each rescue their owners from the cruelty of having to make do with plastic bags. Those without Wellingtons must slosh through high water by tying plastic bags over their shoes, not an attractive look or gait. Without a wheeled shopping bag, it is necessary to carry heavy loads of food and drink in hand-cutting plastic bags, for which, as an added affront, the supermarkets charge extra.

Food and Drink

Eating and drinking present another opportunity to demon-strate Venetian loyalty. Venice has its chic restaurants, or so passers-through say, but specialties of the native cuisine are liver, sour sardines, and rice with peas. This may not sound like much to make a fuss over, but during Carnival one year, a jolly bunch of sodden Venetians roamed about singing, with cheerleading enthusiasm, "Risi bisi! Risi bisi!" in honor of the rice and peas dish. If it's good enough to excite them to song, it's good enough for us Venetophiles.

Other articles of faith are that the Veneto's prosecco is not just cheaper than champagne but better, and that a sgropino is good for the digestion in spite of the drink's ingredients (classically, vodka, prosecco, and lemon sherbet) and its name (which invokes, if not inspires, the unclogging of drains). We are not so far gone in reverse-snobbery as to pass up Harry's world-famous Bellinis, made with fresh white peach juice and prosecco, provided someone else is buying.

Milly Theale ordered a palace with a cook, and the hotel tourists order at restaurants, but the Venetophile gets food where Venetians have gotten it since the fourteenth century: at the open-air market by the Rialto bridge. So much for disdaining parts of town "where all the tourists go." There are other places to shop—open stands in squares, parked vegetable boats, a handful of so-called supermarkets in town, and stores on the mainland where you can buy in bulk—but these are supplementary. Serious shoppers get up early and go to Rialto.

However, foreign foodies may have to relearn their shopping techniques. In Venice, you don't squeeze the produce, and you don't stock up on staples. Feeling up the fruit will anger the greengrocer to the extent that the most profuse apology will not mollify him. That would be a disaster, as you want to visit him every day, along with the butcher, the cheesemonger, the pasta maker, and the fishmonger, not only to pick up fresh food, but to pick up fresh gossip.

Furthermore, you need their help. Many of the names of items are not Italian, but Venetian. Venice is on the metric system (no need to feel bad about having to convert weight to ounces and pounds, because the grocer will still be struggling, after all these years, to convert euros into lire), but fresh pasta, cheese, prosciutto, and other processed meats are sold in etti, an etto being one tenth of a kilo, roughly a quarter of a pound.

Once you are friends—and to any except the most morose of grocers, that only requires going to him several days in a row—you can ask the cheesemonger for a taste and request the butcher to throw in some rosemary and parsley if he has not automatically done so. The latter will cut up your chicken or rabbits for you and offer to give you the head and the claws or paws. The butcher who specializes in donkey and horse meat does not offer head or hooves, but he will give you a free taste of his smoked and shredded delicacy. The fishmonger will clean (but not fillet) your catch as you wish, and ask you if you want the ink gland from your cuttlefish, in which case he will gift-wrap it in a tiny piece of scrap paper.

Any greengrocer will pick out for you the fruits that are ready to be eaten that very day, but your special friend will alert you to which of the five varieties of pears is at the height of its season and which are a bit off. Seasons count. From January to October you can hardly find a fresh mushroom, certainly not one with any taste, but in November every stall will be overflowing with an astounding array. September and October are persimmon season, and the Venetians like them ripe enough to eat with a spoon. Your friend will pack them in a carton, like eggs, but even then a jostled trip home will result in a bag full of mush.

The most charming point of pride in a town where even the drinking water has to be imported is the sign "nostramo" on some produce. "It's ours." Homegrown. It didn't sprout up between the stones of a campo, but it was at least grown on one of Venice's auxiliary islands.

Finally, as a touching gesture of friendship, one of your suppliers might confide with a shrug of the shoulders that indeed, his price is excessive. But, he adds philosophically, there is a big demand and it will sell all the same.

The respectability of regular housekeeping does not preclude promiscuous grazing elsewhere; when has it ever?

For that there are wine bars—bacari—everywhere. Venetians, and therefore Venetophiles, will order an ombra, named for the shade sought by outdoor workmen, or a spritz, which is not our wine and soda but herbal bitters (Select) with prosecco and a splash of seltzer. Hot chocolate and coffee are usually available in bars, although people who imagine Italy as one big Starbucks will find that when they order a latte, they get a glass of milk, possibly hot milk. (Coffee with milk is "caffè latte.") But no one will be surprised if you fortify yourself at breakfast with a "correction," such as a shot of grappa in the coffee and a thick smearing of chocolate goo on your freshly baked brioche.

Wine bars offer succulent, overstuffed half-sandwiches with the crusts fastidiously cut off, and a variety of hot and cold snacks called cicheti, but they are out on display, so one needn't learn their names. Much better to learn the name of the bartender, who will then greet you as a regular on the third visit and begin to prepare your customary order before you give it.

If someone has a small appetite at mealtimes in our big hall, we know where he's been. We also know who has been shopping, because of a boy-girl deal that says that every time she stops at a shop, the next stop is at a wine bar.

Advanced Accessorizing

We do all this, we drink all that, but the palace-mates felt it wasn't enough. If we really wanted to fit in, one of them suggested, we should all go out and buy yappy little dogs.

Tufted in more-or-less-white fur and brimming with attitude, these creatures are a Venetian tradition, adept at insinuating themselves into eighteenth-century scene paintings. Sometimes they are pictured racing crazily among the bewigged and cloaked ladies and gentlemen; all too often, I am sorry to report, they are lifting or squatting.

Perhaps the antique Venetians tired of such antics and decided to breed dogs for no legs. At any rate, the modern Venetian dog is most often seen nestling in his owner's arms, casting superior looks at pedestrians, although there is plenty of evidence that he still hits the streets when necessary. There is also a rougher, sea-going dog population whose job it is to pose on the prows of their owners' boats in the attentive hunting dog position. But this requires a boat.

A pet cat will no longer do. Once haughty and admired for their family resemblance to Saint Mark in his leonine manifestation, cats have fallen seriously out of Venetian favor.

Until a few years ago, feral cats were everywhere. When you looked up, you saw them crossing the rooftops to sun themselves on the terra-cotta tiles. Certain nooks and run-down gardens seemed to be carpeted with cats. You would have thought them safe. It seemed reasonable that a watery town would prefer to put up with cats, rather than rats. And it was unthinkable that a relation of Saint Mark's, even a homeless one, would be run out of Venice.

Suddenly they were gone. Amid dark murmurings, the official word came that they had been spayed and relocated to the

The Ultimate Venetian Accessory (and Artists' Model).

lagoon island of San Clemente. When displaced by a new luxury hotel, the cat sanctuary was said to have moved to the Lido, which had undergone a more gentle change in fashion, down from its heyday of beach pavilions, dressy luncheons, and Thomas Mann. There is also supposed to be a refuge in town for the few feral cats who remain, but the touristic pastime of photographing cats posing near lion statues of comparable size is over. Only the occasional fat house-cat or shop-cat is still glimpsed outdoors, staying close to home in case it is challenged.

The pigeon population would also seem to have had special protection because of the popularity it has with tourists, for whom feeding and dodging pigeons in Saint Mark's Square is a tradition whose charm eludes the locals. No self-respecting Venetian beyond toddler age would give a pigeon the time of day, much less a handful of piazza corn, which would only encourage it to use its benefactor's head as a runway. It is believed that pigeons were purposely imported by the Austrian occupation forces, although presumably for reasons of animation, rather than annoyance. In any case, there is nary a one in the piazza scenes of Canaletto and other view painters.

We Venetophiles should empathize with these creatures, as there is a striking similarity in the way the city speaks of the problems caused by cats, pigeons, and tourists. Yes, they acknowledge, we used to think they were useful, but now there are too many of them and they make too much of a mess. The suggestions for pigeon control are different from those suggested for tourists, as they include putting poisons or contraceptives in the food, yet the results have been no more successful. The street birds' behavior may have tainted the reputations of respectable birds, as there appears to have been a decline in the once-large number of canary cages put out in the morning to get the sun.

So fluffy, feckless dogs it is for the Venetians. In our group house, however, in the absence of a plan for what to do with them after our holidays were up (rent them to other tourists?), this idea had to be abandoned.

We hit upon a simple substitution. Italians were years ahead of Americans in adopting mobile telephones and even now use them openly with more impunity than in the land of cell-phone rage. This enthusiasm may have something to do with the wayward nature of the Italian land telephone system; now they can actually reach one another. So some years ago, in a burst of what turned out to be premature hilarity, we ran out to toy stores and bought ourselves realistic looking toy cell phones that screamed "Pronto!" and other useful Italian phrases ("Who's calling?" "Come get me right away!") at the push of a button.

For two or three years, we were able to amuse ourselves by making these telephones ring and passing them to one another at odd moments with the urgent declaration, "It's for you." Then, as we all acquired American cell phones at home, it got less funny.

Finally the day came when the joke died. We admitted that life in Venice, which meant being out and about all the time, required mobile telephones if we were to warn others of being late for meals and appointments, to announce having come upon unexpected treasures, and to request directions of our hosts while halfway there. Mine is tiny and light enough to be worn around the neck like a locket, and works on a card, which means there is no charge for a plan so it doesn't run up a bill between trips. Sadly, I foresee the day when everyone will have international telephones and I will no longer think it worth bragging about as an emblem of Venetophilia.

Recreation

The chief Venetophiliac recreation is walking around calling out "Oh, look!" to one another. Almost anything qualifies for this relentless expression of childish wonder: a weather-beaten carving of a head over a doorway, a fireboat flashing its warnings, sunlight striking the water, children playing campo soccer, mythological figures on a door knocker, a rowing crew at practice, the trash boat, a corner votive shrine, a swordfish for sale complete with sword, a dark painting one had previously missed in the side altar of a church, a single shoe floating in the canal.*

Next is the delight of doing the boring tasks one does at home. Crossing the street, but pausing at the top of a bridge for the view. Grocery shopping, when it involves vying for the day's aquatic roadkill with the old ladies and restaurateurs who get to the Rialto early. Taking something to be repaired, and having its problem explained and solved instead of receiving the explanation that it isn't worth fixing.

It is not exactly Venetian to make a fuss over crossing the street or discovering that the luggage repairman repairs luggage. Carnival no longer lasts the six months it did during the eighteenth century, and the various regattas and festivals (see chapter eight) are only momentary distractions. So Venetians have to share the daily amusements of the rest of the world—following the soccer games, exclaiming over real estate prices, and asking people on the street to sign petitions. But once they had more original games.

Ever on the lookout for authentic Venetian whoopee, we studied the rules and the Gabriele Bella paintings of these activities, where everyone seemed to be having a jolly time. Wouldn't you know, though, that it turned out that none of these would be feasible for us, as they had long since become illegal or unethical.

Such as pushing one another off bridges, a popular team sport and tourist attraction in the sixteenth and seventeenth centuries. Two rival factions, the Nicolotti (in the black hats), who occupied the half of Venice nearest the mainland and were mostly fishermen, and the Castellani (in the red hats), who occupied the parts toward the lagoon and mostly worked at the Arsenal,

---

*"Oh, look!" is not to be confused with the equally common "Look out!" which signifies danger from dogs below or pigeons above.

Traditional Venetian Whoopee: Fun on Bridges (Outlawed in 1705).

would amass in groups on opposing sides of a small bridge and go at one another with bamboo staffs until weapons were outlawed and fists were substituted. As the bridges at that time lacked parapets, people kept tumbling over, and someone always put a damper on the fun by getting bludgeoned to death. The state vacillated between trying to control these events and, in 1574, proudly featuring a bridge battle as part of its VIP treatment for a visiting dignitary, Henry III of Poland, who was taking a memorable detour on his way to becoming King of France. This fight was not a success, as the king's reaction was to ask them to please stop that, right now.* Bridge fights were banned altogether on Saint Girolamo's Day in 1705, when the two fac-

---

*The Venetian poet-courtesan Veronica Franco was more of his idea of fun.

tions were going at it so intently that nobody wanted to leave to put out the fire at Saint Girolamo's convent church, which was thus destroyed from neglect on its very own saint's day.

After that, the Nicolotti and the Castellani instituted talent competitions called The Strength of Hercules. This took the form of using poles, shoulders, and heads to create human pyramids of half a dozen or more wobbly layers, with the person at the top making triumphant gestures. These competitions, too, led to riots and had to be put under official control.

Then there was a category that might be called Fun With Animals, although nowadays it would be pointed out that this was not Fun For Animals. Chasing bulls through the city, for example, or pitting dogs against tethered bulls or bears. This was outlawed in 1802, because the stands collapsed under the eager spectators. Here is how to play some other Venetian animal games:

1. Shave head. Fasten white, fully clawed cat to wall. Test whether one can batter cat to death with head before it claws one's scalp to shreds.
2. Hang ducks at top of greased pole. Shimmy up pole to capture ducks.
3. String up live goose by the feet. Suspend from window near bridge. Leap off bridge swatting away madly with the object of grabbing goose.
4. Place eel in tub of blackened water. Without using hands, dip head into water and try to grasp eel in teeth.
5. Race around Campo San Zaccaria yowling and pretending to be a lion for the purpose of ensuring that your bride will be faithful (if, indeed, she still wants to marry you).

Even the bloodless amusements have been shut down. The Procession of the Courtesans, in which Venice's human tourist

The Fun Never Stops (note cat bashing at left and goose grabbing at right,
two traditional Venetian pastimes, now outlawed).

attractions went for open-air gondola rides while the rest of the
population hung over the bridges palpitating, have long since
ceased. Although the name of the Bridge of the Tette is retained
(it is where the lower end of the trade displayed their—well, their
tette), Venice lacks common prostitution. Even nuns have turned
respectable. Once convents were a center of lively activity, with
the young noblewomen, who had been coerced into the vocation
to save their families from paying dowries, making the best of it
by putting on plays and entertaining visitors with even jollier
socializing. But that was before church killjoys discovered what a
good time they were having.

Venice does abound in musical offerings. It was always a center of music, with little opera houses everywhere and composers
on frantic deadlines churning out pieces still beloved by audi-

ences today. In a brilliant pairing of supply with demand, Venice provided its orphans, of which the romantic city had more than its share, with music lessons. Vivaldi, the Red Priest (for his hair, not his politics), trained such successful All-Girl Orchestras at the church of the Pietà that a warning to rich and ambitious parents not to abandon their daughters at the Pietà for free music lessons is chiseled into the side of the building.

Vivaldi's posthumous reputation was in eclipse in the twentieth century until he was rescued by a Venetophile. Olga Rudge, the violinist and musicologist who lived in Venice with Ezra Pound, is credited with starting the Vivaldi revival in the 1930s, turning up and publishing lost works, giving Vivaldi concerts, and founding the Venetian Vivaldi Society. We have long since ceased to thank her. As we explain to newcomers, the good news is that there is a choice of small concerts in Venice every night. The bad news is that they all play Vivaldi.

"But I like Vivaldi," newcomers are wont to declare. When they've been treated to him for four or five concerts in a row, and have been several times importuned on the street by teenagers in ill-pressed eighteenth-century costumes to come to a concert at "Vivaldi's church" (he was dead when the present one was rebuilt on the site) by touring high school orchestras, they reconsider. So we check the posters and listings, and offer a prize to anyone who can find a concert that doesn't feature Vivaldi or, failing that, one that at least isn't playing the *Four Seasons*. Once it was "The Worst Works of Giuseppe Verdi," and it lived up to the name.

This aside, finding a Vivaldi-free concert is nigh on impossible, so we have been on the lookout for other evening entertainment. In an exhibition at the Querini-Stampalia museum some years ago, I spotted an eighteenth-century Venetian painting of a genteel indoor crowd wielding chairs onto one another's heads.* One night, when we were about to break down and attend a concert,

---

*If anyone knows the rules of this sport, I would appreciate hearing them.

knowing that it would be weeks before the *Four Seasons* vacated our heads, one of the housemates pleaded, "Can't we just stay home and hit one another over the head with the chairs?"

Adopted Attitudes

As we became acclimated, we found our attitudes changing. It no longer bothers us when candles lean out of their candlesticks in random directions, as they do even when preening for photographs in oversized coffee-table books. Perhaps in homage to Venetian bell towers, there isn't a strictly vertical candle in all of Venice.

Street signs to San Marco or the Rialto or the railway station that feature twin arrows pointing in opposite directions no longer seem unreasonable. Eventually, you could get there either way, and how is the sign painter to know which route you would prefer?

We accept as a matter of course that the church of Saint Simeone Piccolo is about double the size of the church of Saint Simeone Grande, that your motorized water taxi can get caught in a speed trap on the Grand Canal for going five kilometers an hour, and that talk of building a subway system is serious, which is not the same thing as saying that anything will come of it.

Nothing cushions the shock when landmarks are destroyed, but the Venetian custom is quickly to point out whom a fire might benefit. After the Fenice opera house fire in 1996, those who had been doing reconstruction work on it no longer had to offer excuses for their excessive delays. After the 2003 fire at the monstrous nineteenth-century factory on the Giudecca, the ungracefully named Mulino-Stucky, those who had been turning it into a hotel had fewer worries about preserving its historical integrity while meeting the expectations of modern guests.

Against all predictions, we lived to see the full re-functioning of the Fenice, at about the time that the schoolchildren who had donated their allowances to the cause had reached adulthood. What is more, the acoustics are nowhere near as bad as was forecast. So we subscribe to Venetian optimism and determination about reconstruction.

The slogan "Com'era, dov'era," to replace what was lost exactly "as it was, and where it was," was first pronounced after the bell tower in the piazza collapsed in 1902. The four-hundred-year-old landmark had developed a huge crack, and the city's architects and engineers had been asked to evaluate the damage.

"Oh, don't worry about it," they advised. That was in the spring. On July 11, they were called back because the fissure had widened noticeably. "Don't worry about it," they said. On July 12, it was shedding brick into the piazza from an advancing gap, and it occurred to the team that there could be a problem. This being a Saturday, however, they assured everyone that it needn't interfere with anyone's weekend plans, but could wait until Monday.

Well, they were right. It wasn't until 9:47 A.M. on that Monday that the tower collapsed, destroying Sansovino's Loggetta at its base but thoughtfully nicking only a corner of the adjacent library, also by Sansovino. No one was injured by the collapse because a policeman with a layman's view of engineering had decided that since the crack now rent the entire building from top to bottom, it might be a good idea to clear the piazza. When the custodian's wife had to leave, she was in the act of ironing six shirts owned by Mr. Jesurum, whose luxury linens shops were, from the nineteenth century, the place to buy your daughter's trousseau if she was marrying a reigning prince. In the spirit of com'era, dov'era, six gentlemen each wore one of the undamaged (but newly washed and ironed) shirts to the opening ceremonies for the rebuilt tower a decade later.

A dramatic photograph exists of the tower in mid-collapse, but it is a fake, because the film of the time was not fast enough to catch this. When the considerable amount of dust was cleared, some people murmured that the appearance of the piazza had suddenly improved. But the bell tower was reproduced anyway, right down to the Sansovino guardhouse at its base.

Long before this sequence of events, other replacements had been popping up all over town, the most conspicuous of which were all but one of the mosaic lunettes on the front of Saint Mark's basilica and the capitals on the columns of the Doge's Palace. The statues of Saints Mark and Theodore atop the columns in the piazza, and the four horses atop the basilica, are also in their second incarnations. Some restorations were better done than others, but even those most reviled when they were fresh, such as the work on the Turkish Warehouse (now a pokey natural history museum), which nearly gave Mr. Ruskin apoplexy, no longer stand out as impostors.

We have developed a fierce antipathy toward Napoleon, which is bewildering to innocent history buffs, who tend to admire his nerve and dash. To Venetophiles, as to Venetians, Napoleon's crimes are forever fresh. He not only brought an end to the Republic a thousand years into its existence, but he was strangely unenchanted by his new possession and left Venice after spending only nine days there and countenancing massive destruction and plunder. He had the barbarian nerve to steal, as war loot, the very treasures that Venetians had stolen from Constantinople as war loot. He showed no respect for Venetian religious institutions with their proud history of showing no respect for church authority.

He blackened Venice's international reputation as we have never succeeded in blackening his. To justify liberating a republic whose citizens had shown no interest in this service, he painted a

A Badly Behaved Tourist.

picture of Venice as a merciless police state. And he uttered one of the strangest war cries in history: "I don't want any more Inquisition, I don't want any more Senate, I will be an Attila to the Venetian state." Mind you, the Venetian state was founded by people whom Attila had expressly failed to conquer, even if it was only because they ran away and hid.

In a spectacularly misguided form of Venetophilia, the French Committee for the Safeguarding of Venice and a Venetian bank (my bank, I am sorry to say) bought and brought back to Venice an eight-foot statue of Napoleon that had stood, mockingly, in front of the Doge's Palace, where no doge's statue (just a couple of reliefs) had defied the ban on personality cults. Toga-draped, with arm outstretched to imitate Marcus Aurelius's statue in Rome, the pose suggests nothing so much as "Heil, Hitler." The statue had been violently ejected the minute Napoleon's defeat had made it safe to do so.

Never mind that Venetians had commissioned it originally, in a spirit of misguided optimism before Napoleon began ransacking the place and knocking winged lions from their perches. The reaction to the proposed restoration of the statue in 2003 prompted a trial at which Napoleon was convicted (in absentia) of raping, sacking, and pillaging the city. The offending statue is in isolation in a corner of the Correr Museum, which occupies the Napoleonic palace for which Napoleon leveled a Sansovino church.

We don't like Austrians much better, not meaning contemporary fellow tourists but those of the era of muttonchop whiskers and gaudy uniforms. During the noble revolt of 1848–49, when the Venetians momentarily took back their city, the occupier dropped a bomb from a hot-air balloon on the Church of the Scalzi and destroyed its Tiepolo ceiling, the vandals.* We still disdain the Quadri Caffè in Saint Mark's Square, because it was the Austrian officers' hangout, while we favor the venerable Florian Caffè opposite, because it was patronized by loyal Venetians and famous Venetophiles. But since inflated prices and inflated bands keep us from going to either one, this prejudice inflicts no commercial damage.

Most of all, we hate moto ondoso. I found this out at a meeting of the Private Committees for the Safeguarding of Venice, the

---

*All right, Venetians destroyed the roof and much else of the Parthenon in 1687, but how were we to know that the Turks were using it as a powder magazine?

international consortium of restoration societies that now serves as Venetophile Mission Control. A motion was made to condemn moto ondoso, and feelings raged with such heat that I was unable to tug a sleeve and ask anyone what we were so upset about. The cadre of UNESCO translators murmuring into our earphones had offered no English rendering. The vote was heading for unanimity, so if everyone else was against it, I was, too.

Later, I asked a Venetian friend what I had so roundly condemned. I knew that we deplored the motorboats, but that would be motoscafi. So what was moto ondoso?

"Waves," he said.

Oh, waves. Like King Canute, I had condemned the waves.

With about the same effect. Along with condemning motor-generated waves, we had voted to condemn the transformation of houses on the Grand Canal into hotels. Several more have opened since the vote was taken.

Tiresome Remarks

A hazard of loving Venice is that poetic observations keep popping into one's head. These are not harmless oh-how-lovely thoughts, but the sort that suggest philosophic speculation about life and death, truth and duplicity, illusion and reality.

Uttering them should be resisted at any cost. Striking, fanciful, and original as they seem to the person who has them, they have been popping into visitors' heads for centuries, and some of these were heads of people who wrote their thoughts down in books that are still being read.

Take the notion that those narrow black gondolas look like so many hearses or coffins, perhaps with the additional touch that each gondolier, with his aloof posture, is like Charon, who, for two bright coins, such as the euro change collected for the

traghetto ferry, is rowing the dead on the River Styx. Among the
many who published the coffin comparison were Goethe,
Chateaubriand, Mme. de Stael, Théophile Gautier, Byron,
Shelley, James Fenimore Cooper, Twain, Wagner, Benjamin
Britten, and Mann. After visiting Venice, Michelangelo included
a suspiciously gondola-like boat ferrying the dead in his *Last
Judgment* in Rome. Henry James, who likened a gondola ride to
being taken to one's doom (when actually, he noted fastidiously,
one was only being taken to tea), also entertained the thought
that riding in a gondola was like being rocked in one's cradle, the
gondolier having "a little the look of an absent-minded nursery-
maid pushing her small charges in a perambulator."

Nor should the piazza be compared to a drawing room,
although it is all right to say "Venice is a salon" when you repeatedly run into friends on the street, as everyone does.

Other notions to be suppressed:

- That all of Venice is like a stage set (or, for the musically
  inclined, an opera set), and we are just actors acting parts, so
  who is to say what is real, because we may act different parts
  tomorrow?
- That there are actually two Venices, the one of stone and the
  one formed by its reflection in the water, and who is to say
  which one is really the illusion?
- That it is no accident that Venice was world famous for its
  mirrors, and guarded the secret of making them so severely
  as to have ghastly punishment in store for any mirror-maker
  who revealed them. Water had given them the disposition to
  view life in terms of reflections, and who is to say, etc.?
- That it is no accident that Venice is world famous for its
  masks, which remind us that we all wear masks throughout
  our lives, and who is to say which visage is the real one, and

whether the masks grow to reflect us or we grow to become like our masks?*

We have also found it convenient to translate the "pax tibi" part of what is written in the lion's open book (Pax Tibi Marce Evangelista Meus . . .) as, "Oh, chill out."

There are two other conversations about Venice that it is best not to have, although they are difficult to avoid. Revealing oneself as a Venetophile to outsiders inevitably brings them on.

The first questions they ask are, "Isn't Venice unbearably crowded? Isn't it a tourist trap?"

It is the questions that are traps, into which Venetophiles commonly fall, first by accepting the odd notion that they themselves are something other than tourists, and then by declaring that their part of town isn't crowded because it is the real Venice. The true answers are Yes, Venice is full of other tourists and it has no secrets left, if it ever had them, and No, it is not unbearable. The most crowded places are the piazza, the Rialto bridge area, and the shopping street that connects them, the Merceria. There are plenty of less-crowded squares, museums, and shops, and, as in New York City, people tend to favor their particular neighborhoods, where the pace is slower and faces are familiar. Still, to eschew the main parts of town would be to miss the big-time monuments, exhibits, and events. At the Rialto, the souvenir stands are crowded, but after the early shopping hours the food markets just beyond them are not; in the piazza, there may be lines to get into the Doge's Palace,

*If you must have an all-purpose remark, here is one from an Italian phrase-a-day calendar that is practically guaranteed to improve your social life, whatever it is that you wish that to be: "La vedrei bene in questi pantaloni di cuoio" (You'd look great in these leather pants).

but not to get into the Correr Museum, with its exceptional collection of artifacts from Venetian history.

The second question is, "Isn't Venice sinking?"

This is an "Is Broadway dying?" sort of question, to which we have taken to snapping, "No, Venice isn't sinking. The water is rising."

As with Broadway, the real answer is, Well, it is still around, but yes, there are serious problems. Venice has in fact been sinking since its inception, and the recent raising of the pavement of the Molo, the canal edge of the piazzetta, is far from the first such remedy, as one can judge from the truncated look of the columns at the Doge's Palace. What is worrisome is that while the increased rate at which Venice had been sinking has now been slowed by banning groundwater extraction, the rate at which water is rising worldwide has increased.

The result is that flooding is much more frequent than it used to be. (And if that isn't enough trouble, there is now also an occasional problem of low water, when the gondolas stick to the bottom of the canals. But no one asks about that.) When the moon is full or new, the sirocco is blowing, and it is starting to rain, we listen for the warning siren, pull on our boots, and alternately wade on the ground and teeter on the planks. Shopkeepers get busy pushing door-sized floodgates against their ground-level entrances except at the former Hermès shop on the piazza, where, it was believed, someone could push a button that made the furniture rise to the ceiling. (I rushed to see on a flooded day, but a metal covering that had been lowered over the store front blocked the view.) Friends have reported finding fish swimming in their shops.

Within Venice, the topic is a hot one on which everyone has a violent opinion. It's the fault of industry in the outlying cities or of global warming or of the taxis and private speedboats or of tampering with the natural ecology. Or all of those. Never mind that the last named crime is an activity that included the founding of Venice as well as maintaining its historical survival.

The solution is equally hotly debated, although one giant floodgate of Project MO.S.E. (Modulo Sperimentale Elettromeccanico), partly put into place at a lagoon entrance after more than two decades of political debate, is not yet functioning and the other floodgates are missing. Perhaps in 2011, we were told. When the necessity for this system was urgently endorsed by an international team of hydraulic engineers under the auspices of the Massachusetts Institute of Technology, a Venetian professor of urban planning, who was also a leader of the Green Party, scoffed that of course they were bribed to say that. What else would one expect of MIT engineers? he shrugged.

As the arguments rage on through the years and the water crises creep into more of the calendar year, we live with the notion that Venice could eventually slip away and our descendants conclude that we were describing a fantasy. It would be enough to prompt thoughts about the fragility of beauty and love, were it not that others have voiced all that already.

CHAPTER THREE

Great Moments in Venetian History

The pop culture of Venice is her own history, which provides the common references that everyone in town still uses and understands. Until you are familiar with such events as the Battle of Lepanto and the state visit of Henry III of Poland and France to the point of forgetting that you were not present, many Venetian paintings and some Venetian conversation will be mystifying. Unless he or she is a history scholar in a position to clarify and supplement what is believed, the good Venetophile does not argue probability in regard to the general version of events but accepts it, miracles, contradictions, and all.

However, learning history the high school way—by memorizing the names of kings, presidents, and despots and accessorizing them with their battles, sex scandals, assassinations, financial scandals, political brawls, rebellious children, and natural disasters—doesn't work for Venice. The ideal doge for the Republic, with its non-hereditary, anti-personality-cult, and checks-and-balances system, was a malleable old party who didn't get too big for his ermine-trimmed toga. Venice didn't always get such a one, but she got enough doges who were tired and true (tried and true turned out not to be synonymous) that it is hard to distinguish individuals. It doesn't help that doges were elected from such a small pool that even after early attempts to establish dynastic succession had been forcibly repulsed, the same names recurred over the centuries.

The doge everyone remembers is the one who isn't there. Others, in the frieze of portraits in the Doge's Palace, nearly all look alike: a bunch of expressionless seniors, the early ones in brocaded Eastern helmet-shaped hats, the later ones wearing the corno, the horn-shaped symbol of office unique to Venice. But in the 1354–55 slot, where Marin Falier should have been, a black veil is painted. His head is missing because his advisors had it lopped off on his front steps.

Marin Falier is the only doge, perhaps the only chief of state in the history of the world, who overthrew himself. Some doges slunk off to monasteries in search of peace and quiet or were ushered out in that direction, and in the early years, voter dissatisfaction was occasionally settled by assassination. But Marin Falier, at the pinnacle of a long and distinguished career in the service of the state, instigated a conspiracy to topple the government that he enjoyed lifetime tenure to head. He planned to head the succeeding revolutionary government as well, promoting himself to prince, but his motive was to punish the noble class, of which he was a member in highest standing. Thus he toppled from the attempt to kick over his own support system.

What had driven the elderly doge to this was no political threat, but graffiti left on his throne after he had everyone over for a Fat Thursday party: "Marin Falier maintains a beautiful wife while others enjoy her."

Well! It was those feckless young patricians with nothing better to do, always causing trouble. They were plentiful, because the Venetian version of primogeniture was to conserve family property by allowing only one son and one daughter to marry, clapping surplus daughters into convents, where they stirred up trouble, and letting surplus sons loose, where they stirred up trouble. Among them, they produced Venice's unusually high population of alleged orphans.

Marin Falier: The Doge Who Isn't There.

Only a few decades previously, Falier, not yet doge, had helped put down some hotheaded young blue-bloods who had tried to start a revolution. Members of the two other classes, the citizens and the populace, were not generally disposed to attack a system that treated them better than their likes were treated elsewhere, so the upper class was left to do this for and to itself. As in modern America, revolutionary fervor, when it occurred, was a characteristic of the children of the rich and got nowhere. Rabble brought up to feel privileged tend to be loose-lipped, and in Venice, word of a coup would comfortably precede the planned event. Those who made it as far as the piazza were in for an armed surprise.

Watching Where You Walk

The modern Venetophile who is in the piazzetta with presumably peaceful intentions needs to bear in mind the stories of both of these attempted coups. For historical reasons, it is necessary, when entering from the lagoon side, to walk around, rather than between, the columns bearing the lion and Saint Theodore. If entering from the shopping street opposite, the Merceria, it would be prudent to look up.

When Marin Falier made his formal entrance after being elected doge, Venice was enveloped in fog. (Venetian fog can be so thick that passengers on the narrow Grand Canal cannot see either shore, and from the middle of the piazza, the basilica appears only as a wispy dream. It is like living inside of a Monet.) He missed his stop at the entrance to the piazzetta, and was put ashore at the spot where, thoroughly befogged, he unwittingly walked between the two columns.

This is a bad, bad move. The columns are souvenirs from an unsuccessful twelfth-century peacekeeping mission led by Vitale Michiel II, another luckless doge. In his case, he had not only fallen for a delaying trick by the Emperor of the East, but his ships were found to contain a little something for Venice in addition to the columns: the plague. The public did not take this well, and his dogeship was terminated by mob action in the street. This did not prevent a later public from focusing on the loot and making the anniversary of his return into a holiday (see chapter eight).

At any rate, he had brought home three huge and heavy columns. As they were transferred from ship to shore, one got dropped into the canal.

It is still there. There was enough trouble trying to right the two that made it to shore. For forty-five years, they lay there on the quay, getting in everybody's way. Finally, an engineer offered to lift the pair into vertical position. But it happened that he did not gamble in physics alone, and the price he named was the gambling concession in that choice public real estate between the two columns, smack at the then-safe ceremonial approach to Venice. He succeeded in righting the columns and, since it was a point of pride to Venice to keep her word, he got his reward.

This did not mean that Venice was going to put up with high-rolling low-lifes carrying on under her and her state visitors' noses. Her benefactor had forgotten to put in a claim to the air rights over his gambling tables. The government decided that this space between the two columns would be a good place to hang criminals, although presumably not when it was expecting company. Gamblers interpreted the swinging bodies over the tables as bad luck, and the concessionaire soon found that meant bad business. Doge Falier's fate, nearly two centuries later, is proof enough that walking between the columns is still bad luck. Nowadays, however many crowds in the piazza spill over into that space, you do not find Venetians or Venetophiles among them.

Another citizen reward was claimed by an old lady who helped save the Republic from the conspiracy of 1310, when Falier still was on the government's side. This one was led by Bajamonte Tiepolo with members of the Querini family (who had to wait until their own disapproving papa was out of town) and other shiftless patrician scamps. Not only were government forces tipped off and waiting, but at the Merceria entrance to the piazza, old Mrs. Rossi, who lived upstairs in the apartment at the corner, leaned out over her flower box and let go of a mortar. She missed Tiepolo but hit and killed his standard bearer, which so unnerved Tiepolo that he turned and fled. An unattractive reaction in a revolutionary, perhaps, but it saved his life from the fed-

Mrs. Rossi, Counter-Revolutionary, Strikes a Blow for Rent Control.

eral troops waiting in the piazza. He was sentenced to exile and a favorite Venetian punishment: humiliation through real estate. His house was razed, and a column of shame was later erected where it had stood. The participating Querini, who were killed, only had two-thirds of their house demolished, because one of the three brothers was innocent. Another conspiratorial family had its front door chained open day and night for the better part of a century.

What did Mrs. Rossi get? Rent control. It was a cannier request than the gambler's, and it held, way past her lifetime, although Rossi descendents occasionally had to resort to the law to remind the Republic of its promise. Venice still remembers, even if it no longer ensures bargain rent for this prime location, now worth millions. High above two luxury-shop windows, there is a commemorative bust of the dear soul, leaning out of her apartment, fixing to drop a rock on passersby. The Tiepolo column is no longer standing (it is in the Correr Museum, an inscription in Campo San Agostin marking the original site) and the name Tiepolo, which some centuries later became associated with voluptuously painted ceilings, was redeemed.

For even the most committed Venetophile, it seems cheeky to claim a share in Venice's historical glories. We cheer for her triumphs, as being our side, as we lament her losses. But after all, we did not have ancestors who fought at the Battle of Lepanto. (Although . . . see chapter five.)

Where we can feel the joy of identity is in the telling little anecdotes in Venetian history that demonstrate, for better, and even more often for worse, that these were people very much like us. Impossible as it is to distill national character from centuries of individual stories, unreliably reported, Americans can find countless illustrations of qualities we can relate to Good Old American Know-how, or perhaps Good Old American Sorry-About-That. Historically, Venetians were ingenious at improvising—and remarkably accident-prone. How can we not love them?

Politics aside, what we learn from the stories of Marin Falier and Bajamonte Tiepolo is not only the importance of real estate and of thinking through your wishes. They offer some of the most endearing examples of human fallibility and ingenuity—characteristics we shall call Whoops! and What If?

Who were the people who unloaded the great columns and allowed one to fall into the canal, and what did they say when it happened? "Damn!"? "Those things are really heavy"? "It'll look better with two columns anyway"?

The Tiepolo plot was exposed after one of the conspirators,

in the course of getting himself properly done up for the occasion, couldn't help telling his tailor, "You'll never guess what I'm going to be doing." If he survived, what was his excuse? "How was I to know my tailor was a blabbermouth? I've been going to him for years."

The engineer who asked for the gambling concession without securing the air rights probably had a retrospective case of Whoops! but the officials who thwarted him were geniuses at What If? "We have to honor our deal, but what if we scare off his clientele?"

There are a number of instances of such tricks that got Venice out of untenable positions. Still another outlet for this creativity was coming up with inventions, or refinements on ancient inventions, that affect the way we live today. Culling these illustrations from centuries of political, economic, and military history should give the Venetophile the sense of knowing these people and how they think.

Whoops!

A popular show of no confidence in Doge Pietro Candiano IV, in 976, took the form of burning down his neighborhood. Having done everything he could to enrich and aggrandize himself while subverting Venetian republican principles, he probably deserved to be extinguished. And so he was. But Whoops! the punishment got out of hand, and the fire spread to hundreds of buildings, ravaging not only the Doge's Palace, but also the resting place of Saint Mark, which was not yet a basilica but the doge's chapel, adjacent to his official residence.

Then, as now, one of the occupants of Saint Mark's was Saint Mark. Double Whoops! The people had rid themselves of a pesky doge and scorched some prime real estate, but they also appeared to have fried their patron saint.* And they had gone to so much trouble to acquire Saint Mark (see chapter one). His resting place could be rebuilt, and it eventually was, into the bizarre splendor we know today. But how do you reconstruct an evangelist?

The answer is that you cannot, but you can trust him to do it himself. When it would take a miracle to get you out of trouble— isn't that when you need a saint? And Mark, being saintly, was presumed to have no hard feelings about the small matter of having his dwelling burned down when he had been given an explicit and divine guarantee that his posthumous Venetian existence would be peaceful.

A century or so after the fire, it occurred to state and church officials that Saint Mark was still missing. They went off their feed, organized a prayer posse, and three days later one of the columns in the rebuilt church flipped open. There was Mark, sarcophagus and all. This miracle is illustrated in mosaics on a wall inside Saint Mark's basilica. Panel one depicts a large crowd bent in prayer; panel two shows a trapdoor opening in the column and the chief dignitaries offering prayers in its direction. Others who are assembled there are captured forever in glittering tiles as having lost interest and started talking among themselves.

This illustration could have been worse. According to a seventeenth-century historian, there was barely a moment between the time that the dignitaries beheld the miracle of Saint Mark's extended arm and their registering the fact that the hand was wearing a mighty handsome gold ring. Naturally they dove for it. With the attitude of "Welcome back, our patron saint, and you won't be needing that anymore," the doge, the bishop, and others tried to wrench it from his finger.

---

*Unless, as a British historian argues, what they really had there all along was the body of Alexander the Great, who vanished from his Alexandria tomb at about the same time Mark did. But such a colossal Whoops! is unthinkable to loyal Venetophiles.

This did not work. Saint Mark was not letting go. But one of the company tried a less aggressive tack. He prayed for the ring. And he wanted it so badly that he literally prayed himself sick. At that spectacle, the saint gave in and Domenico Dolfin was given the ring, along with an oral guarantee (coming from inside the column) that he had clear title to it. Some years later, a Dolfin heir donated it to the Scuola Grande of San Marco.

It could not have been a great loss to Saint Mark, who had a regular jeweler. Only two centuries earlier, during a wild storm, he had hitched a ride with a reluctant old fisherman to the island of San Giorgio to pick up Saint George and then to the Lido to pick up Saint Nicholas. After the trio took care of the weather problem by zapping a boatload of demons, Saint Mark gave the fisherman a gold ring, telling him to pass it on to the doge.

Let us hope that the two accounts of the doge's acquiring ecclesiastical authority from the evangelist through this symbol derive from a single legend. Otherwise, the doge looks not just grabby but also greedy, going for seconds when he already had one of Saint Mark's holy gold rings.

On the wall of the imposing entrance to Venice's extraordinary ship-building factory, there is a bust of Dante Alighieri, who immortalized the Arsenal in his *Inferno*. Of course he did this by saying the place looked like hell, comparing the boiling pitch used to caulk ships to the substance into which errant souls were cast. But Venice was never averse to spreading the word that her war capabilities were fearsome, and anyway, that was a long time ago. Now Venice is just happy to be associated with Italy's premier poet.

The Whoops! factor occurred in 1321, when the association took place in the flesh. Dante had, by this time, made himself unwelcome in his native Florence, which is now equally happy to reclaim him retrospectively, and was employed on a diplomatic visit to Venice from Ravenna. His mission, which seems to have involved adjusting navigation rights in Ravenna's favor, was not a Venetian priority, and anyway, there was some ill feeling about Ravenna in connection with a sailors' brawl in which Venetians had been killed. So nobody gave Dante the time of day. Even when he admitted defeat, they stonewalled his plea for a safe passage to take a ship back to Ravenna. His only remaining choice was to tramp back through the swamps, where he caught malaria and shortly died. Knocking off Dante has to be counted as a major Whoops! by anyone's reckoning.

Perhaps having learned from this mishap, Venice did better by the second-greatest Italian poet, Francesco Petrarch, who appeared in 1354 as a diplomatic envoy from Venice's old enemy, Genoa, and again, six years later, on a personal mission to escape the plague. The state struck a bargain, offering him a house in exchange for his bequeathing to Venice his famous book collection as the foundation of a state library.

In contrast to Dante, Petrarch was given honor and attention—slightly too much attention, he pleaded, when unable to face a third day in a row sitting next to the doge on a reviewing stand watching sporting events in celebration of victory in Crete, when he had serious work to do, including writing verses celebrating these events. But the honors conferred by officialdom were offset by indignities from those young patrician no-goods. When they declared that they personally had quizzed Petrarch and concluded that he was nothing but an old dummy, he took offense and left town, in spite of the free house and box seats.

The real Whoops! had to do with what became, or did not become, of Petrarch's library. His bequest stated the condition that his books "shall neither be sold or separated; and that they shall all

"Folks, what's holding us up here is that the True Cross was accidentally dropped in the canal. Please be assured that we're doing everything possible to locate it, and we'll soon have this procession under way. We apologize if the delay is causing you any inconvenience."

be placed in safety, sheltered from fire and water, and preserved with care forever." Some of his even-then priceless codices were thought to have been stuffed into storage at the basilica where they moldered, but on later examination, these turned out not to be his. So at least Venice had only forfeited, but not destroyed, his library. Apparently Petrarch took it with him when he left in a huff, and the collection was subsequently dispersed.

An expanse of wall in the Accademia Galleries of Art is devoted to commemorating a Whoops! In *The Miracle of the True*

Cross at the Bridge of San Lorenzo, Gentile Bellini, Giovanni's less-
talented brother, depicts a religious procession for which a fashionable crowd has turned out. There on the right are the artist
himself and his circle—relatives, presumably, and patrons. On
the left, in the black dress, is Venice's only royalty, Queen
Catherine, née Cornaro, who was mailed to Cyprus as a
teenager to be consort to its short-lived king, and yanked back
after years under siege from friend and foe alike. In spite of her
troubles, this Daughter of the Republic had gotten the hang of
being royal and was said to have her eye on the king of Naples,
but the Senate squelched this. They offered her a retirement
package that included a toy court in nearby Asolo. That long
row of partially exposed bosoms lined up behind her in the
painting belongs to her ladies-in-waiting.

The bald chap in the canal, managing to stay decorously and
effortlessly afloat, in contrast to his treading and thrashing companions, is Andrea Vendramin, the Guardian Grande of the
Scuola Grande of San Giovanni Evangelista. He has just rescued
that confraternity's treasure, a fragment of the True Cross, which
unfortunately fell into the canal while they were parading it
around.

We know from the columns episode that such things happen,
but the crowd is taking it remarkably calmly. They are shown
standing around, marking time, some chatting, others playfully
shoving one another on the bridge, and the rest look bored, no
doubt wondering when the procession is finally going to start up
again and how the delay will affect their social plans for the rest
of the day.

What is the matter with them? Don't they understand what
just happened? Someone dropped a piece of the True Cross in
the canal! The True Cross! They took it out for ventilation and
veneration, and somebody dropped it off the bridge!

Who is responsible? How would you like to be the one who
was entrusted to carry the True Cross and let go? What would

you say? "I'm sorry"? "Hey, it was an accident"? "It's his fault, he pushed me"? "Look, I said I was sorry, what more do you want?" Or "Never mind casting blame—someone should just go get it"?

How is anybody supposed to find a piece of old wood mired in all that junk that accumulates in a canal? Take a look some time at a canal that is being dredged, as they successively are being nowadays. Even aside from such large-scale modern trash as defunct washing machines and obsolete computer parts, there is so much muddy mess that it would take a miracle to find anything.

Ah! So the Venetians present were right: There was no use getting all worked up. Thanks to a miracle, the holy relic floated apart from the rest of the canal debris and was fished out by the triumphant Guardian Grande. The parade got going again, and the crowd made it to their lunch dates. The scuola still has its relic of the True Cross.

Gentile Bellini was the inadvertent cause of another famous episode of Whoops! in which he realized too late that one should not argue with a powerful patron. This incident was not an accident and did not take place in Venice. Bellini was doing a stint as painter-in-residence in Constantinople when his patron, Sultan Mehmed II, ventured to criticize Bellini's painting of Saint John the Baptist on the grounds that the beheading did not look realistic. Ordinarily, that is the sort of thing that could be argued all day to no end, but the sultan had resources. He said, "Look, I'll show you," summoned two slaves, and instructed one of them to behead the other.

During the Renaissance, it was not immediately apparent what a spectacularly bad idea it was to immortalize important houses by hiring immortal artists to paint pictures on the facades. Venice had such painters in abundance, and the best of them were willing to take on these jobs. Whoever first thought of

the eye-catching idea of having the outside of his house done—it
might have been planted by Giorgione's daubing his own house
at San Silvestro—must have been tickled to imagine the edge
such painting would give him on his neighbors.

A fad started, and for a while there, the Grand Canal seemed
to be turning into an outdoor picture gallery of world-class art.
Then—Whoops!—the salt air ate it all up.

To the Venetophile, news that a faint trace of such a fresco has
been found during the restoration of a facade is thrilling. To the
homeowner, it is not. That person is disgruntled enough from
the expense of the restoration, knowing that the elements will be
nibbling away on it before it is even finished; from the work and
delay of being officially required to document the earliest color
his house was known to have been painted so this could be
reproduced; and from months, if not years, of having his interior
dimmed and his view blocked by scaffolding. And now work will
come to a halt while the art experts pore over his illegible bit of
colored plaster.

It is said that some years ago, when it became necessary to
paint the facade of the Fondaco dei Tedeschi, the old German
quarters which had become the modern post office, the then-
postmaster loathed pastels and wanted it painted plain white.
When informed that he could not cut through the bureaucratic
demand for historical accuracy with this solution, he replied that
in the earliest known documentation, the front of the building
had been painted by Giorgione, and the street side by Titian. He
declared himself ready to be told how to reproduce this.

"Okay, smartie," was the answer in effect. "Then document
and use the predominant color of those frescoes."

"Flesh pink," he reported. The historical accuracy forces gave
up. The facade was painted white.

For that matter, the Fondaco dei Tedeschi project was apparently not an entirely happy experience the first time around.

Giorgione kept being congratulated by passersby, who marveled at how much his art was improving, as evidenced by the later paintings on the side that were so much better than what he had painted on the Grand Canal side. Giorgione stopped speaking to Titian.

He was not the only one. In a stunning pedagogical Whoops!, Titian went home one day and noticed some unusually good drawings being done in his atelier. When he inquired which of his apprentices was doing such work, he was told it was the dyer's young son. Titian expressed interest in talking to this marvel, and the boy was sent in to see the Master for what turned out to be a very short talk. "Take your stuff and get out of here," Titian is said to have told the boy. Tintoretto, who grew up to manage quite well without further instruction, never forgave him.

Venice had a way of dealing with prominent people whose carelessness led to major cases of Whoops!, and neither meaning well nor having a record of previous triumphs served as an excuse. The latter circumstance may even have had negative value, as Venice was ever wary of personal popularity that might turn political.

It clapped such people into jail. But lest that be considered an unduly harsh punishment for mistakes lacking in malice, two cases show that the jailed celebrities harbored no hard feelings. They had only to be released to go right back to working cheerfully for the glory of Venice.

One was Vettor Pisani, a distinguished admiral who won many glorious victories over Genoa and her allies. But then he lost one. There was no thought of analyzing and perhaps sharing the blame, much less of rallying his spirits and wishing him better luck next time. He lost; they jailed him.

That defeat, at Pola in 1379, had serious consequences, as it enabled the Genoese to take neighboring Chioggia, using it to try blockading Venice into submission by starvation. Considering that Venice lives on imports, it would not have taken long. A somewhat panicked population asked itself who was the best person to lead the defense, and it was not the candidate proposed by the government.

Yielding to popular demand, the government plucked Pisani out of jail, packed him off with cannon-laden galleys, and wished him well. Skipping the opportunity to say "I thought you said you didn't need me," and "But didn't you tell me I was incompetent?" the old admiral pitched right in. He set up a blockade of his own around the Genoese encampments, and, with the aid of timely storms and re-enforcements, used those cannons (although they had an unfortunate tendency to backfire), routed the enemy, and saved Venice. We should all be thankful that he was not a man to bear a grudge.

Another such case involved the great Renaissance architect and sculptor Jacopo Sansovino, né Tatti, who changed the look of downtown Venice (although not as much as he wanted to, his dream being to raze the basilica and replace it with some nice, up-to-date piece of his own creation) and built the largest residence on the Grand Canal. Although he arrived in his middle-age, with more experience sculpting than building, the city had welcomed him enthusiastically, awarding him significant architectural projects and granting him residence on the piazza.

One of his commissions was to build a state library. Venice, which had not learned from the loss of Petrarch's library, had been almost as careless with another famous collection, bequeathed by Cardinal Bessarion in 1468 on the explicit condition that it be housed in a library near the basilica. For the better part of a century, these priceless Greek and Roman manuscripts were shifted around the Doge's Palace, and some had become damaged or lost. Sansovino had friends who were pushing to get a library built, and he landed the job of building what is now the Marciana library, next to the bell tower and facing the Doge's Palace from the piazzetta.

Sansovino was born in Florence and had been living in Rome, but now he was a hotshot architect and not about to take advice from his clients. He was not above learning from other Italian architects, however, and in Rome, his peers were going in for impressive vaulted spaces. Paying no attention to Venetian protests along the lines of "Trust us; we know the terrain; it shifts; you've got to use wood," he decided to do stone vaults. And the first one fell to the ground.

Achieving the dream of ignored and frustrated clients everywhere, Venice threw the architect into jail. He protested that it was only one small section that fell, pointed out that the damages were nothing compared to the total cost of the building, and blamed a host of other circumstances, from the weather to his workmen. Nevertheless, Venice docked his salary and made him pay the reconstruction costs. When his friends Titian and Aretino sprung him, he went about his work again in a somewhat more responsive frame of mind.

What If? (Solutions)

The Whoops! factor is a recurrent note in Venetian history, but not because the people were particularly clumsy. It is that they were so full of wild and imaginative projects that even the inevitable mishaps were dramatic enough to inspire them to commemorations, rather than cover-ups. Furthermore, these are part of the greater story of Venetian brilliance in circumventing difficulties.

That miracles did happen was not seen as an excuse to sit around and wait for them to do so. However many saints Venetians had brought bodily over to their side, they exercised astonishing daring, originality, and ingenuity in solving their problems themselves. Their penchant for thinking outside the conventions of their time—the What If? factor—produced a variety of bizarre political and practical ideas that actually worked.

The most unlikely and brilliant of Venetian ideas was Venice. This was the response to their first and scariest problem, Attila the Hun. "Okay, we're not safe on land or sea," they apparently reasoned. "But what if we lived in the marshes?"

Surely there must have been some among those ninth-century fugitives who screamed, "Are you crazy? There's nothing here but weeds and water! Didn't we come here in the first place because no one in his right mind would want to take this away from us? It's fine as a hideout, but as a city? For starters, what's going to hold up the buildings? Do you want our descendents to be living in rush huts while the rest of the world is lolling in luxury?"

But they went ahead, and one great idea led to another. Planting wooden piles in the muck and letting them petrify so that they could hold up the buildings, for example. Keeping the facades of houses separate from the structural unity of the other three walls, so that when a canal wall sloshes down into the water, as happens from time to time, it doesn't take the building down with it. Going wild with delicate designs and enticing decorations on houses, knowing that the lagoon would offer the protection from invasion that feudal Europe sought, less reliably, from stone fortifications.

The next best idea was to adopt Saint Mark. This is not to say that the Venetians coldly analyzed the problems of the time— ecclesiastical bossiness from the Patriarchate of Aquileia, abetted by the even bossier Papal States, and a lingering vestigial political relationship with Byzantium that crowded their emerging status as an independent power—and came up with, "What if we kidnapped Saint Mark?"

But they did it, and this catapulted Venice into the religious and political big-time. Even the papacy could boast only an apostle. As an added benefit, the ungracious act of demoting Saint Theodore, an Eastern favorite, from his status as Venice's patron saint, gave notice that Byzantium was no longer Venice's ruler but her customer. Not to mention that the lion made a splendid and flexible logo, as the book it holds (or steps on) promises peace. The book could be shown open in peacetime and shut during war, when the lion would also shoot up a paw clutching a sword. That image could not be improved upon, as the modern city found when French designers who were selected to provide a new logo came up with a one-winged lion sticking its face out of a V. It is, perhaps, an only too-vivid reminder that Venice now gets by on a wing and a prayer.

Venetian history is filled with attempts to outsmart, one-up, and patronize those formidable opponents, the popes. Forever being rebuked by the Papal States for being insubordinate and over-tolerant, Venice was nevertheless the place to turn when cunning crowned with ceremony was required. When Frederick Barbarossa was forced to humble himself to Pope Alexander III, concluding years of warfare and schism, Venice provided the stage and served as impresario. High drama was performed, with the emperor kissing the feet and knees of the pope, who, humility be damned, was said to have placed his foot on the emperor's neck before raising and embracing him. This production was months in the making, during which Venice extracted a variety of concessions from both sides. Between the retinues of both parties and the onlookers, she also had a record tourist season.

More often, relations were less happy. Venice was determined to achieve a form of separation of church and state, by which she did not mean separation of the Venetian church from the Venetian state—on the contrary, state permission was required for building churches, founding orders and such—but jurisdictional separation of the Papal States from the church in Venice. "Venetians, and then Christians," goes a Venetian saying that did nothing to endear them to the Mother Church. The popes were equally determined not to let go. That the two sides might come to military blows often seemed possible, but popes also wielded heavy-duty spiritual weapons, the use of which finally led to the most audacious of all of Venice's What Ifs. When Venice was put under an interdict in 1606, a Venetian friar posed this question: What if the pope promulgated an interdict and nobody noticed?

Venice had already suffered the severe inconvenience of three interdicts and the wholesale excommunication of members of its governing bodies; this was to be the test case of how much harassment she should have to take. The immediate issue was who had authority over two lewd and rowdy Venetians who appeared to be monks, although one of them was later found to be only a lewd and rowdy layman. As with so many episodes in Venice's history, the struggles with Rome also had a real estate angle. State control over the ability of the church to buy property, which would become tax-free, was a not inconsiderable issue. (Venice had already flummoxed the church by designating the land for the bishop in the easternmost island, as far as possible from the governmental and social center of town. Therefore, Saint Mark's basilica, which occupies the prime spot in the piazza, appeared to impersonate a cathedral long before the nineteenth century, when it became one.)

Paolo Sarpi was the name of the early seventeenth-century monk who took on the pope in Venice's defense. He was the ideal Venetian—a clever and loyal strategist as well as a renowned theologian and scientist and, as we shall see, a wit. He helped Galileo develop his telescope, he discovered how the eye's iris contracts, and during the volatile years after the Reformation, he supported tolerance for Protestants. As grateful Venetophiles, we go out of our way to greet him, in the form of his statue at Campo Santa Fosca on the Strada Nuova, and offer our respects.

His plan was magnificent in its simplicity. When the ultimatum was looming, Venice refused to receive or acknowledge the fatal communication, and her clergy were ordered to go about their business as usual. Interdict? What interdict? You sent us an interdict? Funny, we never saw it. Our server must have been down.

If Venice failed to notice the interdict, the rest of Europe took notice of this strategy with wonder. The pope's terrifying weapon had malfunctioned. That it required the cooperation of the target in order to be effective was an astounding revelation. In the compromise eventually brokered, Venice did hand over her miscreants and the ineffectual interdict was officially lifted, but the spiritual arsenal of the papacy had been destroyed beyond repair.

Pope Paul V was a sore loser. Some months after this peace had been concluded, Venice's hero, Fra Paolo Sarpi, was attacked on the street by a gang of foreign, knife-wielding assassins. They thought they had left him for dead, but in fact they had killed neither him nor his engaging wit. "Agnosco stylum Curias Romanae," he punned when his surgeon remarked on the messy incompetence of the wound they had inflicted. "I recognize the style/knife of the Roman Curia."

This was a spectacular breakthrough, but Venetians always seemed to have a novel way out when apparently thwarted by someone else's wishes or actions. There was the matter of the hired general Condottiere Bartolomeo Colleoni, who had faithfully fought Venice's land wars until his death in 1475. This

"This is not what I meant, and they know it."

fealty was no small matter. Militarily, Venice had always been incomparable at sea and incompetent on land, so when her Italian neighbors' armies went after her, she was dependent on mercenaries, who are a notoriously undependable lot. Venice had given vast sums, reckless license, and extravagant promises to Francesco Bussone, the fearsome Carmagnola, only to have him play Venice off against his former employers, the Visconti, and when she finally caught on, she convicted him of treason.

Carmagnola's successor, Erasmo da Nardi, called Il Gatta-melata (the honeyed cat), proved more loyal, and Venice honored him by commissioning an equestrian statue of him by Donatello, which is in Padua. Gratitude cannot, however, be said to be the prime motivation when it came to commissioning an equestrian statue of Colleoni, who had served under both Carmagnola and Il Gattamelata before himself assuming command of Venice's land forces. The idea had been Colleoni's, and he had taken precautions in his will to ensure it got done.

First, he left his not-inconsiderable fortune to Venice on condition that the statue be made. This was not a problem, as the cost would come out of the inheritance. Then he stipulated that the statue be erected in front of San Marco. This was a major problem. Nobody had a free-standing (or riding) statue in the piazza other than the two saints on their columns. Colleoni was not even a Venetian, but a reminder that she had to resort to hired help to lead her not-always-successful land wars. Besides, his coat of arms was a dirty joke: balls, to match the meaning of his name.

Yet refusing his request would mean forfeiting his bequest. It was a delicate matter that called for Venetian ingenuity. The discussion must have gone something like this: "Of course we have to honor his wishes; we cannot accept the money otherwise. How unfortunate, therefore, that he is not here to explain his wishes beyond any question. For example, he specifies that the statue should be at San Marco. But which one? The basilica is not the only building dedicated to San Marco. Nor is it the only one that is on a square where a statue could be placed. What if what he really meant was that it should be placed in the square in front of the Scuola Grande of San Marco?"

It turns out that that was exactly what Colleoni did mean, at least to the best that the grateful heirs could determine without his ferocious presence. We know that ferocity from the arresting statue that dominates the pavement in front of the former Scuola Grande of San Marco, which is now part of the hospital. Yet the old warrior must be satisfied, as the design for it by

Verrocchio, finished and cast after his death by Alessandro Leopardi, resulted in a work of art that has commanded respect and attention (and the giggle he expected at seeing his coat-of-arms) ever since.

Outsmarting other Venetians was a harder proposition. Venetian officialdom was no match for Bianca Capello, a sixteenth-century noblewoman whose career of defying authority and the odds began when she was a teenager.

She started out banally enough, by defying her own father, and in the usual way. Instead of allowing him to make a match for her with a rich old nobleman, she ran off to Florence with a young bank clerk who told her, erroneously as it turns out, that he was rich and noble. Once disillusionment had set in all around—the father realizing that he was not able to undo the marriage or lure her back to face disgrace, and the daughter realizing that he had a point about love not compensating for poverty—they might each have settled for a life of regret. But Bianca and her father were not the sort to settle.

Not content to bore everyone with tales of his stupid, ungrateful daughter ruining her life, Papa Capello made a major diplomatic and religious incident out of it. The religious part was easy: His brother-in-law, the Patriarch of Aquileia, joined him in putting a bounty on the couple's heads. He also managed to get the Council of Ten involved to the extent of declaring the couple to be outlaws, pronouncing a death sentence for the bridegroom and demanding of the Florentine Grand Duke, Cosimo de' Medici, that he extradite Bianca so she could face her father's— and by now everyone else's—wrath.

Unbeknownst to them, Bianca was already coming around to the view that her poor plebian husband was no prize. But aside from their having escalated the situation to the point where it would be dangerous for her to return, she was a Venetian, not a quitter. Her father's position was that he would have done better in choosing for her; hers was that she could still do better for herself.

And so she did. A lesser woman, even today, might have become discouraged by her circumstances—married, pregnant, and stuck in a hovel with in-laws who harbored the outrageous notion that a Venetian noblewoman should help with the housework. Bianca treated her legal problem as an opportunity. She charmed Cosimo de' Medici into refusing Venice's official request to send her back, using, of all strategies, a gallant declaration of loyalty to her feckless husband. Next she caught the eye of a decidedly better catch, Cosimo's son and heir, Francesco de' Medici.

What is more, she married him. It took her fifteen years and an astonishing amount of Venetian ingenuity, but Bianca was not one to let anything stand in the way of true love, untold riches, and becoming Grand Duchess of Tuscany. Among the objects she got out of the way were:

- Her first husband, who was happy to profit by her august connection, but whose own extramarital affairs were less well managed, ending with his murder by the brothers of one of his mistresses (who apparently was an ex-mistress of Francesco's).
- Francesco's first wife, the extremely well-connected Giovanna née Hapsburg, who finally caught on that her friendly lady-in-waiting was even friendlier with her husband and in-waiting for her position, which Giovanna vacated by dying in childbirth.
- Her own failure to bear a son to Francesco, which she remedied through faked pregnancy and baby-snatching. Bianca managed this so adroitly that he and other Medici accepted a

bond with the snatched child even after Bianca had voluntar-
ily confessed.

- Francesco's brother, Cardinal Ferdinando de' Medici, who
  was also in-waiting, but for Francesco's position, and more
  actively interested in securing it, which he eventually did,
  presumably by poisoning Francesco and Bianca.
- Florentine public opinion, which grew no fonder of the foreign upstart as she amassed more and more wealth, property,
  and position, but was forced to accept her as their Grand
  Duchess.
- Venetian opinion, which grew ever fonder as she amassed
  more and more wealth, property, and position, but had been
  rash enough to try to run her down as an outlaw and to
  refuse her amnesty when she was merely Francesco's
  mistress.

However, Venetian diplomacy was characterized by flexibility,
as no one demonstrated better than Bianca. At various times she
defended her first husband, her father, her brother, and
Francesco's venomous relatives to an extent that smacks suspiciously of plain good nature.

The Venetian government, no less flexible, had a What If?
inspiration (prompted by Francesco, who wanted his bride to
have a higher pedigree than disowned Venetian and rascal's
widow). What if, instead of declaring her an enemy and outlaw of
the republic, Venice declared her a Daughter of the Republic?
And so the Venetian government did, at the same time that she
was proclaimed Duchess of Tuscany. What is more, Venice threw
in a diamond necklace to show there were no hard feelings.

The best What If? as a one-liner came from Veronese, Paolo
né Caliari. When the Inquisition denounced his stupendous

painting of the Last Supper as sacrilegious, Veronese tried in vain to argue the concept of artistic license, an original argument at the time. It has served succeeding generations of offensive artists so well that many believe it to be a license requiring them to offend. But it did not go over with the Inquisition.

Amid all that indignant spluttering—"It's full of drunks! Women! Buffoons! Dogs! A parrot! Germans! A servant with a nosebleed! You can't have those creatures at the Last Supper!"—Veronese finally agreed to make a change. He did not touch the drunks, women, buffoons, dogs, parrot, Germans, or nose-bleeding servant, of course. The painting was fine the way it was, as you can see for yourself at the Accademia. What occurred to him was "What if I told them that this is not the Last Supper? What if I put the name *Feast in the House of Levi* right there on the painted pedestal where they can't miss it?" And so his picture is known to this day.

What If? (Inventions)

Venice has been credited with inventing practically everything that makes life worth living (or not), including opera, factories, mirrors, quarantines, bleached hair, double-entry bookkeeping, lotteries, paperback books, casinos, regattas, roof terraces, assembly lines, improv comedy, platform shoes, social walkers, and women's team sports.

Many of these, Venetians actually did invent; others they rediscovered, refined, and popularized to the extent that these things came to be considered Venetian. Renowned throughout the known world to be as stylish as she was clever, Venice acted as a major trendsetter.

Bright ideas were popping up with such frequency that inventions were required to protect the interests of individual inventors and of Venetian commerce. In the fifteenth century, Venice invented the patent system, which was, of course, copied elsewhere. Ten-year patents for new techniques were issued in industries such as silk, flour, and glass, and intellectual property rights were included when an historian and critic, Marcus Antonius Coccius, received the first known copyright in 1486.

Long before, Venice had pioneered other methods for retaining the secrets and services of valuable workers. Paying promised wages was one of them. Venice's preponderance of great artists had something to do with the tendency of princes and other art patrons of the time to duck their bills with excuses of disliking the finished product or having spent the money on wars or undergoing defeat or death. Venice could be counted upon to pay for what she had commissioned. And because glorification of Venice was the goal of public and private Venetians, there was no dearth of commissions.

Two other methods were astounding for their time, perhaps for any time: conferring both honor and benefits on employees. Although guilds there and elsewhere were developing their collective interests, spontaneous state attempts to produce happy workers were even more radical. Shipbuilders working at the Arsenal, which employed up to sixteen thousand in its heyday, had health care, retirement pensions, and other working terms unknown, or at least unpracticed, in medieval times and for centuries to come. In eras when other Europeans looked down on working with the hands (as opposed to killing with the hands), the Arsenal's benefit package included respect. The Arsenalotti, as they were called, served as honor guards to the doge.

It was not Henry Ford who first thought, "What if we had huge buildings where workers with particular skills each did their part as the product moved along from one group to the next until it was finished?" The first factory, with the first assembly line, was the Venetian Arsenal, where separate groups of carpenters, sailmakers, and other specialists successively worked on vessels for the Venetian fleets and on ships that had been commissioned by foreign rulers and crusaders. Opening in 1104 and going out of business only when the Republic did in 1797, it was the longest operating factory in the world. Glassblowers, who operate on the island of Murano,* could even marry up. We know that rare cases of individual social mobility existed in Europe through royal favoritism and brute force, but glassblowers as a class were specifically recognized as eligible to marry patricians. They were also subject to another invention for retaining loyalty which, although novel, was more in the spirit of management traditions of the times: threats. Commercial treason was a concept invented to guard the glass industry, and the penalty was death.

The monopoly was well worth guarding. Since time immemorial, people had been wondering how they appeared to others and suffering the inconvenience and risk of peering into ponds. Nobody knew more than Venetians about vanity, the luxury trade, and glass. What if they came up with something more portable than ponds that people could use to reflect themselves in whatever glory they could muster, and to check their teeth after meals?

In the mid-fifteenth century, a Venetian glassmaker invented cristallo, a clear, colorless glass, and fifty years later, two other Venetian glassmakers invented—the mirror! This was such a sensation that a grateful government sought to protect the resulting monopoly by pronouncing a death sentence on any mirror-maker who left Venice to work directly for vain monarchs and aristocrats, of which the world had a plentiful supply. Eventually the most determined of them, who, not surprisingly,

---

*They started out in town, but the population tired of their forever setting things on fire and had the thought, "What if we pack them off to an island where they can set fire only to themselves?"

was Louis XIV of France, broke the monopoly with huge bribes, and got his Hall of Mirrors at Versailles from an increasingly obstreperous band of Venetian outlaws. But without Venice, we would not have had mirrors and possibly not the inventions mirrors made possible, such as fad diets and tweezers.

Never mind that China invented the printed book and Gutenberg the printing press: Renaissance Venice became the publishing center of the world, with some fifteen hundred presses. The city's comparative leniency in regard to censorship was one of the reasons that it attracted innovative and scholarly publishers from around Europe, including the designer of the roman typeface and, when he died and the patent on it ran out, the first printer to use the roman typeface. The first music publisher, Ottaviano Pertrucci, invented a system of three pressings to print polyphonic music. He thus unleashed amateur music upon the world, because the previous scores, which had to be individually hand done, were carefully given out only to court and church musicians.

Venice published the first printed cookbook in 1475, *Frank Voluptuousness*, by Bartolomeo de Sacchi, aka Il Platina, and in 1570, the first illustrated cookbook, whose author, Bartolomeo Scappi, may have been Venetian as well. That the latter book, which ran into multiple printings, identified him as being "the secret chef of Pope Pius V" somehow smacks of the Venetian.

The greatest of Venetian publishers (although neither he nor the others mentioned was born in Venice) was Aldo Manuzio, founder of the Aldine Press, whose dolphin and anchor logo is still used in New York publishing, but not by him. He also ran the Aldine Academy, in which scholars worked on the classical texts he would then publish. Manuzio, whose classical bent led to his going under the name of Aldus Manutius, invented the italic typeface. This was designed as homage to the cursive hand-writing of the monks and scribes he would contribute to putting out of business. Modern publishing would be unthinkable without two of his other inventions: the pocket edition, smaller, cheaper, and sold in greater quantities than his regular editions; and the rejection letter.

Because the great mathematician Fra Luca Pacioli settled in Venice and published the first business school textbook there, it was erroneously assumed that the Venetian practices of banking and accounting, including double-entry bookkeeping, had been Venetian inventions, along with the income tax and the sales tax. Some were ancient practices, some invented by Italian rivals, but there they were, in the textbook and in conspicuous practice by a dominant world trader, so collectively they became known as banking alla veneziana.

However, another way of throwing money around most certainly was a Venetian invention. In 1522, a Venetian merchant of what we now call vintage fashion invented the lottery, throwing the Rialto into a greedy frenzy. The government took note and, within a week, invented state supervision of lotteries. A week after that, it invented the state lottery, complete with taxes on winnings, and abolished private lotteries. This, in turn, ignited ingenuity back on the street. Scalping was invented.

Official ambiguity about gambling—that it was bad for the people but good for the purse—surfaced again when some enterprising noblemen invented the casino. There was action everywhere, but it became fashionable for the nobility to maintain private little hideaways for invited friends to enjoy games of chance and, inevitably, of love and politics. The government then opened its own, the Ridotto, admitting anyone who wore a mask. This became a wild international attraction, but it fed the Venetian passion for gambling so wildly that a century and a half later the government closed it down. Today's casino, also an international attraction, bears a sign that it is not for us (Venetians).

Other practices that stemmed from world trade included resident diplomacy and public health. From ancient times, city-states had sent out special envoys, and Milan institutionalized its diplomatic corps in the late-fifteenth century, but Venice had consulates abroad from the thirteenth century. With volatile rivals close to home and commercial outposts abroad, she had to ask herself how to protect her interests and her merchants on a steady basis. "We can't just react to whatever happens," the government must have reasoned. "We need to know in advance what is being plotted so we can influence events in our favor. What if we had our own government officials living in key places, picking up the gossip, ingratiating themselves with the local power structure, and getting the Venetian traders who live there out of trouble?"

Presumably because one thing led to another, Venice thought of inventing diplomatic ethics. Someone must have noticed that it was not a good idea to allow envoys to be on the take from their host countries, so state gifts, including medals and honors, were routinely confiscated. Extensive written reports were required, as a result of which much of the European history we have of the next five hundred years is based on material written from the Venetian point of view.

Ideas were not the only thing spreading through the global economy. Vehemently hit by outbreaks of plague, Venice invented governmental responsibility for public health. In the fourteenth century, she was running a medical school and employing state doctors who had to take periodic refresher courses. The Republic invented the quarantine, named for the forty days that incoming ships were sequestered in case symptoms of plague should appear, and began isolating the sick.

What If? (Fun)

On the happier side, Venice took up anything that looked like fun and ran with it, adding original touches and enlarging the scale. Others had carnival for a week—but what if that is only just long enough to get the party going? Venice's Carnival, in the eighteenth century, lasted for six months.

Florence had court opera in 1598—but what if we had a full opera season, putting on performances in public theaters and selling tickets? The first public opera house, at Saint Cassiano, opened for the Carnival season of 1637, and by 1700, there were ten opera houses in Venice with a repertory of more than 350 operas. And what if instead of opera's being sacred or classical, we made it funny? Baldassare Galuppi came up with opera buffa.

Improv comedy was another natural fit, although the commedia dell'arte, with its classical roots, had spread through Italy from Naples. Venice had dozens of private, public, cloistered, and open-to-the-street theaters in the eighteenth century. In its early manifestation, the dominant form throughout Italy was what we would now call scripted improv, with sketched plots on which stock characters—foolish lovers, pompous braggarts, insolent servants, domineering wives, sharp swindlers, saucy gold-diggers—improvised. When this began to grow predictable and tiresome, the thought occurred to Carlo Goldoni: "I can do better than that. What if I updated the characters and wrote their lines for them?"

One might say that reality theater was a Venetian invention. Processionals put theater in the streets and regattas put theater on the canals. The very word regatta is of ancient Venetian coinage, only coming into English in 1652 in a description of a Venetian event. Doges and procurators fairly leapt with eagerness to add a regatta and ducal procession to every noteworthy occurrence, whether political, religious, or social. The king of France or the Hapsburg emperor is coming to visit, let's have a regatta; an important dynastic marriage is arranged between merchant families—pull out those skiffs and multicolor jerkins, we're having a regatta. A plot uncovered, a plague ended, a treaty signed, start tarring those hulls, it's regatta time. Eventually, Venetian rowing clubs were organizing regattas without the pretext of a holiday. By the eighteenth century, important events needn't even be connected to a regatta; competitions between rowing clubs themselves became sufficient impetus, and not just for men. From the late fifteenth century, women's crews had a place on the canal as well. Regattas could be professional or processional, cortege or competition.

The odd practice of adopting theatrical masks in everyday life served several purposes: the doctor's mask shielded the doctor from contagion, the aristocrat's mask and cloak subdued a potentially provocative display of luxury, and the philanderer's mask mitigated the consequences of adultery, it being bad form to recognize your masked husband or wife out on the town. Although these conveniences are no longer in practice, Venice does what it can to provide opportunities for the products of its proliferating mask shops. The revived Carnival observes standard calendar limits, but it is lavishly celebrated (see chapter eight). And the American version of Hallowe'en has been enthusiastically adapted, complete with costumes, masks, and New World round pumpkins in the Rialto market, not just the pocked and pimpled green squash that Europeans pass off as pumpkins.

Other innovations in vanity and props for social life included hair in a color now known as Titian achieved by means of a sunbleaching formula and a lot of patience for sitting on a typically

Venetian roof terrace; platform shoes, called chopine, that were often so high that the lady had to lean on the shoulders of two gentlemen; and the social walker, called a cicibeo or cavaliere servente, an adaptation from the Spanish of the designated gentleman with whom a married lady could appear free of scandal, the official Just Good Friend who may or may not also have been her lover.

Of all the Venetian inventions, these may have been the ones most vividly remembered by the privileged youth who used to be sent on the Grand Tour of Europe in the hope that they become cultured and polished, the euphemism for getting scandalous impulses out of their systems out of range of their reputations. However, these may not have been the quaint customs about which they chose to write home.

CHAPTER FOUR

Venice with Your Imaginary Friend

Venetophiles often bring with them people they adore, with whom they yearn to share Venice. The place to look for such a treasure is not in the adjacent airplane seat on the way over, although its occupant may technically meet the criteria and suspect no rival. For evidence of the hidden passion, look in the carry-on bag. Discover what a Venetophile has brought along to re-read, and you will know whom he or she will keep sneaking off to visit.

A college edition of Lord Byron's or Robert Browning's poems? Canaletto's notebooks? Casanova's memoirs? Wagner's diaries? Henry James's essays and novels on Venice? Vasari's *Lives of the Artists*? Ernest Hemingway's *Across the River and into the Trees*?

Imaginary friends: It is embarrassing, but all Venetophiles have them. The magical-historical setting lends itself to the fantasy that if you could only get through that illuminated nighttime window or sneak into that darkened convent, you could be partying or doing heaven-knows-what with Casanova or George Sand. The Byron group speeds off to the Bridge of Sighs, while the Shakespeare crowd trots right down to the Rialto or the Ghetto (see chapter six).

Fans of Donna Leon's mysteries give themselves away by their abnormal interest in mundane places—a counterintuitive desire to visit police headquarters or a sudden cry of "Look! That's where Guido buys flowers for Paola!" For years, we responded to gracious luncheon invitations from friends who cautioned that they lived up ninety-four steps by cajoling them into coming to lunch with us instead. When they let drop that their apartment was used as the home for Miss Leon's hero, we bounded up those ninety-four steps in a flash, brushed past our hosts and tore through the familiar setting.

Dante devotees head for the Arsenal, but unless there happens to be a public art exhibition in the cavernous halls where rope was made, they have to halt at the front entrance. There, on the wall above the Arsenal's zoo of miscellaneous lion statuary stolen from enemies and colonies, is Dante's bust and a plaque of verses from his *Inferno*. But that is it. The great ghost town beyond that, once alive, at boiling temperatures, with whole families of skilled workers speedily turning out those legendary Venetian galleys, requires special permission to visit. Years ago, there was a waterbus going through the canal that separates two lines of vast empty sheds from which the ships were launched, so passing peeks were available, but the route is no longer used. Years from now, if current plans materialize, the Arsenal will be turned into a tourist center with a subway running directly from the airport. For now, it requires wrangling a VIP tour from an admiral to be stunned by the stretch of eerily quiet territory that gave this tiny town a world-shaking war machine and an even more envied merchant marine.

In daylight, you can spot frustrated photographers around town, trying to recapture Canaletto's views. What drives them crazy is that although he used a camera obscura himself, Canaletto was apt to rearrange buildings as if they were furniture, regularly distorting a view for balance or putting San Giorgio Maggiore smack in the midst of the Grand Canal next to the Rialto, and adding buildings that he just thought up. If this is too frustrating, they can pick any of the number of view painters,

*To Taunt the Tourists, Canaletto Moves the Buildings
Around and Sticks in Fake Ones.*

printmakers, and photographers who took up his idea, ranging
from Canaletto's contemporary, Francesco Guardi, to our near-
contemporary, Alfred Stieglitz—and from A (John Taylor Arms)
to Z (Felix Ziem). (See chapter six.)

In another respect, Canaletto's new friends have an easy time
finding him. They are not limited to trailing him around in his
personal life—birth and burial places at San Lio, family property
nearby in the Corte Perini, the place on the Barbaria delle Tole

that he rented when he was on the outs with his sisters, the Accademia where he attended meetings when it was part of the Academy of Saint Luke, and the sausages and salted provisions factory on the Riva di San Baseggio, in which he owned an interest. From his sketchbooks, reproductions of which are readily available, they can identify every spot in town where Canaletto hung out.

The great Venetian painters can be tamely admired through their works in the Accademia, the Doge's Palace, the scuole, numerous churches, and, for that matter, outside of Venice, in the major museums of the world. Breaking into the magical concentric circles where they studied, worked, squabbled, feuded, and partied is different. But if you take one of them as an imaginary friend, others tend to follow.

Titian and Associates

Titian is the best choice because he lived so long (at the legendary age of ninety-nine, it still took the plague to kill him) that numerous other paths crossed his. Also, he gave the best parties.

Like many of his friends and associates—including Giorgione, Veronese, and Jacopo Bassano, as well as his particular pals, the architect and sculptor Jacopo Sansovino and the blackmailing dirty poet Pietro Aretino—Titian can be counted as a Venetophile himself. Artists arrived from Italian towns near and far, drawn by Venice's position as an aesthetic center and, not coincidentally, as a generous and reliable patron. Around 1498, Tiziano Vecellio came from Pieve di Cadore, about seventy-five miles away, at the base of the Dolomites to the north, to study in the dynastic Bellini studio at the time when the renowned sons of Jacopo Bellini, the genius Giovanni and the competent Gentile, were carrying on his tradition.

The young painter—except that one never thinks of Titian as being young—had a state-owned studio in the uncompleted Ca' del Duca near Campo Santo Stefano and lived across the GC on the Calle Ca' Lipoli, in a building no longer there. It was adjacent to the apse of the Church of Santa Maria Gloriosa dei Frari, that repository of the history of art that now houses both Titian's early pivotal work, the *Assumption*, as its central altarpiece, and at the other end of the church, his tomb. Each of these created controversy, as did the painting he asked to have placed over the tomb, his final work, a *Pietà*, which Palma Giovane finished after Titian's death.

The friars who had commissioned the *Assumption* wavered when they saw that instead of the heavenly scene they had imagined, Titian had devoted a good third of the canvas to anxious mortals lifting their yearning hands toward the rising Virgin. His clients managed to avoid a colossal Whoops! by grudgingly accepting it, but they did succeed in ridding themselves of Titian's *Pietà*, one of the most complete representations of grief and misery ever conceived by a great artist, then on the verge of his own mortality. Under a mysterious nocturnal light, the aged Titian, in the guise of Saint Jerome, looks up in horror to the face of the dead Christ; Mary Magdalene shrieks as she flees, in sharp contrast to the poignant acceptance of the Virgin; and flickering torches held by angels cast a ghostly illumination across the scene and on the mosaics of the apse above. At first, the friars complied with Titian's last wish, but after living with the picture for a year or two, they decided they didn't much care for it. It eventually found a home in the Accademia. Titian's funeral monument was made in the nineteenth century by the forgettable sculptor Luigi Zandomeneghi and his son, and is insultingly topped by the Austrian eagle of Venice's military occupier at that time.

By 1531, Titian had moved up in the world. He brought his sister and his children (whose mother he had married at her

"We paid how much for this thing?
Can we de-accession it?"

deathbed) to a spacious apartment he rented on the northern
shore of Cannaregio, and when he was annoyed by the ram-
bunctious prostitutes in the apartment below, he ousted them by
taking over the rest of the house. At the time, it had extensive
gardens and a spectacular view of the lagoon as far as the mainland and, on a clear day, of the white caps of the Dolomites near
his birthplace. But, as happens to prime real estate in burgeoning
cities, it no longer has a view. In Titian's last years, a twenty-year

project began, using landfill to create the Fondamente Nove, from which the waterbuses now depart for the lagoon islands. The house is now 5179–83 Canareggio, an unremarkable flat wall in a narrow area across a canal and behind the present day church of the Gesuiti.

At the time, his lord-of-the-manor residence was in keeping with someone in demand by emperors, kings, popes, dukes, and doges. In addition to commissions for paintings, Titian was collecting noble titles, church benefices, honorary citizenships, and, from the Holy Roman Emperor Charles V, the promise of three hundred wagons of grain. Unfortunately, when he was ready to collect the grain, twenty-eight years later in 1564, he couldn't, because he couldn't find the paperwork. Whoops! The septuagenarian artist must have been banging around that big house in disgust shouting, "Now where did I put that damn receipt? Anybody seen a royal receipt? It's got to be here somewhere."

World renown did not protect Titian from local ecclesiastical critics. The nuns of Santa Maria degli Angeli on Murano rejected the Annunciation altarpiece he did for them in 1537, choosing instead to commission a painting by the infinitely less gifted Pordenone. Whoops! Titian sent the offending painting as a gift to Charles V. For what it's worth, the nuns still have their Pordenone.

In his new setting, Titian became known as a lavish host, and we have an account of a lawn party at which he served precious wines and bountiful food, and deployed gondolas full of singing courtesans. He, at least, was said to keep his dignity, which is more than Aretino and Sansovino cared to do. It seems that they had met those courtesans before.

The style was somewhat different at Aretino's house, on a small canal he liked to call the Rio dell'Aretino (on the right looking east from the bridge of San Giovanni Grisostomo toward the GC). It was crawling with so many guests that some passersby mistook it for an inn, joined the crowd, and when ready to leave, requested the bill. Aretino paid no rent, as the landlady hoped to live on his connections; he shamelessly cadged groceries from his friends, and he inveigled the ambitious young Tintoretto to paint his ceiling for only a letter of praise as payment. When he was thrown out by the landlady's son, he snapped that it was a leaky apartment anyway, and found himself better quarters on the GC, at the Riva del Carbon, where he didn't pay his rent, either. Sansovino also lived rent-free, in the piazza, where he was given state quarters in the Procuratie Vecchie.

Tintoretto did not attend these parties, as he was Titian's archenemy and, anyway, led a pious life. He lived on the Fondamenta dei Mori, nos. 3398–99, spent years working at San Rocco's scuola and church, and is buried in his own parish church, the Madonna dell'Orto.

Defying just consequences, Aretino died happily, and Titian pathetically. The poet keeled over in a tavern, laughing at a dirty joke about his sister. He could hardly have deserved less to be memorialized on sacred ground, but there he is, in a place of honor under the floor of the church of San Luca, not far from the house on the Riva del Carbon. In contrast, after Titian died at home, his house was ransacked and looted, and he was buried in the church of his critics, grand though it is, without the painting he asked to have over his grave. His house has a plaque on it, and the nearby campo is named after him, but now it is just a house where someone else lives. Aretino's bust is more conspicuous: for some reason, it adorns the fruit and vegetable market on the Grand Canal.

The Venetophile Class Picture (left to right: Richard Wagner, John Marin, Wolfgang Amadeus Mozart, Marcel Proust, Titian, Lord Byron,

The Salon Keepers

Strangely, the other cult figures who are most popular as imaginary friends are almost always Venetophiles themselves, rather than Venetians. Perhaps this is because Venice, always nervous about the possibility of a dynastic takeover, disapproved of personality cults. So until foreigners immerse themselves in Venetian history, they tend not to be acquainted, let alone imaginary friends, with Venetians other than Casanova and Marco Polo.

To find the cult Venetophiles, we go through a whole second string of Venetophiles who became famous, if only within the city, for entertaining their world-famous compatriots. They opened their hospitable doors in the late nineteenth century, after military occupation and poverty had turned Venice socially dark.

Before that, the world knew that nobody gave a better party than

*Pietro Aretino, Ernest Hemingway, Peggy Guggenheim, John Singer
Sargent, Henry James).*

Venetians. Sovereigns loved swooping in for state visits of amazing
splendor, and rich foreigners considered Venice the dessert course
of their Grand Tours. Even after the demise of the Republic, in the
early nineteenth century, Countess Albrizzi held forth at the Corte
Michiel, and her rival, Countess Maria Querini Benzon, entertained en masse (and frequently individually) at Ca' Benzon on the
GC. A belle in her youth, Countess Benzon was immortalized in a
still-popular song as "the blonde in the gondola," but she was better remembered around town later as the fat lady who used to tuck
polenta down her bosom to keep it warm for in-transit munching.

The first Venetophile salon was that of the English consul
Joseph Smith in the mid-eighteenth century. A description of his
parties can be found in *A Venetian Affair* by Andrea di Robilant, a
nonfiction romance in which Smith discovers the hero's and
heroine's designs on him just in time to save his virtue and

purse. Not only are they conducting their clandestine affair at his house, but they are plotting to use him as a permanent cover by marrying him and his money to the heroine. Smith, who built and lived at Ca' Mangilli-Valmarana on the Grand Canal, was also doing a booming business supplying foreigners with souvenir paintings by Canaletto, collecting enough books to form the basis of the British Library, and selling his own collection to the British royal family.

A century later, a major donor to the British Museum, Sir Austen Henry Layard, the British diplomat who had discovered the ruins of Nineveh, retired to Venice with his much younger wife, Enid. They maintained a salon, which she kept up long after his death, in Ca' Capello, their GC house opposite the Sant'Angelo waterbus stop. Hordes of foreign royalty came through their doors, as well as the growing expat community, whom the Layards provided with an English church on the Campo San Vio and the opportunity to do good works at a sailors' retirement home they founded on the Giudecca. They also threw themselves into the promotion of Venetian glass- and lace-making, not only for aesthetic reasons but to foster employment among Venetian artisans.

The other key people for newcomers to see for a Venetian orientation during the nineteenth century were also Brits: first Rawdon Brown (until he turned irascible) and then the Scotsman Horatio Brown, no relation to each other but both chroniclers of Venice. Neither is likely to be as much in demand as an imaginary friend as they were as real friends, but both were stalwart Venetophiles who made important contributions to the knowledge of other Venetophiles, in person and through their work.

And then came the Americans. By the late nineteenth century, with Venetian society hunkered down and reduced to peddling its patrimony in chunks, Americans opened GC salons that were frequented by superstar Venetophiles. By then, Venice was teeming with English and American artists and writers. European royals flocked there as well—rarely reigning royalty, as in Venice's heyday, but the ousted, the out-of-favor, and the pretenders for whom rented Venetian houses were as close as they were going to get to living in palaces.*

One American salon was at Ca' Alvisi, aka Ca' Gaggia, which consists of an ill-matched pair of facades—one colonnaded and one plain—next door to the Europa & Regina hotel complex, with a guest suite in Ca' Giustiniani-Recanati out back. Katharine de Kay Bronson of New York presided there with her daughter. The other was Ca' Barbaro, a huge double house near the Accademia bridge, which Daniel and Ariana Curtis of Boston first rented, then bought. From time to time, they sublet to Isabella Stewart Gardner of Boston without disturbing the visiting habits of the guests.

Both Ca' Alvisi and Ca' Barbaro had their own careers in the arts. Mrs. Bronson was given to the impressive feat of writing playlets in Venetian dialect and the perhaps oppressive one of making her household staff perform them. Mrs. Curtis also wrote a play, but not about Venice. However, Ca' Barbaro has starred in literature and film as the model for the house in *The Wings of the Dove* as well as the set for that film, and for other such films as *Brideshead Revisited, In Love and War,* and *Everyone Says I Love You.*

Venetophile hosts were not exempt from the vision of immortality—the longing for a permanent monument and perpetual public recognition of themselves as significant Venetophiles that would allow them to live on in the well-stocked

---

*Even in the eighteenth century, Voltaire's Candide finds that six strangers in his Venetian inn turn out to be the dethroned Grand Sultan, an English king just out of prison, an Emperor of All the Russias who was reared in prison, two deposed kings of Poland, and a luckless king of Corsica.

stream of Venetian history. Two of them accomplished this by willing their houses and collections to become major museums with their names on them. While Mrs. Gardner was subletting in Venice, she gradually bought enough bits and pieces of other Venetian houses, principally the Ca' d'Oro, to construct her own in Boston, which is now her museum (see chapter eight). In the mid-twentieth century, Peggy Guggenheim out-Venetophiled her by bequeathing her house, where she ran a salon and then some for modern artists of assorted nationalities and tastes, to become a museum right in Venice itself.

One hazard of salon-keeping is that all those creative and combustible people begin using the material around them. It was all very well for Monet to paint what he saw from the Ca' Barbaro water steps and for Henry James to populate the house with his fictional characters. But when Edith Wharton wrote "The Verdict," a short story about a painter who gives up art and marries money when he realizes how meager his talent is, the Colt gun heiress who had married the Curtises' painter-son Ralph was outraged. Their entire salon was seething after Vernon Lee set her story "Lady Tal" in the "half-fashionable, half-artistic Anglo-American idleness of Venice, with its poetic setting and its prosaic reality." Henry James was apoplectic because the hero was a fussbudget aging bachelor novelist described as "a kind of Henry James, of a lesser magnitude." Vernon Lee was frozen out of town.

Equally mischievous artists could at least be set sketching. Mrs. Bronson acquired quite a collection when she suggested that her guests draw one another, and Peggy Guggenheim had guestbooks full of such valuable little pictures that they were later exhibited at her posthumous museum.

Depending on when your imaginary friend lived his real life, you can be reasonably sure of finding him and a number of his cohorts at Consul Smith's or at Countess Albrizzi's and Countess Benzon's, or at the Layards', the Curtises' and Mrs. Bronson's. Any time in the last three centuries, you could also find them hanging out at the piazza cafés. Whistler had his mail delivered to Florian's, where Henry James had breakfast before having lunch at the Quadri, and Byron, Goethe, and Balzac had been there before them.

Lord Byron

Lord Byron, Venetophile extraordinaire, frequented the salons of the two Venetian countesses, but he also lost no time in mixing with the less exalted natives. Within a week of his arrival in November 1818, he had rented rooms off the Frezzeria and was enjoying the landlord's wife. When his enjoyment abated, he took a two-year lease at the Grand Canal's Ca' Mocenigo, where he installed her successors and a collection of other wild creatures, of the jungle variety. It was at Countess Benzon's that he met the young Countess Teresa Guiccioli, the mistress who was to take him away from Venice—first in pursuit of her, to Ravenna, and then in escape from her, to Greece, where he expired.

A Venetophile in pursuit of Lord Byron will find his first apartment at 1673–74 on the Piscina de Frezzeria, in the district of San Marco, and his grander quarters at Ca' Mocenigo, now marked by a plaque. His other properties are unfortunately gone. These were two getaway cottages in town, one of them in the Campo Santa Maria del Giglio, near the Gritti Hotel, and another on the Giudecca. Maintaining such places for gambling and other conviviality was a Venetian habit and we get our word casino from these little houses, called casini. However, Byron did not keep them for the usual Venetian gentleman's reason of needing a trysting place away from the wife at home. Byron needed trysting places away from the cat-fighting mistresses he had installed at home.

He could also be found at every gambling house and theater in town, but those places are no longer operating. The last state-run ridotto has been incorporated into the Hotel Monaco, and the one above the Ponte dei Baretteri on the Merceria now houses the Alliance Française. Although Byron kept a box at the Fenice opera house, that was the Fenice from two fires ago. The Grand Canal, in which he swam for hours at a time, is still there, but swimming is not advised.

Following Byron around involves going afield (and a-lagoon). He commuted to the island of San Lazzaro to study Armenian, and the monks piously preserve the workspace of their profligate pupil along with his portraits and a commemorative tablet. He rode horseback on the Lido, sometimes with Shelley, when that poet came to argue the maternal rights of Byron's (and perhaps Shelley's) discarded mistress, Claire Clairmont. And he observed the Venetian summer holiday custom of taking a villa on the Brenta.

Lord Byron's admirers will also want to follow his imagination to the places he depicts in his poems and plays. Most obvious (and easily accessible with a ticket for the Doge's Palace tour) is the inside view from the Bridge of Sighs, as immortalized in *Childe Harold's Pilgrimage* (see chapter six). The recently restored Foscari family house, which Ruskin considered the finest example of fifteenth-century Venetian architecture, is relatively accessible because it is now part of the university. Doge Francesco Foscari (the elder of the Two Foscari in Byron's play and Verdi's spinoff opera, whose duty to office rendered him helpless to quash the ultimately fatal punishment of his beloved but rascally and possibly treasonous son) died there shortly after being eased out of the dogeship and thus out of the Doge's Palace. A copy of the unhappy doge's portrait, kneeling to the Lion of Saint Mark, is affixed over the Porta della Carta, the entrance to the Doge's Palace.

The death place of Marino Faliero, of Byron's play by that name, is on that same tour ticket to the Doge's Palace because he was beheaded on its steps, although this was long before the existence of the Giants' Staircase, which we see there now. Doge Falier's sarcophagus, which was opened in the nineteenth century and found to contain a skull between the legs of the headless skeleton, is under the arcade of the Turkish Warehouse. The Falier family house was across the canal opposite Campo Santi Apostoli.

For the mood of Lord Byron's doom and gloom poem "Ode on Venice," it is not a question of where to look, but when. On high water days, after the plaintive warning of the sirens, as the level creeps up to one's knees and the daily wailing begins about what should be done to save Venice, the mood is set for:

> Oh, Venice! Venice! when thy marble walls
> Are level with the water, there shall be
> A cry of nations o'er thy sunken halls,
> A loud lament along the sweeping sea!

John Ruskin

Hardly anyone is more popular as an imaginary friend than the great Victorian art critic and über-Venetophile John Ruskin, who had no real friends in Venice or anywhere else. True, his mother and father loved him, but even his admirers and protégés didn't much care for him personally. Marcel Proust, who conceived his passion for Venice from reading and translating Ruskin, is said to have delayed going there until he was sure that Ruskin was safely dead.

Ruskin does not make an easy holiday companion. He was given to startling outbursts that would doubtless be accompanied, were he present in the flesh, with flying spittle. He called Titian's *Presentation of the Virgin* (in the Accademia) "stupid and

The Ur-Venetophile John Ruskin and His Nemesis
(Mr. Ruskin is the one pictured at left).

uninteresting." A mere gargoyle on the side of the church of
Santa Maria Formosa prompted him to write, "A head—huge,
inhuman and monstrous—leering in bestial degradation, too foul
to be either pictured or described, or to be beheld for more than
an instant; for in that head is embodied the type of the evil spirit
to which Venice was abandoned in the fourth period of her
decline; and it is as well that we should see and feel the full horror
of it on this spot, and know what pestilence it was that came and
breathed upon her beauty. . . ." Canova's tomb in the Frari (since
the design was not used for Titian as Canova had intended,
Canova's students prepared it for him) was called "consummate
in science, intolerable in affectation, ridiculous in conception,
null and void to the uttermost in invention and feeling."

Don't hold back, Mr. Ruskin. Tell us what you really think.

This sort of thing led Henry James to compare going around with *The Stones of Venice* and especially with later Ruskin works to vacationing with your angry governess. Yet that is what James chose to do, keeping up a one-sided conversation in which he thanked Ruskin for drawing his attention to the "serious loveliness" of the row of women banqueters in Tintoretto's *The Marriage at Cana* at the Salute, took mild and respectful exception to Ruskin's condemnation of the railway approach to Venice, and argued that Ruskin was "pushing matters too far" by calling Veronese deeply spiritual. On sum, he stated that there is no one better than Ruskin for enhancing the enjoyment of Venice.

Many a later Venetophile can vouch for this. Creepy old poop though he was—in a fit of aesthetic Puritanism, he destroyed all of Turner's drawings of nudes—Ruskin was the most zealous and discerning Venetophile of all, and imaginary time spent with him is always rewarding. His detailed analyses and drawings of Venetian architecture are too rich to miss. An entire day just going from one capital of the Doge's Palace to another reading his descriptions can pass so quickly that you are surprised when the print becomes too shadowy to discern and you wonder why your arms ache.

The answer is: from carrying around *The Stones of Venice*. If you form a serious attachment, this is a problem, because there is hardly anywhere you can go where your imaginary friend does not have something interesting and often poetic to say.

An even worse problem can develop from hanging out with Ruskin. One day I looked out of our gothic windows at the Sansovino house next door and mused, "You know, Ruskin does have a point. There *is* something vulgar about the Renaissance."

"Oh-oh," came the response from within the room. "Time for you to go home."

A way to guard against this form of seduction is to open an imaginary friendship with Mrs. Ruskin as well. Euphemia Ruskin had a merrier time in Venice, as we know from her published letters. Because she was so cheerful in spite of her husband's notorious neglect (after five years of marriage, she was able to prove to a mesmerized divorce court that she was a virgin), we forgive her turning to the Austrians for her social life. There was little other social life available, as the Venetians were in mourning for their independence, and it was either Austrians or staying home with Mr. Ruskin.

Imaginary friends who don't find that as daunting a prospect as Mrs. Ruskin did can conjure up the couple by renting their room at the Danieli Hotel (No. 32) or at the Gritti, which was then Ca' Wetzlar, where they occupied the ground-floor front rooms. (Byron had tried earlier to rent from Baroness von Wetzlar, but she drove too hard a bargain for him.) On Ruskin's visits before his marriage, he had stayed at the Danieli, and in 1887, after the divorce, he stayed at the Grand Hotel and then at the site of the subsequently built, plaque-bearing Pensione la Calcina, Zattere ai Gesuati 781.

Robert Browning and Son

According to Robert and Elizabeth Browning, who were the world's most besotted parents, their son, Robert Wiedemann Barrett Browning, known as Pen, came down with a major case of Venetophilia at the age of two. The family was living in, of all places, Florence, when they took a five-week trip to Venice in 1851. Pen Browning was destined to spend his adult life watching people register the thought, "*That's* what those two poetic geniuses produced?" but his parents considered him a marvel of aesthetic discernment and religious piety.

As a sign of his depth of soul, they reported (Mrs. Browning being given to citing his genius in baby talk) that their toddler had shrieked with delight at the sight of the Venetian Customs House and on being shown various churches. Perhaps their interpretation was correct. Pen grew up to be a dabbler, but his love of Venice turned out to be constant.

The widowed Robert Browning had started visiting Venice again in 1878 with his sister. They stayed at the Albergo dell'Universo, which was housed in Ca' Brandolin-Rota, next door to the Accademia Galleries. Then the poet made friends with Mrs. Bronson, whose houseguests they were thereafter, in Venice and at her retreat in Asolo, which also would come to have a great hold on father and son.

But at this time, Pen was at Christ Church, Oxford, rowing, playing billiards, and flunking; then he was in Paris, painting and sculpting with modest success that fell short of Browning family standards. Robert Browning used his influence as a national treasure on Pen's behalf with university and art world authorities, but it was a struggle. He was not getting the dazzling results that his late wife had expected.

Then he got the idea of installing Pen in an important Venetian house. Next door to the Universo, on the other side from the Accademia, was a huge place, Ca' Contarini-Polignac, aka Contarini del Zaffo, which Browning tried to buy. The deal deteriorated into a lawsuit, but Pen loved the idea and managed to discover his own way of financing life as a property owner on the GC.

He married an American heiress. He had spent fourteen years of courtship on the wealthy Fannie Coddington, whose feelings for him were apparently chiefly fueled by her admiration of his parents, and he finally wore her down. With her dowry, they bought Ca' Rezzonico, now the Museum of Eighteenth Century Venice and thus open to visitors. The junior Brownings put a lot of work into it, commuting from their temporary residence at the much-rented Ca' Dario.

They also put into Ca' Rezzonico a beautiful young woman

who was variously rumored to be Pen's mistress or his daughter. Eventually his wife, who had managed to put up with the snakes and birds Pen kept, had enough and left. But that was later. Until his death, Robert Browning dignified the household with his presence. He cut a great figure around town, tootling about in the gondola he maintained, reading his poetry aloud for assembled guests at Mrs. Bronson's, at the Curtises', at Lady Layard's. He attracted groupies down from England.

In earlier years, Robert Browning had dipped into legendary Venice for the adultery and murder of "In a Gondola" and for "A Toccata of Galuppi's," which is not so much a tribute to the composer as an expression of melancholy yearning for the past by a home-bound Venetophile: "I was never out of England—it's as if I saw it all."

Once the poet had gotten to know Venice, the tone changed. "Ponte dell' Angelo, Venice" contains a supernatural fright, but its theme is a modern one—the rapacity of lawyers. His tribute to Goldoni is backhanded praise for the playwright's superficiality. And he went after the other Venetophiles around town, writing a snippy poem about Rawdon Brown's inability to leave Venice on a planned trip home, and an even snippier one about Richard Wagner:

> Wagner gave six concerts: five
> I have managed to survive.
> He announces the other two:
> Stand these—hang me if I do!

Squabbles aside, it was a huge loss to Venetophiliac society when Browning died there in the closing days of 1889. He lay majestically in state at Ca' Rezzonico before his body was returned to England to be buried in the Poets' Corner at Westminster Abbey. Lady Layard rushed over with a hand-picked and handmade laurel wreath to lay on the coffin.

Richard Wagner

Richard Wagner had gone to Venice to get away from noise, only it was the noise being made by his first wife, Minna, and his mistress, Mathilde Wesendonck, whose husband was one of Wagner's many betrayed benefactors. The Wagners had accepted a house on the Wesendoncks' estate, where Wagner wrote the first act of *Tristan and Isolde* before Mrs. Wagner found out that between them, the Wesendoncks were providing him with more comfort than she had realized. Wagner left them to sort this out for themselves as he picked himself up and went to Venice in 1858 to write the second act.

He stayed for just a year, but returned to Venice in 1882 with a different volatile wife, Cosima née Lizst, whom he had acquired from another friend, her first husband and his conductor, Hans von Bülow. The following year, Wagner, like Browning, died in Venice and had a memorable gondola funeral procession on the way out of town to be buried at home.

During the first trip, Wagner quickly moved from the Danieli Hotel into the lower piano nobile (there are two) of the vast Ca' Giustiniani on the Grand Canal. With Ca' Foscari, next door, it (and various other Giustiniani palaces around town, including Mrs. Bronson's guesthouse), had belonged to the Giustiniani family, who claimed to be descendents of the Emperor Justinian. It was a legacy they made considerable effort to keep going. In the twelfth century, the family had petered down to one lone monk who was summarily fished out of his quiet life by dispensation of the pope and married off to the doge's daughter with explicit instructions to continue his line. After he dutifully produced twelve Giustiniani children, his plea to be allowed to return to his monastery was granted, and the family lasted until the twentieth century.

Although they are not open to the public, I know those quar-

ters from both virtual and real experience, difficult as it sometimes is to tell the two apart where Venice is concerned. In recent
years, Ca' Giustiniani was occupied by a friend who gave those
grand balls that made my first Venetian fantasy come true. But I
was already familiar with the front rooms from *Venetian Life,* the
book William Dean Howells wrote when he was American consul in Venice (see chapter five). That post was a reward for writing President Lincoln's campaign biography, and on the last year
of his assignment, five years after Wagner had vacated the building, the Howells family lived there. As a young journalist,
Howells had not considered it worthwhile to take advantage of
the opportunity to meet Lincoln for a mere campaign biography,
but he hit his stride with his delightful account of mid-
nineteenth century Venice. When he regains the reputation he
once had of being one of America's great novelists, I will not be
the only Venetophile to claim him among my imaginary friends.

By the time the Howellses rented six rooms and two kitchens
at Ca' Giustiniani for a dollar a day, the centerpiece of the salon
on the Grand Canal, with its frescoed ceiling and gilded mirrors,
was a nonfunctioning sewing machine. Wagner, who had taken
one room and not always met the rent, imported his piano and
decorated—one can hardly say cheered things up—by hanging
red cloth on the walls.

Ca' Giustiniani is near the big curve in the GC, and when the
composer went out on one of his balconies (balconies from
which we took a breath of night air during those balls), he could
hear the ritual warning shout of the gondoliers as they turned
into the side canal. Although he sneered at the level of formal
music in Venice (except for the piazza bands, which occasionally
played his own work), he was struck by these cries and adapted
them for the shepherd's horn in the third act of *Tristan.*

When Wagner returned to Venice with Cosima and an
entourage of servants and children, they stayed at the Europa

Hotel and then moved into the garden wing of Ca' Vendramin Calergi (the main house had been occupied by the French Pretender), where he hung blue cloth, finished *Parsifal*, and died. The huge Renaissance building is open to visitors as it now serves as the municipal casino, and it has its Wagner commemorative plaque. (Anti-Wagnerites prefer the plaque of Venetian composer Benedetto Marcello, slightly farther down the canal.)

Although Wagner had demanded privacy for work, work, work, Wagner sightings around town were not uncommon. He was sketched at Mrs. Bronson's by the Russian Venetophile, painter and photographer Alexander Wolkoff; seen by Whistler at Florian's; and spotted on the waterbus, in bad shape, by an adoring Gabriele D'Annunzio, who described the incident in his novel *The Flame*. Not long before he died, Wagner conducted a private concert at the Fenice for Cosima's birthday and took the children out to see the Carnival. Franz Werfel's novelized biography *Verdi* contains scenes of Wagner's Fenice rehearsal, his band appreciation in the piazza, and it has Verdi coming to pay a belated call, only to be told that Wagner had just that minute died.

Henry James

It is hard to get Henry James alone. He had John Ruskin as his own imaginary friend, and generations of writers and scholars after James have chosen him as theirs. In addition, there were his real friends and acquaintances, some of whom, especially the expat artists, are other people's imaginary friends. Collectively, it begins to sound like a description he once gave of his sightseeing party's landing on Torcello: "We had two mighty gondoliers, and we clove the wandering breezes of the lagoon, like a cargo of deities descending from Olympus."

But if Henry James's imaginary friends were to be faithful to his strict preferences, they would go out on the town with him alone, using only his purposely published writings about Venice, not the letters and anecdotes that have been churned up since. There are exhaustive biographies that dog his every footstep and fictionalized "biographies" that dog every step he might have taken, but he loathed biographers and feared becoming such a subject.

Indeed, the greatest reward for his Venetophile disciples is to see even the most obvious sights through his eyes—with the bonus of digestible tidbits he repeats from Ruskin. Henry James's essays about Venice, variously published as *Italian Hours* and *Venetian Hours,* contain some of the most memorable descriptions of art and architecture, about which he warned that there was "notoriously nothing more to be said. . . . There is nothing left to discover or describe, and originality of attitude is completely impossible."

Then he describes the Baroque church of the Salute as waiting "like some great lady on the threshold of her salon. She is more ample and serene, more seated at her door, than all the copyists have told us, with her domes and scrolls, her scolloped [sic] buttresses and statues forming a pompous crown, and her wide steps disposed on the ground like the train of a robe."

And he calls attention to the Tintorettos at the Scuola of San Rocco by saying, "Solemn indeed is the place, solemn and strangely suggestive, for the simple reason that we shall scarcely find four walls elsewhere that inclose [sic] within a like area an equal quantity of genius. The air is thick with it and dense and difficult to breathe; for it was genius that was not happy, inasmuch as it lacked the art to fix itself forever. It is not immortality that we breathe at the Scuola of San Rocco, but conscious, reluctant mortality."

And instead of repeating that the Piazza San Marco is a drawing room or an opera set, he calls it "the lobby of the opera in the intervals of the performance."

It is true that even James indulges in the usual railing against other tourists, restoration projects, and public transportation (he derides, or perhaps flatters, the pokey waterbus by characterizing it as New York–style "rapid transit"), and that he romanticizes the Venetian squalor of that time. But there is no more unusual or insightful travel tip than his warning about the Venetian version of cabin fever.

> After you have stayed a week and the bloom of novelty has rubbed off . . . you have seen all the principal pictures and heard the names of the palaces announced a hundred times . . . you have walked several hundred times around the Piazza and bought several bushels of photographs. . . . You have tried the opera and found it very bad . . . you have begun to have a shipboard feeling—to regard the Piazza as an enormous saloon and the Riva degli Schiavoni as a promenade-deck. . . .
>
> If in such a state of mind you take your departure you act with fatal rashness. The loss is your own. . . . When you have called for the bill to go, pay it and remain, and you will find on the morrow that you are deeply attached to Venice. It is by living there from day to day that you feel the fullness of her charm; that you invite her exquisite influence to sink into your spirit. . . . The place seems to personify itself, to become human and sentient and conscious of your affection. You desire to embrace it, to caress it, to possess it; and finally a soft sense of possession grows up and your visit becomes a perpetual love-affair.

The next sources for Henry James's imaginary friends are his novels *The Wings of the Dove* and *The Aspern Papers.* In the former, Milly Theale's dream house is based on Ca' Barbaro, which he also describes in the essays, although not by name, and where he was often a guest of the Curtises' and of Mrs. Gardner's.

The Aspern Papers is set in a Ca' Capello—not the Layards' Ca' Capello on the GC, but a smaller one in Santa Croce, across the canal from the train station and next door to the huge Ca' Gradenigo, with twin gardens in between. I did not realize this juxtaposition when a friend living in Ca' Gradenigo took me to its garden. Such are James's powers of suggestion that I swore I had been there before, although I was unable to say when or how. The Master's descriptions are sparse and atmospheric, but somehow they invoked that particular garden. At any rate, it was not Gabriele D'Annunzio's hot-and-heavy description that alerted me, although that writer uses Ca' Capello in *The Flame* as the residence of the barely disguised Eleanora Duse, long-adoring and -suffering mistress of the barely disguised Gabriele D'Annunzio. James knew Ca' Capello through an American writer, Constance Fletcher, who did, in fact, have a portrait of Lord Byron that she had acquired through romance, although hers had come two generations later, from the poet's grandson.

Actually, I was in the wrong one of the two gardens, which a Ca' Gradenigo resident had cultivated in protest against what had happened to the "real" *Aspern Papers* garden. Ca' Capello has become the quarters of an arts commission office charged with protecting historic sites and—in defiance of its own principles—it filled its garden with its air-conditioning equipment.

James may not have wanted his personal comings and goings chronicled, but he admitted to harboring the impulse to do this for an admired author. He actually used the word "thrill" in connection with knowing that the George Sand–Alfred de Musset–Venetian doctor scandal (see chapter one) had begun in the Hotel Danieli, and was interested to discover the house in which Sand subsequently lived. Then he went on to fret about the strange phenomenon that gives rise to imaginary friends, as well as the more modern and perhaps less decorous forms of groupie-ism:

I am not sure that the curiosity I speak of has not at last, in my breast, yielded to another form of wonderment—truly to the rather rueful question of why we have so continued to concern ourselves, and why the fond observer of the foot-prints of genius is likely so to continue attentive to an alter-cation neither in itself and in its day, nor in its preserved and attested records, at all positively edifying. The answer to such an inquiry would doubtless reward patience, but I fear we can now glance at its possibilities only long enough to say that interesting persons—so they be of a sufficiently approved and established interest—render in some degree interesting whatever happens to them, and give it an impor-tance even when very little else (as in the case I refer to) may have operated to give it a dignity.

Yes, Master. That's why we are following you.

His first trip was in 1869, and he returned in 1872 with his unstable sister, Alice. In 1881 he moved from the Danieli, com-plaining of the waterbus noise, to rooms at 4161 on the Riva degli Schiavoni, which gave him a view of the island of San Giorgio Maggiore and the traffic in the basin when he looked up from working on *The Portrait of a Lady.*

He had also looked up the American salon keepers and on many subsequent trips was the houseguest of Mrs. Bronson, Mr. and Mrs. Curtis, and Mrs. Gardner. He wrote lovely things about them in his essays; his sensitivity to privacy preventing him from naming them until he wrote about Mrs. Bronson after her death.

However, his letters, so many of which managed to survive despite his frantic efforts to destroy them, contain less-flattering references, of the kind that would amuse his designated reader but bruise his hosts. Even his bread-and-butter letters to Mrs. Curtis are a bit odd, just managing to intimate, in his praise of the library, that he appreciated her house more than she did and that he liked it better without her there: "Quite the most thrilling of my experiences since we parted was to go back to the beautiful empty Barbaro and spend thirty-six hours there with a grand usurped sense of its being my own."

The trip when he most didn't want us looking over his shoulder was his 1894 letter-destroying mission after the apparent suicide of his friend, Constance Fenimore Woolson, a popular novelist of her day and a niece of Venetophile James Fenimore Cooper. Depending on which critic you read, Miss Woolson was either hopelessly in love with James or an equal partner in the exchange of literary ideas. At any rate, she settled in Venice at James's suggestion and took up his casually stated wish to have his own Venetian property with such enthusiasm that he began avoiding her.

Melancholy, deaf, and ill, on purpose or in a disorienting fever, she leapt to her death from her top-floor apartment in Ca' Semitecolo, opposite the Gritti Hotel. James declared himself unable to face the funeral or Venice ever again—and then suddenly whizzed down there, going through her papers and, most bizarrely of all, attempting to sink her black Victorian dresses in the lagoon, only to have them catch air and come ballooning up.

Declining to stay with his friends on this occasion, he made a point of obtaining for himself the apartment that Miss Woolson had occupied when she first went to Venice. It was in Ca' Biondetti, next door to the building that today houses the Guggenheim Collection, and it bears a plaque honoring an eighteenth-century resident, the pastel portraitist Rosalba Carriera. Unable to resist the lure of three such imaginary friends, we rented the ground-floor apartment one snowy winter, conjuring James trudging down the dark alley to the courtyard each day, with more material for his grim task.

James McNeill Whistler

Whistler, too, went to Venice because of John Ruskin, but not out of friendship, imaginary or otherwise. Bankrupt from suing Ruskin for a scathing review (Whistler won, but was sarcastically awarded a farthing in damages and forced to pay court costs), he took a commission to make etchings of Venice. Nor was he initially in love with the place he referred to as "a sort of Opera Comique country." In an early letter to his sister-in-law, he carried on about how much he missed London and London club food in contrast to the Italian cuisine. He complained about the Italian language, and how the unusual cold was limiting his progress. Just the sort of thing for which tourists are ridiculed.

But things got better. Contracted to stay for three months and produce twelve etchings, he remained for fourteen months beginning in September 1879 and executed more than 150 prints and pastels. A slight figure with a Yankee accent, a mass of curly black hair with a punky white streak in the front, a straw boater in his hand, a ribbon standing in for a tie, and a monocle in his eye, Whistler makes an exciting, if irascible, imaginary friend. He roamed the city, hitting all the cafés and late-night clubs and dominating the salon at Mrs. Bronson's.

When in the imaginary company of painters and printmakers, the challenging task is to match the visual evidence they left with the reality, checking whether they were faithful to Venice or took wanton liberties with her appearance. Whistler deliberately picked little-known areas in an effort to capture the characteristic local flavor, rarely depicting the major monuments. As a result, the dedicated Venetophile goes mad trying to track down his sites among the many possibilities. There are recent guides that give descriptions, but not directions, and some of the views no longer exist, having given way to age or to the advances of

*To Taunt the Tourists, Whistler Hunts Up Obscure Sites
and Renders Them Backwards.*

modernity. Even those views that remain defy easy identification, which makes it all the more gratifying to his imaginary friends to discover one of those unremarkable buildings, or an obscure Moorish window fronting on a canal.

But there is an additional affliction: Whistler worked directly on the plates, refusing to account for the reversal of the printing process, so the views of Venice he produced are mirror images.

He was taking care to annoy anyone who might want to purchase his work as a souvenir. Presumably, he was also capturing the immediacy of the moment, not to mention saving himself the labor of first making a drawing, and then tracing or reproducing it on the plate. The post-Whistlerian printmakers in Venice, including Mortimer Menpes, Joseph Pennell, Otto Bacher, Ernest David Roth, and John Marin, did the same, although the Scottish artist James McBey dissented and used a rear-view automobile mirror on his easel to etch in reverse.

So we are reduced to fishing out a compact mirror, or carefully lining up a view, then glancing between the sight and a photocopy held aloft, looking at the image backward through the blank side of the paper. Both methods are invitations to public ridicule.

When Whistler first went to Venice, he and his mistress, Maud Franklin, lived somewhere along the Rio di San Barnaba, and he may have had a studio at Ca' Rezzonico, where a number of artists had working space before the building was sold to Pen Browning. (The uncertainty is because unlike John Singer Sargent, who did work at Ca' Rezzonico, Whistler never did views of or from it.) Yet when he moved to the Casa Jankovitz, now the Bucintoro Hotel, he did numerous views from the windows and of the neighborhood on the Riva degli Schiavoni and the nearby Via Garibaldi. (No plaque, although his enemy, Ruskin, got his.) The building is L-shaped, so that all the rooms have remarkable vistas south and west, and it was full of art students under the guidance of Frank Duveneck when Whistler joined the party.

This was not far from the rooms Henry James took on the Schiavoni soon afterward. Duveneck's wife-to-be and her father, Lizzie and Francis Boott, lent much to James's characters Maggie and Adam Verver in *The Golden Bowl* and Pansy and Gilbert Osmond in *The Portrait of a Lady*.

John Singer Sargent

John Singer Sargent led a more luxurious and less exciting life in Venice. Arriving with his parents in 1880, he stayed at the old Hotel d'Italie, which was on the site of the Hotel Bauer, and stayed on after them, taking rooms in the piazza and the studio in Ca' Rezzonico.

He, too, portrayed out-of-the-way places, but they are not so hard to find, and in some instances he kindly put the address in the title: *Campo dei Frari, Ponte Panada: Fondamente Nove, Campo behind the Scuola di San Rocco, Café on the Riva degli Schiavoni,* the last being a favorite artists' hangout, the Orientale, which was where the Danieli Hotel annex is now.

As a cousin of the Curtises', he was warmly welcomed to Ca' Barbaro for many years until he made his hosts a handsome bread-and-butter present. It was a portrait of the senior and junior Curtises in their splendid salon, and it would have been a jewel of the family's collection had not Mrs. Curtis—having acquired the true Venetian spirit—rejected it. She claimed that he made her look old and stodgy, and that it made her son, Ralph, perched on the edge of a gilded table, look foppish. That may be, but she could have accepted it and stashed it in her attic. Since Sargent retained possession, he presented it to the Royal Academy in London as his diploma piece, thus making it possible for untold numbers of people to see those poses as the definitive depiction of the Curtises.

Some Poor Prospects

Some imaginary friendships are not going to work. The people may be extraordinary, but they don't make good traveling companions, at least not in Venice.

Shakespeare, for starters. He wasn't there. Remember? And for all the speculation about the models for *The Tragedy of Othello, Moor of Venice* (see chapter two), most of the play takes place in Cyprus. You could people the Ghetto and the Doge's Palace with characters from *The Merchant of Venice,* but turning Venice into one of Shakespeare's stage sets does not feed hunger for knowledge about Venice.

Marco Polo wasn't there much. He was either in transit, in China, or at a war with Genoa, most of which he spent in a prisoner-of-war camp, dictating his memoir. The house from which he set off and famously returned, unrecognized until his relatives understood how rich he was, burned down in 1596. Much is made of a fragment of a thirteenth-century arch in the Corte Seconda del Milion and other bits incorporated into the nearby Malibran Theater. Besides, he was born in Dalmatia. At any rate, he is reputedly buried in San Lorenzo church, and if you are in Venice, you have probably already visited his new airport.

With Casanova, there is the opposite problem. Although he spent lots of time elsewhere on the lam, there appear to be no places in Venice that he did not frequent. Special Casanova tours are regularly offered, and gondoliers point randomly to houses all over town as places where Casanova slept, which may be true. We do know that he was born on the Calle Malipiero, baptized at the church of San Samuele, moved into Ca' Soranzo at the east end of Campo San Polo when he hoodwinked its owner into becoming his protector, and that he escaped from The Leads prison, located on the top of the Doge's Palace.

Proust's Venice is mostly in his imagination. He thought about it all the time, but made only two trips there, both in 1900, one in May with his mother and the other all by himself in October. Even then, he seems to have been in a daze. Here are the instructions to his favorite part of Venice (Moncrieff and Kilmartin translation):

I had plunged into a network of little alleys, or calli, packed tightly together and dissecting in all directions with their furrows a chunk of Venice carved out between a canal and the lagoon, as if it had crystallized in accordance with these innumerable, tenuous and minute patterns. Suddenly, at the end of one of those alleys, it seems as though a distension had occurred in the crystallized matter. A vast and splendid campo of which, in this network of little streets, I should never have guessed the scale, or even found room for it, spread out before me surrounded by charming palaces silvery in the moonlight.

The next day, I set out in quest of my beautiful nocturnal piazza, following calle after calle which were exactly like one another and refused to give me the smallest piece of information, except such as would lead me further astray. . . . And as there is no great difference between the memory of a dream and the memory of a reality, I finally wondered whether it was not during my sleep that there had occurred, in a dark patch of Venetian crystallization, that strange mirage which offered a vast piazza surrounded by romantic palaces to the meditative eye of the moon.

Good luck.

It would be better, although expensive, to let Proust steer you to Fortuny, the dressmaker with product placement in *Remembrance of Things Past*. Mariano Fortuny y Madrazo was a second-generation Spanish Venetophile, his widowed mother having moved the remaining family to Venice when Fortuny was eighteen. She maintained a small salon for artists in their quarters at the sixteenth-century Ca' Martinengo-Tron, near the Rio di San Luca (later bought by Count Giuseppe Volpi, who brought electricity, the CIGA Hotel chain, and the Venice Film Festival to Venice, industry to nearby Mestre and Marghera, and served as

Mussolini's finance minister). A painter, engraver, theatrical set and lighting designer, and interior decorator, Fortuny hit it biggest with his narrowly pleated Grecian dresses and sumptuous velvet capes, the materials for which were made in a fiercely guarded factory on the Giudecca. Proust's Mme. de Guermantes and Albertine wore Fortuny dresses, as did Eleanora Duse, Peggy Guggenheim, and every other real-life lady of the period who aspired to artistic chic and could afford them. His studio and heavily decorated fin-de-siecle residence at Ca' Orfei now form the Fortuny museum, which is the current record-holder (the Ca' d'Oro museum of art having preceded it) as the museum longest closed for restoration. The expensive part of bonding with Fortuny is that his clothes have become cult objects, the originals going for thousands of dollars, and the copies sold in Venice for sums that are less but not inconsiderable.

Even more expensive would be making Ernest Hemingway your imaginary friend. If you have followed in Hemingway's footsteps before—say, staying up all night in Pamplona drinking cheap wine on its Calle San Nicolas, barhopping in Key West or Havana, or even hitting the cafés of Paris—you would be in for sticker shock. Hemingway liked luxurious Venice. He stayed at the Gritti Hotel and the Cipriani, ate and drank at Harry's Bar and the Locanda Cipriani on Torcello, and was suspiciously knowledgeable about the hushed atmosphere of the ultra-expensive antique jewelry shops around the piazza (see chapter six).

Imagining New Friends

It is not as though all the interesting people who were ever in town were from out of town. The advanced Venetophile will soon want to cozy up to characters he or she has discovered in Venetian history.

The great Venetian monk, scientist, and strategist Paolo Sarpi is irresistible. He lived in a Servite cell on the Fondamenta della Misericordia; the famous stabbing by the pope's thugs took place at the bridge at Santa Fosca near where his statue now stands (see chapter three), and he was finally buried—after his body had been carted about hither and yon for years—near the entrance of the church on the cemetery island, San Michele.

Scarcely a generation younger is another towering Venetian theologian, Rabbi Leone da Modena: scholar, teacher, playwright, sonneteer, composer, cantor, translator, and compulsive gambler. With the help of his agonized autobiography, he can be traced in the New and Old Ghettos and on the sorties he made outside them for purposes of business, gambling, and promoting understanding of Judaism. He is buried in the Jewish cemetery on the Lido.

We have some highfalutin' testimony that Veronica Franco was also irresistible, although perhaps not in the same way as the aforementioned gentlemen. When Venice wanted to do its best to welcome Henry III, it sent her over, as Venice's best courtesan and one of her best poets. Montaigne had disparaged the beauty of the famed Venetian courtesans, so Franco sent him her poetry instead. Her letters show a startlingly modern feminist sensibility, and she left money to establish a refuge for prostitutes at 2590 Santa Maria del Soccorso, which now houses—university women.

Also appealing, in yet another way, is the portraitist Rosalba Carriera, who created the vogue for pastels and miniatures on ivory and indeed, with her friend and mentor Antoine Watteau, for the Rococo style itself. In contrast to the Venetian ladies she depicted and the other lusciously ripe subjects that fix upperclass eighteenth-century life for us as a time of playful and untroubled sensuality, Carriera was a working-class worker. Her journals are not filled with beddings, but with sittings. Although she became celebrated and sought after throughout Europe and was admitted to important academies during a period not favorable to women, she seems to have led a quiet personal life among her sisters. Sadly, her career came to an end when she lost her eyesight.

Venice was as short on writers as she was long on painters, but she has her diarist, Marino Sanudo, and her playwright, Carlo Goldoni, whom Venetians consider the answer to Molière (while the French refuse to recognize that there could be a question). Sanudo lived behind the Turkish Warehouse at the corner of the Calle del Spezier, and Goldoni now has his own museum in Ca' Centani at San Tomà, the house in which he lived as a baby, and a jolly statue in the Campo San Bartolomeo.

A personal favorite is Tommaso Rangone, a Venetophile from Ravenna who made it to being Venetian by breaking the rules. Blatant self-promotion was not generally a good idea; an individual Venetian was expected to submerge his personal glory in that of the state. So rich gentlemen who wanted their portraits done would have themselves depicted in the corner of a picture, kneeling to one of Venice's sainted protectors, or to one side of a statue, kneeling to Saint Mark.

Not Rangone. He commissioned Tintoretto to do three scenes from the life of Saint Mark in which the central figure is not Mark, but—Rangone. He got himself into the well-located church of San Geminiano (it faced Saint Mark's, across the piazza, until Napoleon decided that the real estate could be put to better use and knocked down Sansovino's church to build himself the royal palace that is now the Correr Museum) in the form of a bronze bust by Alessandro Vittoria. The bust has since been moved to the Ateneo Veneto, near the Fenice theater. Rangone had his résumé sculpted in symbols surrounding a statue of himself on the Sansovino facade of San Giuliano. It is an impressive résumé, even if not exactly relevant to the church's function: Rangone was a doctor who advised Venice about the plague and dabbled in the other sciences, and the author of books on staying healthy, one of which was called *How a Man Can Live More than 120 Years.* He was eighty-four when he died of the unhealthy plague.

Yet his life should be an inspiration to all Venetophiles. His success as one who started late yet made good is second only to that of Saint Mark himself.

CHAPTER FIVE

Adopt Your Landlord

Why stop at imaginary friends? Don't you want Venetian relatives?

Real ones would be more practical, and there is no denying how attractive it makes even the least prepossessing of people to be discovered to own a house on the Grand Canal. But marriage being a bit of a long shot, Venetophiles settle for imaginary relatives. We adopt our landlords.

Not our living landlords, of course. These people might object, or they may have disagreeable habits, such as raising the rent or lowering the heat. It is our ancestral landlords whom we adopt.

How genealogical pirating works is explained in the Gilbert and Sullivan operetta *Pirates of Penzance*. When Major-General Stanley expresses the fear that he may have disgraced his ancestors who lie buried in the chapel of his estate, young Frederic points out that actually, the general had bought the estate only a year ago. This opens the question of whose ancestors, in fact, they were, to which General Stanley replies, "Frederic, in this chapel are ancestors: you cannot deny that. With the estate, I bought the chapel and its contents. I don't know whose ancestors they *were*, but I know whose ancestors they *are*."

To those who may protest that there is nothing lower than a "descendant by purchase," as the general calls himself, we submit the Venetophile, who is more likely to be a descendant by rental. No sooner do we find somewhere to stay and hand over the rent than we begin to think we own not just the few rooms we have contracted for, but the entire building they are in and everyone who ever lived in it before and all their relations.

Dead Ancestors in Living Rooms

It is a phenomenon that puzzles even those who succumb to it. In *Venetian Life*, William Dean Howells describes this creeping up on him:

> The gondoliers used always to point out our palace (which was called Casa Falier) as the house in which Marino Faliero was born; and for a long time we clung to the hope that it might be so. But however pleasant it was, we were forced, on reading up the subject a little, to relinquish our allusion and accredit an old palace at Santi Apostoli with the distinction we would fain have claimed for ours.
>
> I am rather at a loss to explain how it made our lives in Casa Falier any pleasanter to think that a beheaded traitor had been born in it, but we relished the superstition amazingly as long as we could possibly believe in it.

That was just an early stage. Then Mr. and Mrs. Howells moved across the GC to Ca' Giustiniani and started referring to that as "our own palace" (although he scrupulously added, "as we absurdly grew to call it") and identifying with generations of Giustiniani. He writes fondly of the once-and-future twelfth-century monk who performed the job of repopulating the family, and of the first patriarch of Venice, who became a saint. Then, with a flourish of family pride, he introduces his favorite, an eighteenth-century Giustinian who refused to concede his post as governor of Treviso to Napoleon. This was in contrast to the rapid acquiescence of his peers to the collapse of the Republic. That down-with-the-ship hero even spurned the impressed conqueror's offer of immunity from the general disaster being inflicted on his countrymen.

In a more recent example, *Palladian Days* by Sally and Carl I. Gable, their purchase of a country villa originally owned by the Cornaro family rapidly engendered a proprietary feeling about every Cornaro villa, town house (there are several on the Grand Canal alone), chapel, fresco, painting, statue, and tomb for miles around and the Cornaro family history to go with them. We would consider the Gables major property owners just for having bought a Palladian villa, although it turns out to be the ultimate fixer-upper. When you consider that they have, by extension, acquired a real estate empire and taken on such distinguished Cornaro relatives as Queen Catherine of Cyprus and Elena Cornaro, the first woman to receive a doctoral degree, it becomes a bargain. Ultimately, the Gables assumed use of the Cornaro family crest on a china service that they commissioned.

Another contemporary example is in *Venetian Dreaming*, in which Paula Weideger recounts targeting Ca' Donà on the Fondamente Nove as "my house" after having merely spotted it from the waterbus. She later realized her dream when she was able to rent an apartment there for herself and her partner. The next step inevitably followed:

In a way, I set about adopting the Donà family. The conceit that the story of the Donà and their house, unlike histories of other families in Venetian palaces, was "ours" soon became our private joke. We laughed at ourselves but at the same time we were serious. When, for instance, I read that there was a bust of Leonardo Donà in the church of San

Giorgio Maggiore where he was buried, we took the
vaporetto over to the island to have a look. On previous visits neither Henry nor I had noticed this carving perched over
the church's door. But why was it important to see him
now? What was this all about?

What, indeed?

Venetophiles are, by definition, enamored of history. Each
tends to have a favorite period, usually the Renaissance or the
eighteenth century, rather than the flight from Attila or one of
the plagues; and a favorite type or person, almost always a member of the ruling class and not one of their servants. To any but
the most socially minded, it hardly seems worthwhile to project
oneself into the past for an inglorious life and miserable conditions. Fantasies being free, we might as well make ourselves aristocrats, royalty, or heroes, not the peasants or peddlers that our
actual ancestors might have been.

To narrow that interest to a particular Venetian clan is to have
the frequent joy of stumbling over its traces. Coats of arms are
strewn around on outside walls almost as freely as graffiti, tombs
abound in churches, portraits in galleries. If you have obelisks on
top of your house, it means that one of your ancestral landlords
was an admiral, no small position in the major sea power of its
time. In the long line of doges, as pictured in the Doge's Palace
and on coinage in the Correr Museum, finding "yours" produces
a swelling of family pride and affection.

You can even play when you pay by the night, because Grand
Canal hotels were once private houses and their histories are
known. Visitors staying at the Gritti Hotel can be spotted by the
significant, if not smug, way they register any mention of the
sixteenth-century doge Andrea Gritti. Never mind that it was
the Pisani family who owned that building in its heyday, when its
facade was painted by Giorgione, and that a Gritti only bought

the building in the early nineteenth century, centuries after the doge's death, and held it for a mere few years, after which it became a German baroness's boardinghouse. In the lobby of the hotel, in the place of honor where a Marriott displays a copy of a portrait of J.W. Marriott, there is a copy of a portrait of Doge Andrea Gritti. Only the Gritti's portrait is by Titian.

Then there is *A Thousand Days in Venice*, whose author, Marlena de Blasi, actually does marry a property-owning Venetian. The apartment he owns turns out to be what looks like a storage closet in a concrete, postwar bunker off an alley out on the Lido. Her next book was called *A Thousand Days in Tuscany*.

Foreground Check

Even after you have acquired its property, adopting a family from the Venetian oligarchy can be dicey. There are a limited number of names that trail through Venetian history, a surprising number of them into present times, and every Venetian knows what and whose they are. Thus there are too many people walking around who can trump a poetic Venetophile's identification with particular famous Venetian historical figures by the crude fact of being their descendants by blood.

The proprietary way Venetophiles come to feel about their adopted landlords becomes embarrassingly clear in their reaction to such rival claimants. Such a person has the unfair advantage of being the legal proprietor of the surname and sometimes also of the premises.

At Ca' Donà, Ms. Weideger conducts bitter tenant-landlord feuds with two generations of the Donà dalle Rose family: the young brother and sister who live in the house and the largely absentee older generation who own it.

Mr. Howells did not seem thrilled to meet a Falier at Ca'

Falier, or a Giustinian at Ca' Giustiniani. There was a living Falier
occupying the apartment above the Howellses in Ca' Falier, an
old priest who was a lineal descendent of the beheaded doge
who had not been born there. When the Howellses were in residence at Ca' Giustiniani, a living Giustinian showed up and tried
to buy back their rented apartment out from under them. The
living Falier and Giustinian each get only passing mention in
Venetian Life, in contrast to the charming anecdotes about unrelated tenants of those houses.

The Gables tracked down a living Cornaro, who was apparently happy to be their guest in his ancestral home and to
exchange family stories with them on an equal basis. But then,
his branch of the family had turned Austrian during the occupation, and he turned out to be not only an Austrian but an
Austrian ambassador.

As a rule, it is better not to try to adopt families who are
already in the custody of their descendants. If you are taken with
the audacious romance of Bianca Capello or the finely featured
portrait of Doge Leonardo Loredan by Giovanni Bellini or the
family tragedy of *I Due Foscari* or the gruesome story of
Marcantonio Bragadin—the Venetian captain who was flayed
alive in 1570 by Turks, who then stuffed his skin with straw to be
paraded around on a cow—forget it. There are extant Capellos,
Loredans, Foscari, and Bragadins* who might consider their
claims to be stronger. Gradenigos, Veniers, and Marcellos are
also among the living.

So before contemplating adoption, it would be a good idea to
check out the list published by the Corpo della Nobilità Italiana
of 860 noble families with descendents in Venice, a volume only
slightly larger than the Venice telephone book. The names you

---

*We don't count Bragadin's stuffed skin, which was stolen bac' and now resides in the
church of Santi Giovanni e Paolo.

want are the ones that are not there. You will not find represented the historic families of Pisani, Barbarigo, Mocenigo,
Dandolo, Sagredo, Contarini, Falier, or Giustiniani. So help
yourself.

Wait—not Barbarigo. They are taken. Our household has
adopted them.

Packed Houses

There are many more choices than there are houses. This is
because never have so many people and events been packed into
so little space. With few exceptions, the major houses, which
sheltered whole clans at a time for generations, were built on
canals where waterfront space is so limited that the owners of
these splendid digs were legally required to allow members of the
public free passage to walk through their ground floors, to the
public thoroughfares carrying their boats.

The most the city can manage in the way of urban sprawl is to
shore up the edge of a canal for a few extra yards here or there,
or to fill one in to provide more space for walking and less for
floating garbage. The only people who seriously undertook
urban renewal were Napoleon and Mussolini, and you know
what we think of them. Venice may have more than its share of
buildings leaning at precarious angles, but she does not go
around tearing down buildings.* An old house is one that has
been there for more than seven hundred years; those from the
sixteenth-century building boom are thought to have a touch of
the nouveau about them. (The term case nuove refers to houses
in the sense of families. "New" means that the family was not

---

*One might observe that she doesn't need to, since they fall down. Occasionally they
are torched. But we are not counting accident or crime.

around in the eighth century, when the twenty-four "old" families organized themselves, but had nevertheless made it into the ruling class by 1297, when the patricians first closed ranks. There are also "very new" families who made the cut in 1381 and the really nouveau types who bought their way in later when Venice needed the money.)

If you could do the math, dividing the number of historical personages over the years by the number of houses, you would understand why there are multiple historical associations for each. And if you did the math that the present owners have to do to heat these places and to maintain them, even in the shabby state we temporary tenants find romantic, you could see why you can pretty much pick your rental target.

A prime example is the same Ca' Mocenigo complex on the Grand Canal (there are family houses elsewhere by that name) that has already come up in connection with Lord Byron. It has lots of other interesting residents among whom to choose:

There were seven Mocenigo doges, including Tommaso, who defeated the Turks in 1395; Giovanni, who was painted by Gentile Bellini, and Alvise I, who won the Battle of Lepanto in 1571, and was painted by Tintoretto.*

Giordano Bruno, philosopher and priest, was granted refuge at Ca' Mocenigo in 1591 by Giovanni Mocenigo when Bruno was wanted (in the uh-oh sense) by the Church of Rome. The host cherished hopes that his guest might repay him by confiding the secrets of alchemy. When he found himself stuck with a guest who could neither move on nor teach him how to turn base metal into gold, he did what any exasperated host might do: He denounced Bruno to the Inquisition, which first removed

---

*As doges were drawn from the limited numbers of families in the oligarchy, living representatives of the descendents are prone to telling you how many doges they had. They might consider using tiny drawings of the doge's horned hat after their names, adding one, two, or three, in the way that stars are used to rate hotels or movies.

him from the premises and subsequently burned him at the stake. However, the priest's ghost bounced right back and is living there still, rent-free, long after Mocenigo's demise.

When Antonio Foscarini was caught sneaking into Ca' Mocenigo, disguised and under cover of night, he was arrested, strangled, and, for good measure, hanged by one foot from a gibbet. This was in 1622, when Venice was in a precarious world position, and tenants of that Grand Canal house included various diplomatic representatives from suspicious quarters. Obviously, Foscarini must have been holding traitorous discourse with one or all of them.

Well, no, as it turned out. They had overlooked the obvious, which another tenant of Ca' Mocenigo drew to the Council of Ten's attention. "Of course he had to sneak in, and of course he was disguised," a furious Lady Anne of Shrewsbury, Countess of Arundel, let it be known. "We were having an affair." The abashed officials apologized for having interrupted them and gave Foscarini's worse-for-wear body a state funeral.

In 1793, one of the tenants was Lady Mary Wortley Montagu, the distinguished English lady of letters whom Alexander Pope started referring to as "lewd Lesbia" and "filthy Sappho" when their friendship cooled. She went to Venice in pursuit of a Venetian lover of hers, Francesco Algarotti, a collector, art critic, and philosopher with an unusually busy life since his other lovers included King Frederick the Great of Prussia. He failed to take up Lady Mary's offers, expressed in her poems, to give him another taste of what she said she "could well express between your sheets." But by that time she had also fallen in love with Venice itself—except for her fellow British Venetophiles, whom she called "the greatest blockheads in nature"—and remained there almost until her death.

Ca' Mocenigo was also where the love letters were discovered that form the basis of *A Venetian Affair*, the book about the eighteenth-century couple with designs on Joseph Smith's virtue and money (see chapter four). Andrea Memmo, the hero of that long, passionate, and clandestine, not to say immensely devious and complicated, romance actually lived much farther along the Grand Canal, where he threw one of the last extravagant parties of the Republic upon assuming the august office of procurator of Saint Mark's. But the love letters he received passed down through a Mocenigo connection of his and were discovered at Ca' Mocenigo by a Mocenigo descendant who grew up in that house and whose son, Andrea di Robilant, wrote the book.

These are just a few of the people who passed through one house, and nearly every great house yields a collection of stories. Even with a much smaller property, you should at least be able to get a two-fer. I had always wanted to rent a certain apartment on the Rio dei Mendicanti because I have a painting by Washington artist Jack Boul of a passageway beneath it—but that was before I discovered that a previous tenant was Nietzsche.

A Foot in the Door

We have rented or borrowed numerous apartments, each with its smorgasbord from which to choose a tasty bit of history. Moving around has also given us a sense of belonging to a dozen different neighborhoods, surely deserved after each time making the pleasant effort of getting to know the nearby baker, church chimes, and dead-end streets. But for many years, when there were enough of us to support it, we have also stayed once a year at Ca' Minotto. It is Ca' Minotto we meant when we threatened to hang a sign on our Stateside porch that said OUR OTHER HOUSE IS A PALACE.

That it is unavailable to us when under a long-term lease for a commercial venture only makes us feel more securely Venetian.

To be excluded from the ancestral home is a fate typical of the old families.

This delusion had started innocently enough, when my family and I had worked our way up to going to Venice once (now more likely to be four times) every year. Annoyed by the artificiality of life in hotels and restaurants, to say nothing of the ruinous expense, we had been grateful to find that the Gritti Hotel ran an annex with apartments for rent. We were told these were generally taken by singers at the Fenice and others coming for short stays who wanted, as we did, their own meals and privacy at well below hotel prices.

The duplex apartment we took there was cheerful, comfortable, and clean, and therefore exactly what we did not want. We wanted Milly Theale's thoroughly Venetian digs, but, unlike her, we lacked a majordomo to find them for us. Worse, it was a time when, although there were empty properties everywhere in Venice, there was not much opportunity to rent. Among the things that stood between landlord and tenant were fear of not ever being able to evict those having long-term arrangements, annoyance at having to register short-term ones with the police, connivance about taxes, and concern about rickety furniture and valuable paintings.*

Dead ends kept appearing at the end of the inquiries we made to international real estate agencies, former Venetophiles, and anyone who knew someone with a northern Italian boyfriend who had a cousin living just outside of Venice. There seemed to be an impenetrable barrier that left us out on the pavements and bridges, our hearts filled with the anguish of unfulfilled real estate yearning.

---

*Then the world went on the internet. All it takes now is plodding through the endless advertisements and photographs and maps and remembering that the stars that rental agencies award their various properties are more generously given than stars dispensed from a disinterested source.

Stories of American sorties into the wilds of Venetian housing laws and customs did not help. An American family we knew had been trying for years to buy a certain house and had agreed on a price, but they finally had to admit bureaucratic defeat and decamp for London.

A young American was in the office of his real estate agent (and just securing an agent was considered a triumph), in the very act of closing on the apartment he wanted, when he inquired idly whether he could pay with a check on an American bank, rather than with cash. His agent championed him by announcing over the telephone that that was what they planned to do, and when the landlord balked, the agent screamed, "Then we don't want your damn apartment!" and hung up. A contretemps followed, in which the American tried without success to get the agent to call back and agree to the landlord's payment terms.

It was too late. Pride was now involved, in more than one place, as it turned out. When the agent kept refusing to make another call, the American client himself grabbed the telephone, called, and said, "I'll give you cash tomorrow." The landlord replied haughtily, "I don't have an apartment for rent."

We gave up and again rented the apartment in the Gritti annex. Two weeks before six of us were setting off to Venice, that too slipped away. Management was sorry, but they had sold the building.

That did it. We could resign ourselves to the idea that it took forever to complete a real estate transaction, or we could resign ourselves to an unforeseen, last-minute sale. But we refused to do both at the same time. The Gritti graciously conceded the point and made the handsome offer of three double rooms at one of its sister hotels, the Europa and Regina, at the same price as the rental. This would work out to fifty dollars a person per night—Days Inn prices, or better, at a major Grand Canal hotel.

While my support system was cheering the bargain, I stopped

them dead by taking on the character of a proud Venetian and refusing. It had to be the Gritti Hotel itself. Granted.

I refused again. It could not be back or top-floor rooms at the Gritti, but three double rooms facing the Grand Canal. Granted. Renewed background cheers.

I refused. Background hysteria: "Are you crazy? Do you know what those rooms go for?"

Heady (so as not to say crazed) with my progress, I trotted out Milly Theale's want ad, suggesting that the management of the Gritti surely knew everyone in town and could find just the place that I, or rather Henry James, described. Acknowledged.

Thus I acquired the free services of a modern majordomo. And that is who fulfilled my dreams by finding us an eight-hundred-year-old pink fixer-upper, 3 BR, 3 LR, 3 BA, incomparable view, historic district, handy to transportation.

As a visiting Venetophile declared, "It's a stinkin' pink palazzo!" The quotation is from Venetophile Cole Porter's *Kiss Me, Kate*, where Petruchio bemoans having given up, among others of his bachelor lady friends,

> Venetia, who loved to chat so;
> Could still she be drinkin' in her stinkin' pink palazzo?

If she is a member of our household, the answer is "Yes."

House Pride

The pretentious way to describe Ca' Minotto would be "unpretentious." It is nowhere near the size of Ca' Barbaro, the house on which Henry James based the Palazzo Leporelli, the answer to Milly's dreams. It is especially dwarfed by being next door to the largest Renaissance building on the GC, which Sansovino built for Queen Catherine Cornaro's nephew, but

The Ancestral Home (Adopted Retroactively).

which now houses the prefecture of police and is commonly known as Ca' Grande. Ca' Minotto was there first, however, and appears on the map that Jacopo de' Barbari made in 1500. To those of us who live in American historic districts that date back to the 1920s, this is mind-boggling.

Ca' Minotto was first built in the twelfth or thirteenth century and took its present form in the fifteenth. Extensive renovations and embellishments were begun in 1707, finished in 1720, restarted in 1741, and concluded in 1766, an experience with contractors' promises that we understood only too well. The actual bills from this makeover are in the Correr Museum, presumably already paid.

For whatever reason (money), Ca' Minotto escaped the major nineteenth- and twentieth-century infusions of decorators, antiquarians, and plumbers who made many of the great houses chic and comfortable. Walls are still smoky from when the rooms were heated by fireplaces. There is said to be a replacement heating system, but winter there is chilly. Many of the paintings are dark to the point of being indistinguishable, and one should probably not wish them to be made clean and visible. The antique furniture is innocent of refurbishment, and there are chairs best left alone.

In sum, it is the dearest house in Venice (not a reference to the sinking dollar), and we are not the only people who think so. Our Venetian visitors invariably declared it to be a rare surviving example of "the real thing." When the extended family of the present owners also owned the larger and more grandly furnished adjacent house, Ca' Barbarigo, they preferred Ca' Minotto. A cousin of the family commented that when they threw open the doors between the two houses to celebrate weddings* and other

---

*A Wedding at Ca' Minotto

On February 28, 1601, a wedding banquet at Ca' Minotto turned into a brawl during which Sire Polo Leon, official lover to Lucrezia Baglioni, courtesan, was dispatched by Leonardo Pesaro, of the distinguished family that made its fortune in a surf 'n' turf transportation system of wagons and ferries. For this scandalous murder, Leonardo was de-ennobled and exiled for life or until Venice needed cash, whichever came first; he was welcomed back in 1616. His relationship to Ca' Minotto was through Lucia Barbarigo, who married his brother Giovanni, the builder of Ca' Pesaro on the GC, which is now the museum of modern art. Giovanni also had a notable career as a general, capped by his being imprisoned for plundering paintings, which he had every reason to suppose was the Venetian national sport. When Lucia died, Giovanni married their governess, Maria, thus inspiring a popular song (in Venetian dialect) during his campaign for doge:

> Viva el Pesaro del caro
> Che xe sta in person per laro
> E per ultima pazzia
> G'ha sposa dona Maria.

(Long live Pesaro of the wagon, / who was imprisoned for theft, / and as a final bit of nuttiness, / went and married Ms. Maria.)

P.S. He won the election.

grand family events, they all noticed that the atmosphere changed
when crossing from one to the other: Minotto was magical.

The building is situated in the midst of what Somerset
Maugham considered the most sublime view in the world,
except that he was under the handicap of only being able to see it
in good weather and while nursing drinks from the Gritti's terrace restaurant. We could see it any time we wanted from our
stone balconies, which are guarded by cat-sized lions, and from
an enclosed balcony furnished with chairs and a discreetly
placed pair of binoculars.

We faced Santa Maria della Salute off to our left and the
Guggenheim Collection, with a good view of who is attending its
rooftop parties, to our right. Smack ahead is one of the most
famous facades on the GC, that of Ca' Dario, a house that has
been on the market for years and years, possibly because it has a
curse on it and its residents tend to meet violent deaths. For a
long time, there were rumors that Woody Allen was trying to buy
it, which led to a lot of hand-wringing on our part about "There
goes the neighborhood," but he didn't.

Taking in Boarders

Perhaps the neighborhood goes during the annual week or
two that we have been taking over Ca' Minotto's piano nobile, in
all its decayed, frescoed, and stuccoed splendor, and turning it
into a sort of slapdash boardinghouse. "Dormitory living, but
with Tiepolo ceilings," we warned those who proposed to join us,
in case the word palace was floating around in their heads and
conjuring a luxury hotel or house party. Even good friends
were not asked to participate if they were suspected of being
high maintenance.

We could fit eight or nine people. After that, palacemates were
told to check to make sure that they are in love before proposing

anyone else, as we would have to start doubling up the beds. They were allowed to bring luncheon or dinner guests, providing only that 1. they notified the chef before he went to Rialto that morning, and 2. the guests were amusing. As a result, even when we were only six or eight staying in the house, we seldom sat down with fewer than ten people, often twelve, at lunch and again at dinner. Breakfast, which occasionally featured discussions of the amount of hot water available in relation to the number of people who wanted to take baths, or exchanges between someone reading the newspaper and someone else who was trying to read it at the same time, was too sordid to expose to outsiders.

The only other house rule, when we roomed with friends, was that the kitchen is men's work. The executive chef, who doubles as my husband, turned out lunch and dinner every day, sometimes creating masterpieces that he couldn't name because the fishmongers could only give him the Venetian, not the Italian, words for the ingredients he had chosen. When there were plans to develop a biological station on the island of San Giorgio, he got overexcited, envisioning what he, a molecular biologist, called the ideal life: fish market in the morning and laboratory in the afternoon. But alas, the laboratory plans floated away, as so many grandiose Venetian plans seem to do.

Other men were conscripted as sous-chefs, chef's-day-off chefs, wine stewards, butlers, waiters, and busboys. When the executive chef once wandered into the living room with his glass of prosecco, announcing that he had the sous-chefs taking care of the rest of the meal and sociably asking the women lounging there what they were talking about, he was told, "Football. So go away."

Communal life, such as dining, showing off purchases and asking if anyone has seen one's eyeglasses, takes place in the huge hallway that Venetian houses have running through the middle. Venetians don't have to go outdoors to take long walks.

At Ca' Minotto, bedrooms and other sleeping quarters were allotted according to reverse seniority, which is to say that new-comers got to sleep in the master suite, consisting of a room so enormous that the bed alcove alone, at one end of it, is the size of a normal bedroom. Another bed at the opposite end of the room is so far away as to undermine our claim that the accommodations would be suitable for a ménage à trois if only we knew one. The suite comes with a large dressing room, a narrow room housing a floral-painted toilet, and a bathroom with the other fixtures on the opposite side of the suite—thus creating a hygiene dilemma for those who may get up during the night. It also created a class dilemma, as these facilities were in the exclusive use of the occupants of the suite, while the rest of the household shared two bathrooms, and thus they were occasionally the object of hysterical petitions from the less privileged.

Decorating the arch of the bed alcove is a shield being held up by two cherubs; when you lie in bed, you see the back of those fat baby legs dangling down from the other side of the arch. A Venetian architect friend says that the space behind the bed was probably once the traditional passageway that served as an exit for the traditional lover when the traditional husband showed up for his traditional breakfast. Then the business of the day would begin, and the lady's milliner, hairdresser, and such would fill the room with their goods and services. You have seen it all in the first act of *Der Rosenkavalier*: the Marschallin hides her lover, directs her servants, entertains her friends, and receives trades-people and petitioners, all in her bedroom. We have never been able to watch that opera since without commenting on how piti-fully cramped and unadorned the set is.

These splendid quarters once had an anteroom, which was later made over into a spacious separate bedroom. On its ceiling is a Francesco Fontebasso fresco, *Venice in the Form of Justice*, which features a huge sad lion peeking from behind personified

Venice's skirts. Someone once chopped a big hole in the middle of the fresco to install a chandelier, but there is no light fixture there now, just a hole. The doors of a wall-length closet have pictures of Ca' Minotto and other presumed family holdings in an incongruous pastoral setting. Under crowded conditions, this room has been declared a superannuated girls' or boys' dormitory, although the latter once voted out an occupant for snoring and made him go sleep in a spare salon.

The third real bedroom is in the front of the house, and while it is small, it has a Pompeiian motif on the walls and ceiling, and access to the enclosed wooden balcony, which is just the place to wait out jet lag in the middle of the first night. Fortunately, there are three salons, so we could use two of them, the Tiepolo room and one decorated with stucco animals, to stash snorers and people who show up when the bedrooms are occupied. And we would still have left the central salon at the end of the grand hallway, for hanging out.

We are saved the shame of being the first to use Ca' Minotto as a boardinghouse. A letter from the American modernist artist John Marin, who was in Venice with his parents for five weeks in 1907, is in the archives of the National Gallery of Art, and you can imagine the excitement with which we beheld his letterhead from "Pension Gregory." Gregorio is a favorite given name of our ancestral landlords', and on the paper was printed a picture of our own Ca' Minotto. Only then, Marin and his fellow boarders no doubt thought of it as their own.

Perhaps while pausing from waving to the visitors in the gondolas down below, as we do, Marin did several views from these windows of the expanse of buildings facing us. Visiting artists in Venice were prone to work close to home, and he also executed an etching of the back of the Church of Santa Maria del Giglio—

coincidently, perhaps, of the rear wall of the chapel that is devoted to a member of the house's ancestral family.

This is only one of many thrills of discovery we have had since we took imaginary possession. Among the others:

- A sliver of the house, tucked beyond Ca' Grande next door, is depicted by Canaletto and other Venetian scene painters as part of a favorite view of the canal looking from Campo San Vio toward the church of the Salute.
- The original central Tiepolo from our ceiling is in the Museum of Eighteenth-Century Venice at Ca' Rezzonico (a contemporary copy is in its place, but we can still boast of a genuine Tiepolo room because the original Tiepolo medallions are where they belong, at Ca' Minotto), credited to our house in the museum label. In the gift shop, the fresco is reproduced on postal cards and mugs. Some of the eighteenth-century boudoir furniture from the house also found its way to the museum.
- One of John Singer Sargent's watercolors of a corner of Ca' Grande shows the bunched, second-floor columns we see from one of our windows, and could even (we argue among ourselves about this) have been painted from our second-best salon.
- After the fabled romance in *A Venetian Affair* has ended, it is casually mentioned, toward the end of the book, that Andrea Memmo then began a long-term affair with—a daughter of our house. In our house, no doubt. I gasped when I got to that page; I felt as if I had walked in on them.
- Friends who had stayed there with us were back home watching a made-for-television film called *In a Dark, Adapted Eye*, based on a novel by Ruth Rendell, when they noticed a familiar bridge, a familiar staircase, and finally—Helena Bonham Carter in our very own kitchen. We subsequently

bought the video, but have never seen it all the way through because we dwell exclusively on the scenes photographed in our house.

- One night, a neighbor who was one of our dinner guests walked in the door exclaiming that he had always been curious to see the place because many decades ago his father had had an affair with a lady who lived here.

I am sorry to say that the excitement of these discoveries has led to unseemly public behavior; the cry of "Look! There's our house!" effectively stops a crowded American museum room dead. The declaration, "That's really ours," made to other visitors in Venice about an object or coat of arms seen elsewhere around town comes out sounding huffy, as if honest people would have had the decency to give it back to us.

Taking in Ancestors

Obviously this was a suitable home in which to think about adoption. Especially adoption of people who you have reason to know would feel at home. The only question: Which ones should we choose?

Although ours is not the only house in town named Minotto, it is the only one on the Grand Canal, so we presume that our earliest known ancestral landlord was the distinguished Girolamo Minotto. In 1453, he had the honor of serving as Venetian bailo, something between a governor and an ambassador, in Constantinople.

However, there was an embarrassing slip-up at the end of his diplomatic career. He lost Venice's Byzantine empire.

He was last heard screaming for help from home. The valiant Venetians prepared to mount a rescue mission to save him and the empire, and they had a plan. If they cunningly disguised themselves as Turks, they figured that no one would notice that they were mounting a counterattack. In the event, this fooled exactly no one, but they took so long to get themselves done up in costumes and makeup that by the time they arrived in Constantinople, Minotto and his son were no longer screaming, having also managed to lose their heads.

We had to turn him down for adoption. At the other end of Ca' Minotto's history was our late landlady, whose husband had bought the building after World War II. She would have had to turn us down, had we had the unlikely nerve to offer. By birth she was a Donà dalle Rose, and therefore she had already unknowingly been adopted by Ms. Weideger and her Henry.

We shifted our benevolent attention to the Barbarigo clan, which had owned the house for most of the centuries in between, from 1514 until the branch died out in 1804. Originally from near Trieste, the Barbarigos arrived in Venice in time to become one of the new families who made it into the first draft of what was to become the Golden Book, the official register of patricians. Thus they were part of the crowd that wrested power from the original families and ran Renaissance Venice. Our adoption yielded us two doges, two naval commanders, numerous merchants, the mother of a pope, a saint, a submarine, and a mother-daughter team of notoriously spirited intellectual beauties.

They had assumed the name "Barbarigo" as a triumphantly snide reference to their own Harry's having made himself a necklace from the beards he cut off half a dozen Saracen invaders in 880 (barba, beard; arrigo, Harry: Barbarigo). Chronicles exist with different theories about the family's origins, including that they came from the Levant, where they were executive sheep- and goat-herders to a sultan, but we are much too fond of the Harry's Barbershop (as opposed to Harry's Bar) version to let go. And sure enough, there are six unattached beards on the unattractive Barbarigo coat of arms.

By virtue of our holiday rentals, we feel kinship to all members of the Barbarigo family, indeed to all Venetians of that name whether or not there is a traceable connection to the chief family. We take pride that many were prominent in war, in commerce, and in patronage of the arts, although they had their share of mistakes and misfortunes. In 1417, Niccolo Barbarigo was commander of the Alexandria fleet, but he unfortunately abandoned one of his ships when it was wrecked by a storm and looking to him for help. Instead, he sailed off in his flagship either to safety or to beat others to nearby marketing opportunities. He was convicted of having ignored the cries and flares of his shipwrecked subordinates and fined ten thousand ducats. His sons took up his zest for international trade with more success. One of them is the title character of *Andrea Barbarigo, Merchant of Venice 1418–1449,* a business biography by the distinguished historian Frederic C. Lane.

A later commander was Agostino Barbarigo, who led the left flank at the Battle of Lepanto.* Unfortunately, the admiral had to relinquish command before the victory, as he was hit in the eye by an arrow. A highly active World War II submarine bore the glorious name *Barbarigo*. Unfortunately, it was on the wrong side. It sank in 1943.

In peaceful activity, we have Pierfrancesco Barbarigo, who helped Aldus Manutius set up the Aldine Press (see chapter three) by supplying both money and political influence, and Cristoforo Barbarigo, who got the young Titian his commission to help paint the Fondaco dei Tedeschi (see chapter three), had his youthful portrait painted by the young artist, and ended up, after Titian's death, with a major collection. Cristoforo was not among those who looted Titian's house. He bought it five years later, along with the pictures that had been left behind. Tintoretto had already

---

*He may not have looked so far down the ranks to notice, but this put him nominally in charge of a quirky sailor named Miguel de Cervantes.

picked them over and taken a Christ Crowned with Thorns, a
Diana and Callisto, and a Venus and Adonis, but there was plenty
left for Barbarigo, including a Penitent Magdalen, a Christ
Blessing, a Saint Sebastian, a Christ Carrying the Cross, a seated
Portrait of Philip II of Spain, and a Venus with a Mirror.

But as far as we know, these people were not directly connected to us. In addition to the seventeenth-century Ca'
Barbarigo next door, joined and unjoined to Ca' Minotto as family feelings and finances dictated, there are three sixteenth-
century Barbarigo houses on the Grand Canal that pertained to
various branches of the family:

- Ca' Barbarigo della Terrazza opposite the waterbus stop of
  Sant'Angelo, which was bursting with Cristoforo Barbarigo's
  Titians until 1850, when his descendents sold them to Czar
  Nicholas I. Most are now in the Hermitage, although *Venus
  with a Mirror* was bought by Andrew Mellon in 1931 and
  given to the National Gallery of Art in Washington.
- Ca' Barbarigo way down the GC, opposite San Stae, which,
  like us, once had a Tiepolo ceiling that is now at Ca'
  Rezzonico.
- Ca' Barbarigo right across the street from us to the right, deco-
  rated with much maligned nineteenth-century mosaics that
  nobody cares to remove from the facade and put in a museum.

We are more nearly connected to the ducal line, if you please.
These were two brothers, Marco and Agostino Barbarigo, who
served successively, from 1485 to 1501. That they were of different temperaments is reflected in the rooms dedicated to each in
the Barbarigo Villa at Noventa Vicentina, known as the Villa of
the Doges. Marco's frescoes are all sweetness and light: allegories

of prudence and peace, abundance and obedience. Agostino's have a gimme theme of glory, fortune, war, and more fortune.

Modern rulers might want to thank Marco Barbarigo, as during his dogeship he took questions and comments from the public one day a week, thus inventing the press conference. During a certain session of the senate, Marco had a frank exchange of opinions with his brother, the immediate outcome of which was that Marco had to be buried, and the subsequent outcome of which was that Agostino ended up doge, the opposing candidate, Bernardo Giustinian, having made the gallant mistake of voting for his opponent. A fulsome post-election display of reluctance on Agostino's part forced the loser to accept the gracious but galling task of insisting that the winner take office, which Agostino was able to be persuaded to do.

The new doge commissioned Giovanni Bellini to do a picture (now the altarpiece at San Pietro Martire on Murano) of brother Marco being introduced to the Virgin Mary and Saint Mark, as a monument to the love between the Barbarigo brothers, if not the act that had made this introduction possible. His own sculpted portrait, kneeling to the Marcian lion, adorned the clock tower in the piazza until Napoleon ripped it off, and two painted portraits, one by Veronese and one by Marco Basaiti, are in the Museum of Fine Arts in Budapest. The National Gallery of Art in Washington has four bronze medal portraits of the two Barbarigo doges, and an oil of Commander Agostino by a follower of Veronese.

Agostino's official achievements included initiating the custom of (other people's) kissing the doge's hand, losing Venice's last grip on Cyprus, and practicing financial sleights-of-hand, for which—once he was safely dead—the Inquisition slapped the bereaved Barbarigo family with a bill for seven thousand ducats. By way of eulogy, the diarist Sanudo mentions that Agostino died cursed by everyone for his arrogance, rapacity, tenacity, and avarice, and by the way, he was also heavily on the take.

Doge Agostino Barbarigo: "Show me the money."

It was Marco's son, one of many Gregorios in the Barbarigo line, who acquired Ca' Minotto through marriage. Among his descendants, the ones we chose for adoption were the saint who was born in the house and the two beauties who presided there, although not at the same time, of course.

The Household Saint

Gregorio Giovanni Gaspara Barbarigo was born in the Minotto-Barbarigo compound in 1625. Although he is buried in the cathedral at Padua, we can visit him around the corner in the

Santa Maria del Giglio church, where he was baptized, and where there is a large standing statue of him. At his feet is a glass locker, but without permission to attack it with some window spray and soft rags, we can't see the clothes that he is said to keep in it.

Perhaps we should apply as researchers, now that we have purchased, through eBay, a modest relic. It is a small rectangle of burgundy cloth, enshrined and labeled in a silver frame along with equally small tatters from four saints who are not related to us. The research would consist of checking to see whether one of his robes has suffered a snipping.

At a grander altar than this one, actually at the Frari, way above and to the right of Titian's altarpiece, there is a stained-glass portrait of Gregorio Barbarigo at the beatified stage. A painted portrait is in Ca' Pisani-Moretta, for the edification of international fun-seekers who flock to this Grand Canal party rental site.

Gregorio Barbarigo seems to fit right into the Ca' Minotto household, cheeky as it may be for us to welcome him, considering that he got there first and that he is, after all, a saint. Various members of our group share his interests in international relations, higher education, publishing, and medicine, even if we don't pursue them in quite the same way. He was involved in the negotiations for the Peace of Westphalia, which ended the Thirty Years' War, and he was a leading promoter of the reforms of the Council of Trent and in favor of peaceful coexistence with the Eastern Church. He worked to raise educational standards and founded a seminary that he provided with a printing press and a library. He organized care for plague victims.

We are also grudgingly proud of the friendship and support he eventually provided to his fellow Venetian Elena Cornaro, the doctor of philosophy who was among those recently adopted by Mr. and Mrs. Gable. It took him a while to get it, but in the end he came through.

Gregorio Barbarigo: The Household Saint.

Elena Cornaro was the smartest girl on their block, perhaps on any block. Although there is a Corner house next door to Ca' Minotto, her birth in 1646 was in another GC family property, which is now called Ca' Loredan and is joined with Ca' Farsetti to comprise the modern Venetian municipal offices. As you step off the San Silvestro traghetto at the Riva del Carbon, you can see the plaque marking her educational achievement.

Given to hysteria, anorexia, self-flagellation, and extreme shyness, Elena was not your chipper college girl, even if there had been such a thing at the time. But there seemed to be no subject she could not master—modern languages, ancient languages, history, literature, art, mathematics, physics, medicine, astronomy, and theology. And that was all by her midteens. Her father wanted her to make a brilliant marriage, she wanted to enter a convent, and the compromise was that he would get to display her as a virginal intellectual wonder. She became famous all over Europe for her speeches and debates on scientific, philosophical, and theological subjects at academies, courts, and in public forums.

This is where Gregorio Barbarigo comes in. Elena was aiming at a degree from the University of Padua, where Gregorio, by then Padua's cardinal, had been chancellor of the theological faculty. When visitors ask what she got her 1678 doctorate in, we are fond of replying, "Baroque cinema."

That might not have rattled our saint as much as the fact that she wanted it in theology. We are embarrassed to say that he spluttered that the idea of a woman doctor was ridiculous, that women were made for motherhood, that they would probably get everything all wrong, and so on. Including that it would set a bad precedent—if Elena got a degree, all the girls would want one, and it would upset the boys no end.

All the same, he apparently listened as Elena's father kept up his campaign, for which Cornaro senior was amassing powerful support and world opinion. Cardinal Barbarigo suggested the compromise of her getting a doctorate in philosophy instead of theology, and so she did. Later, he was won over to the extent of supporting her candidacy for a second degree in theology, but by that time she was in the late stages of torturing herself to death. She died at the age of thirty-eight.

Gregorio himself died a few years later, in 1697, was beatified in 1771, and was canonized as recently as 1960. Although we feel certain that he rose through his own merits, the fact that he was not unconnected in Venetian circles was a help to his career. The

pope who beatified him, Clement XIV, was the immediate successor of Clement XIII, né Rezzonico (of the family who first occupied the house that Pen Browning later bought), whose mother
was Vittoria Barbarigo and whose uncle was Pietro Barbarigo, a
patriarch of Venice. The pope in whose reign he was belatedly
canonized, John XXIII, had also been a patriarch of Venice.

The Household Sirens

By comparison to his (collateral but legitimate) ancestor,
Gregorietto Barbarigo can't help seeming like a lightweight. But
he captured a whirlwind, and it is to him, and that lady's influence and taste, that we owe the aesthetics of the house today.

The beauteous, scholarly, outrageous, and acquisitive Caterina
Sagredo Pesaro, called Cattina, was already a young widow when
she married Gregorietto in 1739. He went all out to have the
house fixed up for her. The last major renovation, including the
interior unification of Ca' Minotto with Ca' Barbarigo next door,
had begun on the occasion of his parents' marriage in 1707 and
been completed two decades previously, but Gregorietto hired
the best painter and the best plasterer in town to begin again and
turn the place into a celebration of his own bride. What happened to the paintings that Mamma and Papa commissioned,
including a portrait of the procurator Antonio Barbarigo by
Sebastiano Ricci and work by Nicolo Bambini and Antonio
Balestra, nobody seems to know.

The plasterer whom Gregorietto hired was Carpoforo Mazzetti
Tencalla, a stuccoist whose fanciful white (now whitish at best)
urns, shells, garlands, scrolls, bouquets, flags, and deities spread
themselves over the ceilings and walls not only of Ca' Minotto,
but of many important buildings in town. He populated one of
our salons with adorable colorized animals—rabbit, piglet, owl,
beaver, hedgehog—tucked among the ceiling decorations.

The painter was Giambattista Tiepolo. In the salon that he decorated, he surrounded his central ceiling panel with large gray monochrome medallions. Three more of them are over the doors, all set in elaborate stucco work by Tencalla, who often worked with Tiepolo.

The grand theme for this project was Caterina, who was described (in sonnet form) by her equally saucy pal, Caterina Dolfin Tron, as possessing the virtues of "humanity, courtesy, prudence, greatness without pride, womanliness with education and virtue." Accordingly, Tiepolo's central ceiling painting represents *Virtue and Nobility Vanquishing Ignorance* (and includes a minor character who is thought to be the artist himself or his son). The medallions represent Caterina's personal qualities of merit and abundance, and her intellectual and artistic interests—history, astronomy, geography, astrology, painting, sculpture, architecture, music, and poetry.

That was not all there was to her, however. Caterina had a famous library, partly inherited from her mother, of more than a thousand books, mostly in philosophy, including English and other foreign works. She was a sportswoman who defied social disapproval to follow the nearby hunt. She owned a private club on the Giudecca, at the Fondamenta del Rio della Croce, for the purpose of philosophical discussion and a little harmless gambling, for which it was raided by the Inquisition. The Inquisition turned out to be no match for Caterina, who had her club up and running again in no time. Her other illegal hobbies included overdressing, traveling, shopping on an amazing expense account, and hanging out with ambassadors. When the Abbe de Bernis, the French ambassador, left Venice, Caterina wrote, "I shall be constant to you always, Mr. Ambassador, and never faithful."*

The two Caterinas, Barbarigo and Tron, must have been quite

---

*But then, Casanova claimed that the abbot often preferred to be a witness, rather than a participant, in the act of love-making.

a pair, and I keep meaning to write an opera about them called *Le Due Caterine*. Caterina Tron, who wrote poems under the name of Dorina Nonacrina, had her marriage to a member of a nonpainting Tiepolo family annulled, and then married the immensely rich old Andrea Tron. Although he was elected procurator of Saint Mark's, he is believed to have been bypassed as doge because her feisty involvement in politics made him enemies. On the arts scene, she egged on her friend Carlo Gozzi to satirize a Venetian statesman in a play that the subject tried to have closed. Caterina Tron enlisted state support to keep it open, thereby putting the finishing touches on ruining the victim's career.

Both Caterinas were chosen for the series of portraits Frederick IV of Denmark commissioned Rosalba Carriera to do of the twelve most beautiful women in Venice. Caterina Barbarigo is painted with a catch-me-if-you-can smile, and, in defiance of the sumptuary laws, a wealth of huge pearls. In another portrait, now at the Detroit Institute of Arts, Carriera pictures her in a tableau rôle, with a gigantic pair of scissors, astonishingly caught in the act of calmly lopping off her split ends.

Pietro Longhi painted her out hunting, toting a formidable rifle. This is one in a series that also included a portrait of her husband Gregorietto as a florid master of the hunt, looking as if he is doing a George Washington impression, and a possible portrait of their short-term son-in-law. In Longhi's *The Sagredo Family*, a sedate Caterina is pictured in a domestic setting with her sister Marina Pisani, who was also a renowned belle and also possessed of a gambling casino closed by the Inquisition; their mother, Cecilia Grimani Sagredo, who had started that library; three small children (Caterina's girls, Cecilia and Contarina, and Marina's boy, Almorò II); and a footman who looks as if he knows he is not supposed to be in the picture, but is waiting at the side to step in and serve them coffee or chocolate. These

Caterina "Cattina" Barbarigo: The Household Siren.

paintings are all at the Querini-Stampalia museum off the Campo Santa Maria Formosa. Another Longhi painting, in Padua, shows the two girls, Cecilia and Contarina, studying geography at Ca' Minotto, as we know from the portrait of the Blessed Gregorio Barbarigo hanging on the wall behind them.

After Gregorietto's death, Caterina Barbarigo, who had divided the property with her brother-in-law, stayed on at Ca' Minotto until her death in 1772. But by then, we had—Contarina!

Contarina Barbarigo, Caterina's beauteous, scholarly, outra-

geous, and acquisitive daughter, was not supposed to be back in
the house, having been duly married to another patrician. But she
was not satisfied with the marriage, and she was not shy about
saying precisely why not. When she made public her bridegroom's
physical ineptitude, he slunk off to the priesthood and she
flounced home to Ca' Minotto. However, we do not need to worry
about her being lonely. Her wedding had not interrupted the affair
she had previously begun with Andrea Memmo.

We know that Contarina was a spellbinding, so as not to say
relentless, talker from the stunned testimony of the Austrian
emperor, Joseph II, who had paid a visit to Venice. At a party
given for him at Caterina Tron's, Contarina fixed him in conversation for five hours straight without giving him a chance to sit
down. He babbled about this extraordinary incident to every
monarch he knew, yet some came to hear for themselves.

All Venice was also talking about Contarina. She inherited her
mother's proclivity for defying the sumptuary laws, and even in
luxury-loving Venice, the shopping haul of sumptuous fabrics
she ordered from the Rue St. Honoré in Paris was legendary.

The affair with Memmo ended badly. The great love of his
youth, another lady of beauty and intellect but of questionable
birth, was aware of the competing attractions of the Barbarigo
women. In the early stages of their romance, that was a joke
between them, but later, Memmo began to show a callous side
that was to leave both mistresses reeling.

His first love had gamely accepted the fact that they both had
to marry others since they were not allowed to marry each other.
But after agonizing years of yearning and plotting, when she
finally expected to be reunited with him, he coolly consulted her
on the choice of a new and more convenient mistress, in keeping
with his rising status as a government official.

Similarly, when the wife he had dutifully taken was dead, he
consulted Contarina about the choice of a new wife, a position

for which she would have been eligible. But not eligible enough, apparently. Memmo is quoted in the di Robilant book as having written his friend Casanova that Contarina was "not as rich as she was" and that he was "not very keen on all that flabby flesh."

After twenty-five years as friends and lovers, they thus broke up over what Memmo described as "a trifling matter." He passed the rest of his life bragging to Casanova and others about his multiple conquests.

Thanks to Contarina's husband's problem, there was no issue to inhabit Ca' Minotto when Caterina and Contarina were gone. It passed from one collateral branch of the family to another until 1896, when the house and its contents were inherited by Count Antonio Donà dalle Rose. As this is the maiden name of our first landlady, we initially assumed that direct inheritance had resumed, but such was not the case.

The Household Goods

Another one of those astonishing discoveries was to explain the downfall. In a pile of as-yet-unsorted acquisitions in a sec-ondhand bookstore near the Ghetto, I found an oversized, disin-tegrating, unbound book labeled as the collections of Count Donà dalle Rose at Venice. It was the catalogue of his yard sale.

According to the introduction to this document, the count was such an extremely generous man that at the time of writing, 1934, he found himself in extreme circumstances. Extreme, that is, for someone who had two palaces on the Grand Canal, Ca' Minotto and Ca' Michiel dalle Colonne, named for its eleven Byzantine columns, where he lived.

He had lost little time in turning Ca' Minotto into a pension around the turn of the century. But this was no longer enough, and now he was selling off the contents, along with things from the house where he lived. There it all was, in page after musty page: mythological and historical tapestries, porcelain figures, carved chests, inlaid tables, painted desks, gilded sofas, crystal chandeliers, filmy laces, the golden hat of a doge.

Some of it seemed too grand for little Ca' Minotto. The more imposing Ca' Michiel dalle Colonne, now the registry office, had been built by the Grimani family and renovated by the Zen family, and the Michieli alone had three doges. Other inhabitants of the house had included the duke of Mantua, who had been in the habit of treating his harem of big and fat women (chosen for these attributes) to Venice's Carnival, and who moved there with his other artworks when the Austrians conquered Mantua. This was also where the eloquent Venetian historian Giustina Renier (whose husband's family, the Michieli, bought it in the eighteenth century) told Chateaubriand to stop running down Venice, because he just didn't get it. Royalty had been entertained there. So perhaps we could concede that the Bellini *Pietà*, the Sansovino *Madonna and Child*, the Sansovino caryatids and the Canova portrait busts being offered for sale might have come from the other house.

But there was our Tiepolo ceiling painting. And the portraits of Caterina's Sagredo family and of Barbarigos. And the Longhi hunting series with both Caterina and Gregorietto. And their combined coat of arms with his horrid beards offset by what appear to be prancing lionesses. And there was our Meissen dinner service—platters, pots, and plates with charming little scenes of Venice on them, and the bearded coat of arms stuck right over them. (Not the best choice: Waiter, there's a beard in my soup.)

It was very sad: dear Caterina's treasures, being hawked to the public, scattered hither and yon. And when we think what loving care we would have taken of them . . .

CHAPTER SIX

Venice Depicted

A possible source of Venice's high water that has not been investigated is the Archimedes' Principle Problem: the number of dead bodies that filmmakers and mystery writers have been slipping into cold canals under cover of night.

Using Venice as a crime scene, a notoriously impractical idea to criminals, is an irresistible one to crime fans. Murder mysteries and sinister cinema have surpassed even the Napoleonic regime in picturing Venice as a legal and moral disaster area. To Napoleon's success in convincing the world of the evils of a government that was (unlike his own) staffed by rotating public servants with strictly limited terms and checks and balances, they have added the evils of a menacing citizenry skilled in sadism. The result is that Venice's considerable presence in literature and drama is as an unpoliced police state, as it were, where officials vie with the population in committing and concealing atrocities.

The natural result ought to be that honest folk from elsewhere would be anxious to escape its contaminated clutches. As we know, that is hardly the case. It could be the attraction, of course. Still, word must have gotten around by now that Venice is disappointingly safe.

No matter. Nothing would discourage Venetophiles from going to Venice. Or from reading about it or from going to see

All Those Years That Mystery Writers Have
Been Dumping Bodies into the Canal Seem
to Have Affected the Ecology.

dramas about it in any medium. Flash that winged lion, and you have us.

Murder is not the only Venetian theme that springs to the literary mind. Where the painter sees the gentle play of pastel light on shimmering surfaces and the poet sees the melancholy denouement of a gloriously decayed civilization, the novelist and the dramatist see adultery, despotism, conspiracy, jealousy, and miscellaneous forms of sexual depravity.

This disconnect between Venice in song and story and Venice

as the longtime Pursuit of Happiness Capital of the World is only one of the peculiar problems besetting the Venetophile seeking related entertainment. There are technical problems as well.

It is impossible to organize books about Venice, or even, in a large collection, to know what one already owns, because just about every nonfiction book about Venice is named *Venice* or *Venice Something*. There is *Venice Observed*, *Venice Desired*, *Venice Revealed*, *Venice Transfigured*, *Venice in Peril*, *Venice Preserved*, and *Venice Forever*. *Venice Triumphant* and *Venice the Most Triumphant City* are two different books. Ruskin's title, *The Stones of Venice*, is also the title of a book about Venetian carvings in rock.

An opposite problem occurs with some of the big picture books about Venice, especially those with tantalizing glimpses of the interiors of houses—so handy to show off the houses one has rented or to keep track of those one has not yet managed to charm one's way into. The titles may be changed when new printings appear, luring Venetophiles who had hoped for a fresh addition to the familiar material to spring for expensive books they already have. Nor can you judge Venice books by their covers. Pretty much all of the jackets feature Canaletto views or moody shots of the lagoon with the church of Santa Maria della Salute in the background, and the endpapers are all maps of Venice.

With movies, the problem is false advertising. Venetophiles will go to see any movie with Venice footage, and since movies with brief Venetian scenes always use a Venice photograph in the advertising, we are frequently lured to ones that no one but a Venetophile would dream of enduring. Even then, we sometimes get cheated because there is no Venice footage at all, only primitively and inaccurately rendered backdrops. In *DeLovely*, a film biography of Cole Porter, the Porters appear to use as their outdoor terrace a small-scale version of the fish market. Not only is the house where they lived, Ca' Rezzonico, represented by a gaudy imposter, but the filmed Mrs. Porter mispronounces its name. And in the irksome *The League of Extraordinary Gentlemen,* the city has been callously re-generated by computer, complete with automobiles.

Literary Venice

Venetophiles who can't draw are unable to resist writing about Venice, as the existence of this book attests. It is a symptom of Venetophilia, but then, so is reading anything with any mention of Venice. So the market continues to grow and the Venetophile's shelves to groan.

Many authors admit up front that there is nothing new to be said about Venice, including the statement that there is nothing new to be said about Venice. But since this was frankly put by such nevertheless successful writers as Henry James and Mary McCarthy, it only encourages others to believe that fresh enthusiasm will overcome that handicap. An alternative is to pick through the splendor for a detail that is generally mentioned in passing, and do it for all it is worth. Thus we have *The Decorative Floors of Venice, The Bell Towers of Venice, The Stairs of Venice, The Bridges of Venice,* and, no doubt one day, *The Commodes of Venice.*

It would seem reasonable to start one's Venetian reading with Venetians—original source material, perhaps, or at least history. Plenty of that exists, although it is not casually accessible. Serious research begins with the fact that state documents could be written in Latin, Italian, Venetian, or some combination of them all. The Venetian diarist Marino Sanudo turned out fifty-six volumes (in contrast to Samuel Pepys's paltry ten volumes a century later) on governmental, diplomatic, mercantile, and street life from 1496 until his death in 1536, written in Venetian. (The Council of Ten then lost them, Whoops!, but they turned up again in the eighteenth century, only, Whoops!, to be carried off by the Austrians.)

On an easier-to-handle level, Renaissance documents regulating Venetian life have been published in English in paperback, as *Venice* (of course) with the subtitle, *A Documentary History, 1450–1630*. These range from overly optimistic attempts to reform convents and regulate the wearing of pearls to Pope Paul V's interdict and the Council of Ten's suggestion that Doge Foscari resign "for the necessary and most evident convenience of our state and government." For the full story of Venice from its watery beginning, there are excellent histories by Horatio Brown, Frederic C. Lane, Manfredo Tafuri, and John Julius Norwich, among others. Another book called *Venice,* with the subtitle *Fragile City, 1797–1997*, is a comprehensive modern cultural history.

But one doesn't generally start there. Venice being a vacation spot, its visitors proceed from guidebooks to personal travel literature and fiction.

Travel Impressions

There are several ever-fresh and fascinating impressions of Venice by Venetophiles, Mr. James's and Miss McCarthy's among them. There are also an overwhelming number of others. One useful test is to skim through to see how many words are in italics. Italics may have been invented in Venice, but they are the hallmark of the Venetophile who is so overexcited at having picked up the local vocabulary as to have not yet gotten around to searching for meaning.

When you think of how writers carry on about Tuscany and Provence, whatever it is that people see in such places, the I Love

Venice literature is not so bad. There is no bonding with the earth, because Venice doesn't have any. There is none of that yearning for the peasant life, because Venice never had peasants; at most, Venetophiles can aspire to climb into the skilled artisan class (see chapter seven). But anyone with the urge to restore an old house finds himself in line for services behind all the locals, for whom this is not a hobby but an inherited, never-ending struggle to keep the family roof over their heads and out of the canal.

Whatever leanings our predecessors may have in these directions had to flow into established Venetian channels. Venetians also longed for a bit of nearby earth, and cultivated pocket gardens near their houses or plots on the Giudecca or kept villas, sometimes with real farms, in the Veneto. Venetophiles in the nineteenth century did the same, although most of them missed the point of maintaining such hideaways and spent all their time there tending plant life, instead of gambling and trysting. In 1903, Frederic Eden, great-uncle of the British prime minister Anthony Eden, published a book about the still-famous garden he kept on the Giudecca. Although his place is inevitably called the Garden of Eden, Mr. Eden had the restraint to entitle his book simply *A Garden in Venice*.

Because everyone who lives in Venice is automatically in the preservation business, the plentiful number of interested foreigners are organized into a UNESCO consortium of committees who do civic restoration projects under the supervision of Venetian authorities (see chapter eight). Therefore, the written material produced consists of progress reports, rather than cute accounts of exasperation with colorful local workmen. The British committee Venice in Peril has produced a book about Venice's ecological problems, *The Science of Saving Venice,* which lays out, in a comprehensive and readable way, what emergency measures ought to be taken if only politics didn't keep getting in the way.

————

Thus deprived of the popular travel genre in which the jaded foreigner rediscovers himself amid the simplicity of the Old World, the Venetophile is reduced to pointing out the well-known wonders. The hope is to spot something hitherto unnoticed.

Those earliest on the scene had the best chances. After the era of pilgrim travel tips came Thomas Coryat, who wrote *Coryat's Crudities: Hastily Gobled up in Five Moneth's Travels* after visiting Venice in 1608. He noticed that Venetians had a peculiar way of eating. Rather than grabbing food with their God-given fingers, or genteelly stabbing it with their pocketknives, Venetians used a dainty little pronged thing to carry pieces to their mouths. (The fork had been brought to Venice from Constantinople by a doge's bride in the eleventh century, a refinement that Peter Damien, a future saint, announced had prompted a wrathful God to give her—along with hundreds of forkless Venetians— the plague.) Coryat brought news of this invention back to England—slowly, because he used his God-given feet for round-trip transportation, but it was another two centuries before the English really got the hang of using the fork. Perhaps because Coryat was a former jester at the court of King James I, his readers thought it must be a joke. After all, he had also written that Venetian women ran around town topless.

John Evelyn kept an equally sharp eye on the 1645 fashion scene in his travel diary, reporting streaked hair, huge sleeves tucked up to the shoulder, squirrel-lined capes, and enormous pearls. But he found the proud Venetian ladies ridiculous because of the odd gait dictated by those extreme platform shoes he called "wooden scaffolds." And speaking of scaffolds, he also had the luck to observe an execution, complete with rolling head.

During his travels in the 1770s, Dr. Charles Burney, musicologist and father of the novelist of manners Fanny Burney, was rating audience manners. He, too, noticed a Venetian peculiarity. In general, he found Italian music fans' "inattention, noise and indecorum" to be "quite barbarous and intolerable." He also reported an audience response to special circumstances in Venice, where he attended concerts by the famous choirs and orchestras of girl foundlings. "At the Hospitals and in Churches, where it is not allowed to clap in the same manner as at the Opera, they cough, hem and blow their noses to express approval," he noted in *The Present State of Music in France and Italy.*

A decade later, Johann Wolfgang von Goethe observed that there was nothing new to be said about Venice. But there were an ever-increasing number of visitors who kept diaries and wrote letters, many of which were published. Excerpts from these appear in a variety of anthologies, including those by John Julius Norwich, Milton Grundy, Michael Marqusee, Toby Cole, John and Kirsten Miller, and Michelle Lovric. All these anthologies are entitled *Venice.*

Early writers could count on its being enough to describe at length the visible wonders of Venice—the buildings with their amazingly mixed styles and the canals, with the novel living arrangements they entail. (Robert Benchley's telegram to *New Yorker* editor Harold Ross three centuries later: "Streets full of water. Please advise.") But in the mid-nineteenth century, John Ruskin came along and described all the buildings so thoroughly and masterfully that he now owns that literary prose territory. You could quote him or you could argue with him, but only poets and fools would offer totally independent descriptions.

All the same, there was no stopping each and every visitor from writing a What I Saw in Venice book, and secondhand bookstores are still amply supplied with Victorian and Edwardian versions. This may be because unlike the travelers who preceded them, such as Coryat, Michel de Montaigne, and Jean-Jacques Rousseau, they no longer had a stylish and flourishing courtesan scene to offer their readers.

Whose Venice Is It?

To be sure, a new market for descriptive prose about Venice had appeared. The Grand Tour created the modern guidebook, or perhaps, as the early guidebook authors claimed, it was the other way around: Guidebooks created the tourists. Pilgrims had passed around written tips; Francesco Sansovino, Jacopo's son, had written an architectural guide to the city in 1581, and in the seventeenth century there were aides for foreigners by the poet Marco Boschini and Father Vincenzo Coronelli.

Then Cook's, Murray's, and Baedeker's took over. When the Ruskins went to Venice in 1849, Mrs. Ruskin instructed her mother to buy Murray's *Hand-Book of Northern Italy* (and charge it to her) so that she could follow the references to be made in Mrs. Ruskin's letters. "We use it constantly," she wrote, while her husband was working on the book that conscientious Venetophiles have used constantly ever since. "Murray is invaluable and we never turn a step without its being useful." Now there are a multitude of guides, of which the most thorough and most maddeningly indexed is Giulio Lorenzetti's *Venice and Its Lagoon,* reprinted from the 1926 version, and new guidebooks appear all the time.

With ever more people coming to see Venice for themselves, keeping their own diaries and blogs and writing their own letters, postcards, and e-mails to those left at home, literary descriptions have to offer more. So the author's sensibility became more important, and a genre of travel writing developed that we can call My Venice.

This should not be confused with travel guidance labeled or advertised as My Secret Venice. Those are safe to skip, as the authors are apparently unaware of the literature. When *National Geographic Traveler* emblazoned the teaser "My Secret Venice" on its final 2005 cover, the reporter declared himself "on a quest to find a Venice I was convinced lay hidden, a city unseen to all but local eyes." The secrets turned out to be the Accademia Galleries, the Salute church, and the Gritti Hotel. He recommended taking a gondola ride on the Grand Canal to see the palaces. (Not good advice: You can see them much more cheaply by taking the waterbus, and save the gondola splurge for an exploration of side canals.) Under the heading "Locals in the Know Give Their Don't-Miss Recommendations," his Venetian contacts also recommended a Grand Canal gondola ride, along with the Bridge of Sighs, the Frari basilica and the Cipriani Hotel. Perhaps "don't miss" was meant in the sense of "can't miss if you try."

A *New York Times* travel writer advised the reader to "get off the treadmill that can be Venice tourism" by visiting mask shops. Never mind the fact that to Venetians, mask shops are the very symbol of tourism, driving out fruit stalls, hardware stores, and other such residential necessities to sell merchandise of interest only to tourists.

In contrast, books by Venetophiles who have spent time living in Venice do have secrets to spill. They are just not very nice ones. Such books could carry the subtitle of *Guess Whom I Hate in Venice*. Often their enemies have been fictionalized, and you have to get your own Venetian friends to tell you who they really are. But sometimes their actual names are given, and you run into them on the street and wonder why they are not wearing paper bags over their heads.

The true version of My Venice is distinguished by the personality of the writer, whose skills of observation and description are presumed to compensate for the failure to impart secrets. It is usually someone who already has a reputation as a writer, although some, such as James/Jan Morris (who wrote under both names) and Hugh Honour became known because of the charm of their books on Venice, even if Morris did later write, "My own solution for the problem of Venice is to let her sink." William

Dean Howells's career as a novelist and editor eclipsed his first book, *Venetian Life,* but it was that account of the customs and habits of mid-nineteenth century Venetians that launched him.

Charles Dickens wrote *An Italian Dream,* in which he was afraid he would wake up in Verona finding that he had only imagined Venice. Max Beerbohm, writing as "A Stranger in Venice," questioned whether Venice is a dream, but found that the nightmare was being awake in Padua, panting to go back. Mark Twain wrote *The Innocents Abroad* in the voice of an earnest but overtaxed tourist pushed to his sightseeing limits, but along with the wisecracks he offered his admiration, not only for the art and architecture, but (attention, anyone who has condemned him as a racist for his use of the N-word) for his discovery that "Negroes are deemed as good as white people, in Venice." Mary McCarthy was commissioned by the *New Yorker* to write *Venice Observed* and lived there for three months. Joseph Brodsky was commissioned by the president of the Consorzio Venezia Nuova to write *Watermark* and died there.

The best My Venice books deftly mix the past with the personal present in a spirit of light scholarship. Scores of others have been written in that style, and the personal approach has its hazards. Gore Vidal did a book and television show presenting "his own personal view of Venice," spurred by the desire to "trace his own Venetian ancestry." He found no such traces, because it seems that he did not have Venetian ancestors. The aunt who had told him that the Vidal (or Vidale or Vitale) family boasted three doges had failed to realize that Vidal was the given name, not the surname, of these distinguished gentlemen. (She also had trouble with either history or arithmetic. A Candiani doge, a Falier doge, and two Michiel doges bore the given name of Vitale.) Nor were there any Vidals in Venice's Golden Book, which lists the ruling aristocracy. Vidal went ahead with his book and television show anyway.

———

Those who do have pedigreed relatives have pulled rank and written a small body of Venice travel literature that we might call No, It's MY Venice. Unless you consider that unauthorized adoptions count, you have to admit that they have a point.

Another television show and lush book combination was done for the British Broadcasting Company by Francesco da Mosto. Paolo Barbaro wrote a bittersweet book about returning to his native Venice, facing its problems, and wanly hoping for a better future. Both the da Mostos and the Barbaros are from illustrious (although doge-less) Venetian families. Their names remain on two of the most famous Grand Canal buildings that passed out of their families long ago. Ca' da Mosto, which Ruskin called "the most original and perfect" thirteenth-century building on the GC, passed out of the family in the fifteenth, becoming, for the following two hundred years, The White Lion, a famous hotel where visiting royal Venetophiles stayed. Next door, a White Lion has appeared again to take in visitors, but as a modest bed-and-breakfast. The Ca' Barbaro compound, combining fifteenth- and seventeenth-century buildings, was at times the French Embassy, the Hungarian Embassy, and the residence of Isabella d'Este, before becoming the nineteenth-century Venetophile Central under the ownership of Mr. and Mrs. Daniel Curtis.

A third genre might be called It's Your Venice and You Can Have It. Not all travelers who wrote about Venice gushed. Some of them were so uncharmed as to quibble about minor inconveniences. Some of them just plain hated it.

Albrecht Dürer gave it a mixed review in his 1506 letters from Venice. He considered Giovanni Bellini a painter of taste (Bellini not only talked him up around town but asked to buy a picture), and then groused that the other painters ridiculed his work and then copied it themselves and found excuses to get him hauled before the magistrates. Furthermore, prices in general are terrible, he wrote; vendors are dishonest and everything good is snapped up by (the other) Germans. Edward Gibbon, who stopped off on his way home from Rome in 1775, declared that he was disgusted with Venice. Saint Mark's Square is "decorated with the worst Architecture I ever yet saw," he wrote, and the rest of the place filled with ill-built houses and stinking ditches trying to pass themselves off as canals. Ralph Waldo Emerson, who didn't care for Venice when he visited in 1833, later wavered, and then declared, in his 1837 journal, that it was a city for beavers and that he had had enough of it.

Venice-bashing is something of a French specialty. Venetians do not understand the rudiments of hospitality, Charles de Brosse complained in the eighteenth century. They serve that horrible vegetable, pumpkin. They use funny playing cards that no one can understand. The domes on Saint Mark's look like kitchen kettles, and the mosaics inside are pitiful. The Rialto bridge is nothing compared to the Pont-Neuf. The ladies, including nuns and abbesses, carry daggers to deal with problems in their love lives. Nobody appreciates my friend Vivaldi. The doge makes funny noises when he kisses. The only comfortable house in town is Ca' Labia, where the doyenne is a Francophile.[*]

Montaigne declared Venice a disappointment. Rousseau confessed that he found the women opera singers ugly and that an apparently lovely courtesan turned out to have mismatched nipples. Furthermore, she turned sarcastic when she realized that he wasn't joking about how much that upset him. Stendhal, who worshipped Napoleon, acknowledged the greatness of Venice's

---

[*]When this lady showed him her massive jewelry collection, he offered to give both her and it refuge in France. Apparently, she did not jump at the chance.

past and deplored her being traded to the Austrians, but he found contemporary Venetians incompetent, insolent, and stupid. He thought they should consider it to their glory that it was Napoleon, and no one else, who conquered them. Napoleon's general Pierre Daru wrote a long history to prove that Venice had committed suicide. Théophile Gautier claimed that Venetian mosquitoes targeted foreigners on purpose.

Jean-Paul Sartre and Régis Debray were infuriated by the very existence of Venice. Decaying in a pretty, romantic way, instead of an ugly, nitty-gritty way, Venice is inauthentic, they charged. Also effeminate and castrating, Sartre added. Venetians are the sort of people who admire Titian, they both pointed out scornfully, and Idiots of Venice (Debray's term for Venetophiles), with their worship of art, are as bad as church-goers. Worst of all, being in Venice is not conducive to philosophical and political discontent leading to depression or, in the case of Debray, guerrilla warfare.

Poetry

Ultimately the city belongs to the major poets. This accounts for the people at various sites around town who exhibit visible mental struggles: They are trying to remember the words to the poems that brought them there.

> I stood in Venice, on the "Bridge of Sighs";
> A Palace and a prison on each hand . . .

someone will begin bravely, while actually standing on the Bridge of Straw on the riva near the Danieli Hotel that gives a view of the Bridge of Sighs. Inside the Bridge of Sighs itself, it would be hard to linger for poetry while the rest of the tour group visiting the Doge's Palace pushed ahead through narrow passageways into the prisons.

The open Bridge of Straw is also congested. In addition to the busy pedestrian traffic on the Riva degli Schiavoni, it attracts two kinds of romantics. There are the Byron fans and then there are the pairs of lovers who have themselves photographed there under the mistaken impression that "sighs" refers to lovers' sighs, rather than to the suffering of the condemned. A Venetophile could make the argument that the reference is, indeed, to lovers' sighs, in that it refers to the realization that a quick glimpse through the high window on the bridge is the last that the prisoners—who, incidentally, were apt to be petty felons and not the noble political prisoners Byron imagined—will see of their beloved Venice.

There might be time—for the Venetophile; not, alas, for the prisoner—to flatten against the balustrade and continue:

> I saw from out the wave her structures rise
> As from the stroke of the Enchanter's wand!

But Byron's Canto the Fourth from *Childe Harold's Pilgrimage* is one hundred and eighty-six verses long, and busy people have to be able to get to various waterbus stops along the riva.

Meanwhile, someone at the entrance to the Arsenal is intoning,

> As in the Arsenal of the Venetians
> Boils in the winter the tenacious pitch
> To smear their unsound vessels o'er again . . .

but probably not much more of Canto XXI from Dante's *Inferno.*

Over on the Rialto bridge, just about every visitor has, at one time or another, asked, "What news on the Rialto?" Yes, we all know this is from *The Merchant of Venice*, but whose line is it? Yes, it is Shylock's in act one, but in act three, it is posed by Antonio's friend, Salanio. Apparently Shakespeare considered it Venetian for "Wassup?" For the rest of the play, check out anyone lingering and murmuring in the campo of the Ghetto or the council rooms in the Doge's Palace.

Poets have also supplied words for the dominant Venetophiliac moods, which would otherwise be expressed only by 1. "Wow, this is beautiful"; 2. "Too bad the good old days are over"; and 3. "I really hate to leave."

1.   Fayre Venice, flower of the last worlds delight . . .
                              —Edmund Spenser

            White swan of cities, slumbering in thy nest
            So wonderfully built among the reeds
            Of the lagoon . . .
            White phantom city, whose untrodden streets
            Are rivers, and whose pavements are the shifting
            Shadows of palaces and strips of sky . . .
                              —Henry Wadsworth Longfellow

            And the beauty of this thy Venice
               hast thou shown unto me
            Until its loveliness become unto me
               a thing of tears.
            O God, what great kindness
               have we done in times past
               and forgotten it;
            That thou givest this wonder unto us,
               O God of waters?
                              —Ezra Pound

2.   Once did She hold the gorgeous east in fee; . . .
            Men are we, and must grieve when even the Shade
            Of that which once was great is passed away.
                              —William Wordsworth

As for Venice and her people, merely born to bloom and drop,
Here on earth they bore their fruitage, mirth and folly were the crop;
What of soul was left, I wonder, when the kissing had to stop?
"Dust and ashes!" So you creak it, and I want the heart to scold,
Dear dead women, with such hair, too—what's become of all the gold
Used to hang and brush their bosoms? I feel chilly and grown old.

> —Robert Browning

> Sun-girt City, thou hast been
> Oceans's child, and then his queen,
> Now is come a darker day,
> And thou soon must be his prey . . .
> > —Percy Bysshe Shelley

3.
> Only to live, only to be
> In Venice, is
> enough for me . . .
> > —Arthur Symons

> If I had been an unconnected man,
> I, from this moment, should have formed some plan
> Never to leave sweet Venice . . .
> > —Shelley again

Fiction

Thomas Mann and Ernest Hemingway are to blame for most of the modern novels set in Venice, which is saying a lot because there are huge numbers of them with more coming out all the time. But there on the jackets are moody pictures of the Salute or the Lion of Saint Mark on his red and gold flag, and we can't help dipping into one of the same old stories recast.

Mann did not invent the Creepy Venice novel, but before *Death in Venice,* the scary roles were played by internationally recognized villains: ghosts, brigands, and government officials. James Fenimore Cooper's *The Bravo* is about hired assassins and an even more vicious, blood-thirsty government. In Wilkie Collins' *The Haunted Hotel,* the heroine freaks out when her late husband appears to be joining her in an insufficiently renovated Venetian house being run as a hotel.

Mann's contribution was to transform ordinary, cheerful, apparently helpful Venetians—the hotel clerk, the hairdresser—into harbingers of doom. Never mind the fact that the novel's hero, stalking an innocent child, fits the classic definition of a creep; he is the victim.

And so fictional Venice began to be peopled with criminals disguised as service providers. Two that garnered literary respectability were Robert Coover's surrealistic *Pinocchio in Venice* and Muriel Spark's *Territorial Rights,* both of which feature villainous hotel clerks, among a population poised to cozen visitors.

Mann's title, *Death in Venice,* solidified the strange tendency of foreigners to associate the mortality of the Venetian empire with their personal mortality. Although every Venetian is an historian to much more of a degree than the average citizen of other countries, modern Venetians do not mope the way so many of their literary visitors do. They are no more subject to historical depression than modern Greeks are because the Age of Pericles is over. You might think that the German and the English, if they are so inclined, would have their own defunct empires to brood about.

Ernest Hemingway used the dying hero in his less-than-acclaimed novel, *Across the River and into the Trees,* but he provided two consolations that have been a staple of less-than-acclaimed novels ever since. This genre may be called Masculine Fantasy Venice, so as not to give it a cruder name.

It, too, has its earlier roots. A genuine Venetian, Giacomo Casanova, who may or may not have been writing fiction, stemmed the tide of outpourings about the wiles and ways of Venetian courtesans to establish the idea that their sexual power was nothing compared to that of an irresistible, not to mention dapper, man. *Across the River* is the modern prototype, toned down for more sober times.

Even before feminist literature struck back, sexual conquest in terms of great numbers had its glamorous veneer damaged when it collided with the age of analysis. If the great lover was just a neurotic unable to manage true love, he was less exciting than pitiful. Hemingway provided a monogamous love story. There has been no shortage of steamy novels with Venetian scenes, notably Madame de Staël's *Corinne, or Italy*; George Sand's *Consuelo,* which was inspired by *Corinne*, Camillo Boito's *Senso*; *The Desire and Pursuit of the Whole,* by Frederick Rolfe, who styled himself Baron Corvo; and *Profane Friendship,* by Harold Brodkey. And there are a slew of bodice rippers and shopping novels.

Romance in Venice is such a staple that the most interesting fictional relationships are about people who, although in Venice, fail to fall in love: Henry James's *The Aspern Papers* and *The Wings of the Dove,* about gentlemen who inspire love when their real interest is in the lady's papers and money, respectively; Franz Werfel's peculiar novel, *Verdi,* speculating about that composer's jealousy of Wagner; Edith Wharton's short story, "The Glimpse," about two apparently passionate, quarrelling lovers who turn out to be merely professionally competitive musical partners; and Mary McCarthy's short story, "The Cicerone," in which a barely disguised Peggy Guggenheim is puzzled by a pair of ordinary lovers because "she was used to a mercenary circle and had no idea that outside it lovers showed affection, friends repaid kindness, and husbands did not ask an allowance or bring their mistresses home to bed."

Hemingway's contribution had no such originality, but it resonated with modern writers. His heroine is a beautiful, rich, teenaged Venetian countess with an historic name who, for reasons best known to herself, falls hopelessly in love with a sickly, middle-aged American has-been. Not only does she surrender her perfect young body to this passion, but she tries to press her family fortune upon him as well. They will not marry, so she resorts to slipping her heirloom emeralds into his pocket. And forever afterward, the beautiful, rich, young, titled heroine with a surname that appears in the Golden Book and a strange predilection for over-the-hill foreigners became a staple of Venetophile fiction.

Another convention from Hemingway's novel is the modern equivalent of being adored by the citizenry. A Venetian immigrant, Gabriele D'Annunzio, might seem to have written the ultimate version of Everybody in Venice Loves Me. In his novel *The Flame,* it is not only women who adore the faithless hero. Officialdom covers him with accolades and the entire populace is driven to hysteria in its show of loyalty and devotion to him.

But in Hemingway's postwar novel, the simple and adoring folk are those who serve the tourist: the taxi driver, the concierge, the waiter, the bartender. (Yes, the same folks who lay in wait to betray the tourist in the Mann genre.) The young countess's passion for Hemingway's hero is matched by that of the help at such luxury establishments as the Gritti Hotel and Harry's Bar.

Their adulation is made to seem unrelated to the warmth routinely accorded everywhere to regular patrons who tip well. But it set a whole new category of lavish tipping—the literary endorsement. Not just in My Venice books, but in novels and mysteries set in Venice, you now find the names of real restaurants at which the eager owners and staff are depicted greeting the narrator as a friend and plying him with special treats for which payment in money, they insist, would be an insult.

Innumerable spin-offs of the Mann and Hemingway prototypes have been written since. In them, apparently ingratiating Venetians turn out to be creeps with sinister agendas to snare the foreigner, or apparently cynical Venetians turn up to fawn over the foreigner. Countless young countesses, and the occasional handsome young count or tycoon, surrender to inexplicable passions, and aging men follow the trajectory of the Venetian Republic's decline from glory to a graceful death.

This combination of foul deaths and fine restaurants, both of which are scarce in Venice, has enraptured mystery writers. A single one plants the body near the Bauer Grunewald, the sleuths at the Cipriani, their friends at the Gritti, and the path leads through Da Fiore, Harry's Bar, the Caffè Orientale, and Da Ivo and includes course-by-course descriptions of the meals. In others, there are tricky old countesses as well as beautiful young ones and the occasional painted old count. Startling sexual practices serve as a prelude to killings. A high number of foreign art restorers turn into victims or detectives. The few bodies that are not slipped into canals are walled up in ancient structures.

And then there are the Commissario Brunetti novels, by Donna Leon, beloved even to Venetophiles who don't otherwise like mysteries. Her detective is a salaried, happily married Venetian who likes best to eat at home with his family. Except for the number of people who get murdered—Venetians think of murder as something that happens in Milan or Mestre—life goes on about him normally. He reads history, his wife tells him about faculty squabbles at the university where she works, the children have problems with school or friends, the family visits his aristocratic in-laws, he deals with both competent and incompetent colleagues. In each book, the crime leads him to a major institution or problem, from the church to the nearby American base to the Africans who sell illegal handbags on the streets. And although the detective always solves the mystery, the criminal is not apt to be punished: He is well connected, or the institution moves in to cover things up. Miss Leon, who has a great following in England, the United States, and Germany, does not allow her books to be published in Italian. She lives in Venice.

It should be noted that it is not easy to write even bad fiction about Venice, although many have made the effort. All the other Venetophiles are ready to spot the smallest error of geography or culinary judgment. Thus it is that the most avid consumers of books about Venice are the least tolerant critics.

Film

Movies about Venice make Venetophiles even more cantankerous. And we can't stay away from them. Innocent people should never accompany a Venetophiliac friend to any film that has so much as a quick scene set in Venice. The Venetophile is bound to explode in outrage, unable to stop from setting straight matters that nobody else cares about:

"What? They left the piazza through the Napoleonic Wing, and now they're already at the train station?"

"That waterbus is going west—how can they possibly end up on the Lido?"

"Wait a minute—that glass shop is in the piazza—how can he emerge from it and be in Murano?"

"Casanova was never sentenced to death! That's an outrage!"

That last outcry came from a distinguished Venetian who was objecting to the city's practice of allowing film companies to inconvenience the population while a film is being made.

"Why do we sell our patrimony?" he thundered, presumably rhetorically, because everyone present knew the answer, itself a Venetian tradition. Money.

Annoying as it is to find that half the piazza has been blocked off for a film shoot, location shooting provides amusing moments when you are going about your life in modern Venice and suddenly do a double-take. You notice that the house across the street is sporting two footmen in powdered wigs and breeches posted by its water gate. Cutting through the Rialto market late at night, you spot a crowd of bravos on break having a smoke. A glance from a bridge reveals not just the usual motor-boats, gondolas, and garbage scows but a fully rigged eighteenth-century ship.

We can hardly wait for each movie to come out so we can point out what it got wrong. Good films, such as the Italian *Bread and Tulips,* we have to see at least twice: once to call out "That's the alley near our apartment" and "There's no flower shop in that campo!" and another time to get the story line. The only instance I witnessed in which the irrepressible Venetophile was not considered a nuisance was when *The Talented Mr. Ripley,* a portion of which is set in Venice, was shown on a flight from the Marco Polo airport to JFK. Nobody on the airplane was listening to the dialogue; they were all providing their own: "That's our hotel!" "Uh-oh, they're going to the Florian—do they know how much coffee is going to cost them?"

We even watch all those portentous and pretentious docu-mentaries that lecture about Venice being overrun by floods or tourists. A recent example of the latter was actually the work of American tourists—presumably of the kind who would respond indignantly that *they* are not tourists: We and all the other visi-tors are.

Yet we are grateful for all the films. Cinematography of Venice provides a fix that helps sustain us between trips. We only wish they would get around town more (without interfering with our getting around town). Virtually every film shows the same views of the same monuments: The basilica, the pigeon-filled piazza, the churches of Santa Maria della Salute and San Giorgio

Maggiore, the Rialto, the Bridge of Sighs. In this way, movies have adopted the tradition of Canaletto, Guardi, and the numerous other view painters of the eighteenth century who responded to the foreign demand for recognizable views of the most significant buildings and spaces.

Feature films starring Venice (and maybe also some actors whom we don't much notice) fall into four broad and frequently overlapping categories: Costumed Venice, Romantic Venice, Scary Venice, and Cameo Venice.

Costumed Venice began in 1906 with a silent Italian production of *Otello* in which the Shakespearean drama was enacted, start to finish, in eight minutes. Then, as now, this genre adapts stories from significant literature set in the heroic days of the Republic. The choice of leading men is Marco Polo, Othello, Shylock, or Casanova.

Early examples, such as *The Adventures of Marco Polo* in 1938, with Basil Rathbone and Gary Cooper, and the Bob Hope farce, *Casanova's Big Night* in 1954, were made on Hollywood sound stages. This gives Venetophiles no geography to complain about. To make up for that, it gives us stupendous travesties of history. The laughter of Venetophiles inspired by the Bob Hope movie was not from his jokes and antics but from the idea that the Venetian Republic was preparing to march on Genoa. March? In the old days of their rivalry, Venice and Genoa were both sea powers. And by the eighteenth century, they were both exhausted.

The budget movie we forgive for not showing us much of real Venice is *Dangerous Beauty,* a film about the sixteenth-century Venetian poet and courtesan Veronica Franco. This is because it managed to catch us, instead of the other way around. Having pegged as anachronistic a stirring speech the heroine gives to warn against the supposedly glamorous life of the courtesan and decry the fact that women were barred by lack of education from making their way respectably, I found that this had been taken verbatim from the real Veronica Franco's letters.

More recently, Venetian characters have been moved back to the real Venice, improving not only the view but the historical perspective. In the latest *Merchant of Venice,* which opens with boats plying the Grand Canal just north of the sixteenth-century Rialto bridge, and moves to the costumed crowds in the market, care was taken to position the cameras to avoid anything that has popped up subsequently. No taxis, no barges delivering cases of soft drinks, no shots of us trudging over the bridge with our wheeled grocery cart. The newest *Casanova* made up its own story about the tireless adventurer, but occasionally pictured him romping through real neighborhoods. In both of these twenty-first-century movies, we were reduced to complaining that although the exterior shots of the Doge's Palace were stunning, the interior rooms were wrong—to the extent, in *Casanova,* of passing off the Scuola of San Rocco as the doge's ballroom. And wondering why, whether it was supposed to be the seventeenth century or the eighteenth, the buildings had already decayed to the state they are in now.

Except for these larger-than-life characters, Venice is in film, as in literature of the nineteenth century and beyond, a city where foreigners are the stars and the Venetians are pettier-than-life. At best, they are supernumeraries, at worst, charlatans and the butts of jokes. Perhaps we Venetophiles should be flattered to have become the object of so much interest. But unlike Napoleon and apparently Hollywood, we never wanted to take over Venice and humiliate and banish its citizens.

Romantic Venice, which refers to love stories, rather than to the atmospheric anguish of the Romantic era, is about foreigners coming to Venice to pursue, solidify, or ruin love. Such steamy films include not only Visconti's *Death in Venice,* about an old German musician (not a writer as in the book) madly in love with a young boy, but the wonderfully kitsch *Wagner,* about an old German composer madly in love with himself. With Richard Burton as Richard Wagner and Vanessa Redgrave as Cosima, and Laurence Olivier, John Gielgud, and Ralph Richardson as a trio of knights deploring "this Ring thing," the movie is a condensed version of a television series. The shots of Venice are sparse but splendid: Wagner's piano dangling above the Grand Canal on its way to his apartment in Ca' Giustiniani (someone please tell him that the house has both a garden entrance and a side street from which this would have been easier) and his ornate funeral barge making its way to the railway station.

In the film of Henry James's *The Wings of the Dove,* Venetians have pretty much abandoned the city to the English. But the city itself is lusciously revealed, with reflections playing off water, windows, and mirrors—even if a gondola ride passes the Turkish Warehouse going toward the train station and then passes the fish market and the Rio of Santi Apostoli, which are in the opposite direction. As extra treats, we get some tantalizing shots of the interior of Ca' Barbaro, the very house that served as a model for Milly Theale's palace in the book, and the ladies wear Fortuny dresses. The latter required advancing the period in which the story is set to one that was more sexually free, which wrecked the story, but the dresses are sublime.

In mid- to late-twentieth-century films, Venetians appear as menials gouging for tips or as bourgeois adulterers. The cult movie in this category is David Lean's 1955 *Summertime*—so much so that the heroine's hotel, played by the Pensione Accademia, and the Rio of San Barnaba canal that she falls into, have both achieved the landmark status of being pointed out by guides. Just don't ask for her room at the Accademia, because when she is there, it has views of both the Grand and Giudecca

Canals, a perspective otherwise enjoyed only by the statue of Fortune on top of the Customs House.

The feisty spinster whom Katharine Hepburn plays is a rare cinematic example of an American tourist with charm and dignity in spite of her ever-present guidebook and camera. To compensate, there are bumpkin American tourists to absorb the sneers. But the Venetians she meets are a conniving bunch: sexually and commercially aggressive men, a predatory woman, a greedy porter, a saucy singing maid, an urchin who lies and sells

Katharine Hepburn Creates a New Venetian Landmark.

pornography, and a suitor who lies and sells faked antiques. But because this is Romantic Venice—and because she is learning what passes here for European sophistication—she comes to overlook these drawbacks.

The pesky Venetophiliac moviegoer is unable to overlook the jumbled way that she careens around town. From the train station she takes a waterbus heading west, although her hotel is in the opposite direction; it cuts into the Rio Nuovo, then used as a short cut; the church of the Salute immediately looms before her, although it is on the GC nowhere near the train station and way beyond her hotel; the boat takes the Rio of Ca' Foscari past San Pantalon, with fireboats dashing out from the firehouse; goes back onto the GC, but then turns left toward the Rialto and away from the hotel. You may not care, but Venetophiles are smacking their fists against their foreheads.

And the trip is not finished. It takes her past the church of San Geremia, which is near the train station where she started; past the nineteenth-century mosaic facades of Salviati, which are in the opposite direction; and then passes under the Rialto bridge, after which she gets off at the Ca' d'Oro stop on the wrong side of the Grand Canal and arrives on the right side by walking through Campo Santo Stefano.

Apparently the lady is better than she claims at finding odd ways to get around. At another time, she runs west from the Bauer Hotel and yet emerges into the piazza, which is east. Perhaps she picked up this magical skill from the Venetian playwright Goldoni, whose jolly statue mysteriously migrates, in this film, from its usual place at the Campo San Bartolomeo to the piazza itself.

How did we Venetophiles manage to do all this detailed nitpicking? Well, it's this way: In contrast to a silly film such as the 1991 *Blame It on the Bellboy,* which opens and closes with brilliant aerial sequences of Venice but has nothing worthwhile in between, *Summertime* is so visually evocative that we see it every chance we get.

It is easy to understand why moviemakers are unable to resist Scary Venice. The vocabulary of visual symbols signaling danger are all there for the shooting: dark alleyways, unexpected dead ends, echoing footsteps, masked strangers, decayed buildings, rickety furniture, wavering mirrors, garbage-strewn waters, disorientating fogs, scampering rodents. That these are homey touches, rather than menacing ones, to anyone familiar with the city is irrelevant; moviegoers are trained to interpret them as frightening.

Venice is fetid enough in Visconti's film versions of *Senso* and *Death in Venice,* but for sheer horridness, the honors go to *Don't Look Now* and *The Comfort of Strangers.* This is Brutal Venice (Venezia Brutta would be more properly translated as ugly, but the emphasis here is on brutality), where you are not only doomed, but likely to wish for death to put an end to the tortures to which Venice subjects the unwary.

In the 1972 film *Don't Look Now,* based on a Daphne du Maurier story, a couple whose daughter has drowned is tantalized by a small figure who appears to be she, but who turns out to be a murderous dwarf. Ominous accidents and forebodings pursue them everywhere in Venice. In *The Comfort of Strangers,* an Italian-British production made in 1990, a relatively innocent young couple are the prey of a rich and evil couple who have been stalking them, with sado-sexual designs on the man. On the other hand, they do put the young couple up for free in their Grand Canal palace.

Cameo Venice, in which Venice may appear for twenty seconds or twenty minutes of a full-length feature film, is a major

Scary Venice: Old Perversions in a Grand Canal Palace.

category for Venetophiles, simply because there are so many
such films. In a previous career as a film critic, I remember seeing
filmmakers filing into Harry's Bar for their tax-deductible
Bellinis and beef Carpaccio and overhearing with dread what
they would be subjecting me to a year or two hence.

Sometimes they were taking only a few precious shots of the
real Venice to indicate an exotic locale, when Hong Kong, Rio, or
Singapore could have been substituted without much change in
the plot. Really, we should be able to get a discount if we promise
not to watch the non-Venetian parts of these films. But if there

are no travel expenses, we shouldn't be watching them at all, because Venice will be represented only by makeshift scenery. Films of the 1930s and '40s, including King Vidor's *Unfaithful, Anna Karenina,* Rogers and Astaire's *Top Hat* and Orson Welles's *Black Magic* are in this category.

Venetophile Woody Allen is responsible for the shortest and most anonymous Venice appearance: in *Zelig,* Susan Sontag holds forth with the unidentified church of Santa Maria della Salute behind her (and Venetophiles craning to see around her). But he is responsible for a goodly segment in his musical *Everyone Says I Love You,* where jogging takes him slightly off the most thoroughly beaten paths. He has also noticed, as films rarely do, that Venice has Renaissance paintings, as well as buildings. We were pleased to see a scene in which Julia Roberts visits the Scuola of San Rocco, only to have it misnamed the Tintoretto Museum.

Another couple is off to find romance in Venice in *A Little Romance.* Two teenagers are encouraged by a rascal in the guise of Laurence Olivier to believe that if they kiss under the Bridge of Sighs at the exact moment of sundown—as if one could measure that—their love will last forever. So off they go to Venice, running away from their parents and hiding out from the police in the old Malibran Theater (as it looked before the Fenice fire, when it was spruced up to something of its former glory to serve as an alternative opera house).

To be carried away by their charm, you have to be charmed by the way they carry out their goal. Having doped out that to be under a bridge, they have to be on the water, they hire a gondola they cannot afford. When the defrauded gondolier attempts to put them ashore at the nearby fondamenta of the deconsecrated church of San Apollonia, they shove him into the water, seize his gondola, and, lacking a paddle, utilize the walls of the adjacent buildings to propel themselves under the infamous bridge at the propitious moment. Where are the police when you need them?

Romantic Venice: Young Love in a Hijacked Gondola.

Cameo Venice also appears in adventure films, where the heroes are both foreign and destructive. Our horror at seeing thieves blow through a ceiling in the remake of *The Italian Job*, destroying what appeared to be an eighteenth-century fresco, was mitigated by its not appearing to be a very good eighteenth-century fresco. The showroom glass that James Bond destroys wholesale in *Moonraker* is not particularly to our taste; still, the age and fragility of Venice makes this wantonness a poor joke. What strikes us as even more shameful is that some Venetian footage shown in the trailer for *The Talented Mr. Ripley* never made it into the Venetian section of the film.

One might think that the staple of such films, the car chase, would be a challenge, but this has been overcome, most notably by James Bond. Rather than a mere motorboat in *Moonraker*, he uses a motorized, amphibious gondola to get around. In *The Italian Job,* the boat chase goes down the Rio di San Barnaba, where the *Summertime* heroine fell in. The Campo San Barnaba is also where Indiana Jones goes to track down his lost father in *Indiana Jones and the Last Crusade,* with a boat chase ensuing after the hero does some sleuthing in the basement of a library (actually the church of San Barnaba), is chased through tunnels, and has emerged from a manhole in the campo.

Basement? Tunnels? Manholes? What city is this?

Plays and Operas

Venetians adored live entertainment, street theater and opera alike, as was not surprising in people who at one time wore masks half the year and whose city reminds everyone of a stage set. Reams of material were written to satisfy this appetite. Venice may not have invented opera, as is often said (Monteverdi's *La Favola d'Orfeo* is not the first, but only the first surviving opera), but it invented the public opera audience. Check your opera programs, and you will find that many viable operas had their premieres in Venice.

Venetian historical themes attracted such playwrights and composers as Thomas Otway (*Venice Preserv'd*), Lord Byron (*I Due Foscari, Marino Faliero*), Victor Hugo (*Angelo, Tyran de Padoue*), Rossini (*Otello*), Verdi (*La Battaglia di Legnano, I Due Foscari*), and Donizetti (*Caterina Cornaro, Marino Faliero*) among others. Yet little that is set in Venice remains prominent in the international theater or opera repertory. Shakespeare's two plays, Verdi's *Attila* and *Otello,* Ben Jonson's *Volpone,* Goldoni's *The Servant of Two Masters,* the Venetian courtesan act in *Tales of Hoffmann* by Jacques Offenbach (who also wrote *The Bridge of Sighs*), and the denouement of Leonard Bernstein's *Candide* are about it. Others, including such modern works as Benjamin Britten's *Death in Venice* and Dominick Argento's *Casanova's Homecoming* (he moved his *Aspern Papers* from Venice to Lake Como) pop up now and again. But Venice's stage career has not had the staying power of her screen career.

Anyway, the live stage, for plays or opera, is an odd way to get a Venice fix. It was hard not to cheer when a huge Venetian flag unfurled behind the doge in a production of *Othello* at the Shakespeare Theatre in Washington, which is run by a Venetophile. And when allowed to tour the set of a production of *La Gioconda* at the Lyric Opera of Chicago, I was asked why I kept peeking behind the flats. It was because the rendering of the piazza was convincing enough that Harry's Bar had to be just behind there at stage left.

Pictorial Venice

In the end, the most satisfying of the arts that depict Venice is painting. It is no accident that Venice's most famous view painter, Canaletto, painted for the tourist trade and that most of his work left town in Grand Tour luggage. He understood that what Venetophiles most need is a sunny picture of Venice to cheer our landlocked homes.

But earlier Venetians also loved depictions of Venice. Furthermore, for as long as it was plausible, they loved to have Venice looked upon as important and powerful. So no matter what the subject—history, mythology, religion—such elements as the Doge's Palace, the basilica, the bell tower, the clock tower, and the columns of the piazzetta make it clear that Venice was the center of the universe. At the time, this also served to remind its leaders of their loyalties, send out symbolic taunts to rivals, and, happily for us, to document the way the city looked at various times in the past.

The earliest examples appear in the fifteenth century, in altarpieces or in grand commissions from civic and government institutions, so most of these are still in Venice. Bonifacio de'Pitati painted *God the Father Appearing over the Piazza San Marco* (now in the Accademia Galleries). In the Sala del Collegio of the palace, Mars and Neptune—that Venetian combination of war and water—are pictured by the bell tower. What better proofs that sooner or later, everyone goes to Venice?

The Doge's Palace is practically wallpapered with pictures of the urban scenery right outside. Cityscapes are worked into renditions of Venetian history, allegories attesting to Venice's power and glory, and even portraits of doges praying to the Virgin or to Christ, such as Tintoretto's painting of the *Dead Christ with Doges Pietro Lando and Marcantonio Trevisan*. In the doge's own apartments, Carpaccio's *Lion of Saint Mark* shows the patron saint stepping onto the land of an imaginary landscape but with the Arsenal off to one side—symbolizing the equally imaginary hope that for all Venice's troubles with the League of Cambrai, she had the strength to reassert herself as a major territorial power.

It doesn't matter who the star of the scene is supposed to be, the point is always made that this is happening in Venice. The palace itself appears in Paris Bordone's *Donation of the Gold Ring to the Doge,* originally in the Scuola of San Marco, and in Francesco Bassano's image of Alexander III's *Blessing of the Sword of Doge Ziani against the Fleet of Frederick Barbarosa.*

Not only buildings but Venetian secular life dominated notable fifteenth-century religious paintings. In the series executed for the Scuola of San Giovanni Evangelista but now in the Accademia, Gentile Bellini's *Procession in Piazza San Marco* has the procession winding around to the front, but an immense depiction of the basilica in the back and wandering onlookers in the middle. The facade of the original procurators' offices can be seen on the south side, and the pavement is the one the piazza had in the 1490s. His *Miracle of the True Cross at San Lorenzo* (see chapter three) puts even more emphasis on that neighborhood and the distinguished crowd that the procession attracted. Carpaccio's painting from the same cycle limits the actual miracle to the upper left part of the canvas, while the rest concentrates on who is out and about near the Rialto (then a wooden bridge) that day.

By the end of the seventeenth century, large-scale allegorical scenes calling attention to the greatness of the city were dubious. It was just too much of a stretch to portray Venice as a major power. Pompeo Batoni's 1737 *Triumph of Venice* (now in the North Carolina Museum of Art in Raleigh), featuring a great baroque machine in which Venice personified is pulled forth in a lion chariot, surrounded by ancient gods and philosophers and with the ducal palace and surrounding buildings in the distance, was, by then, politically pathetic.

Fortunately, Venice still had her looks, and her popularity was soaring. Panoramas of the city appeared as ceremonial backdrops for the visits of important foreigners, such as those of the French ambassadors and of King Frederick of Denmark, in the works of Luca Carlevaris. The Arsenal and other bellicose symbols gave way to the invitingly picturesque—the graceful churches of San Giorgio Maggiore and the Salute, and the ever-appealing Rialto Bridge and Grand Canal.

A whole new foreign market had opened for paintings as souvenirs. The Grand Tourists were doubtless all remarking to one another that Venice looked like a stage set, and it was the son of a painter of stage sets, who had trained by doing opera sets, who became the greatest of Venetian view painters.

Antonio Canaletto's earliest paintings were of neither Ceremonial Venice, nor Grand Tour Venice, but of the more humble areas of the city, such as his *Rio dei Mendicanti* (now in Ca'

Rezzonico). It was when he started producing pictures of the city's showcase sights, the Piazza San Marco, palaces along the Grand Canal, the great churches, and other tourist destinations, that he hit it big. With the British consul, Joseph Smith, acting as his agent, Canaletto was avidly collected by English patrons, so that the great majority of his work is now in English collections—including Consul Smith's own collection, now known as the Queen's Collection because he got twenty thousand pounds for it from her predecessor George III. Canaletto was such a success with Venetophiles that he is barely represented in Venice itself. Only his academy acceptance piece, a fantasy that hangs in the Accademia Galleries, and a couple of works in Ca' Rezzonico are left.

When they got home, his clients must have thought that their memories deceived them. Canaletto's Venice is most often pictured on a sunny day, but didn't it rain a lot? And was Palladio's church of San Giorgio Maggiore really next to the Rialto bridge on the Grand Canal? But despite this sort of jumbling in paintings that seem to be so meticulously faithful, Canaletto was the consummate Venetian view painter. Even his paintings of other cities look like Venice.

However, he had two chief rivals in his time: his nephew Bernardo Bellotto and Francesco Guardi. Bellotto found it easier to make a living away from Venice and Uncle, working first in other areas of northern Italy and later in Saxony and Poland. Guardi had a more atmospheric approach than Canaletto, emphasized by the flickering quality of his brushwork, but as he painted many of the same subjects he was doomed to be confused with him anyway.

While Venice remained a republic, her native painters had a monopoly on views, but with the loss of independence came an influx of British and French artists and, later, Americans. Wouldn't you know—the foreigners soon dominated the field. Many, such as Felix Ziem, whose work is in museums world-wide, continued the tradition of Canaletto. More or less accurate Venetian topographic painting was being churned out well into the twentieth century. If you count the sidewalk vendors in Venice, it still is.

As the city itself evolved, so did the methods that artists used. J.M.W. Turner, with his extraordinary interplay of color and light, explored the new possibilities of atmosphere then so much in vogue in French and British art. For someone who only visited Venice three times, for a total of less than a month, Turner had a huge Venetian output. Sometimes he took on Canaletto's precise and measured clarity of atmosphere, as in the National Gallery of Art's *Venice: The Dogana and San Giorgio Maggiore*. In other paint-ings, he conveyed only the most abstracted qualities of form and substance. He also took on Canaletto's habit of tinkering with the geography, something we are more ready to forgive in painters than in filmmakers. He got the Custom House to move closer to the Bridge of Sighs and the Doge's Palace so he could get all three into the great canvas now at the Tate Gallery in London. Turner's one great heir in his coloristic approach was the American artist Thomas Moran, as can be seen in his 1892 *Fisherman's Wedding Party,* now at the Detroit Institute of Arts.

With the social and political upheavals of nineteenth-century Venice came a change in subject matter for art. Patricians had figured in Renaissance scenes and the view painters had put in tiny figures doing all sorts of things, including urinating against the walls. Now bourgeois and working-class life in the lagoon became of interest to artists who viewed this with nostalgia or trepidation.

Then, in 1879, James McNeill Whistler arrived, determined to distinguish his work from Canaletto and Guardi, and from the anecdotal sentimentality of Victorian imagery. He turned his attention away from the stagy areas of Venice to the long vistas, the back alleys, the quiet canals, the isolated squares, the obscure palaces, the idiosyncratic bridges, the humble passages where everyday life was lived. His work was radically to revise the artistic approach to Venice—except, of course, for the sidewalk artist-vendors. Whistler did few images of the Piazza San Marco, the basilica, or the Grand Canal, preferring close-ups of a palace fronting on a small canal, seen straight on from across the water, with no visual indication of the size or structure of the remainder of the building. He focused on the inherent geometric shapes of the openings in the facades of the buildings, and the decorative patterns on the surface—an emphasis on formal elements that would influence the work of Monet, who later worked in Venice, as well as of other nineteenth-century artists.

John Singer Sargent's early watercolors reflect Whistler's aesthetic sensibilities and interest in back-street Venice. But Sargent went a step further, peopling his views of narrow alleys with figures that glance furtively at one another, creating a tangible, if indefinable, narrative.

Whistler's approach to Venetian subjects was as important an influence on photography as it was on printmaking. Some of the photographs by the American photographer Alfred Stieglitz, who visited in 1887 and 1894, bear a clear resemblance to Whistler's formats and presentation. And Stieglitz himself influenced untold numbers of later photographers. Whistler, who went to Venice to rescue his career and finances after a disastrous lawsuit with that other Venetophile John Ruskin, ended up rescuing much of Venice from pictorial oblivion.

CHAPTER SEVEN

Going Overboard

There may come a time—after your friends and relations have become concerned about you, but before you admit that you are getting strange—when you cross the line from being a mere Venetophile to being a total lagoonatic. We are no longer talking about a mild infatuation; we are talking about the civic equivalent of stalking. Maybe it is Venice who should be worried that she keeps hearing our footsteps. Here are some of the symptoms:

Wondering why people ask if you had good weather when you were there—as if rain could dampen your love and as if Venice in the nastiest cold and damp of winter or in the oppressive heat of summer were not better than any place else in mild sunshine.

Accepting the idea that stealing the dead bodies of saints was a deeply religious and patriotic act.

Feeling just as outraged when the waterbus routes are changed as John Ruskin felt about the introduction of gaslight and Henry James felt about the appearance of waterbuses.

Heading for the Canaletto and Guardi paintings immediately upon visiting any art museum, and pointing out the houses in them, naming who lived there historically and who lives there now to people who were enjoying the art until you started talking.

Paying $35.8 million for a Turner scene painting, which carried an estimate of $15 million, and of which similar ones exist.

Forgetting to wish friends a happy trip when they announce that they are going to London or Tokyo or Buenos Aires, and instead blurting out "Why?"

Keeping the Venetian tidal calendar on your refrigerator and, even when at home, contemplating a full moon with no thought of romance, werewolves, or maniacs but only of whether the piazza will be flooded.

Being willing to pass time in the Frankfurt or Paris airports if that is the only way you can afford to get to Venice.

Showing so many visitors around that you can't pass through the Campo Santo Stefano without wanting to tell someone the naughty nickname of the statue of Nicolò Tommaseo (a leader of the 1848 rebellion), acquired because the pile of books behind him appears to have been expelled from under the back of his long coat.

Comparing yourself with Titian in that he proves that one needn't be born in Venice or be in residence there all the time in order to be a good Venetian.

Refusing to carry a map when in Venice, because you know your way around, but carrying one when at home in case you need to check a location when coming across a reference in a book or when grilling other travelers about where they stayed.

Setting the weather on your home page at home to show the weather in Venice.

Attending the Venice Biennale not because of the chance to see new art, but because a number of Venetian buildings that are otherwise closed can be visited then, ostensibly to view the art.

Celebrating April 25 as Saint Mark's Day while the rest of Italy has the effrontery to call it Liberation Day.

Sympathizing with the Venetian Serenissima Army, eight activists who hijacked a waterbus and briefly took over the bell tower to mark the two-hundredth anniversary of the fall of the Republic by espousing Venetian independence from Italy, even though the extremist Northern League, which tries to sever northern from southern Italy, denounced them as crazy.

Flashing your waterbus pass for identification in the States where you know it isn't going to work and you will have to produce your American driver's license instead.

Keeping track of the white peach season to make fresh Bellinis at home and failing to keep track of the amount of prosecco you consume while testing for the right proportions.

Calculating your route in Venice to take traghetto gondolas across the GC instead of bridges.

Announcing that obelisks symbolize the rank of Venetian admiral, even if the obelisks in question happen to be in Egypt or Central Park, or on someone's coffee table.

Claiming that polenta is a perfectly edible food.

Finding that you are being given Venetian-related presents by friends, and actually building the model gondola and the three-dimensional puzzle.

Saving paper bags from Venetian shops to use as wrapping paper.

Imagining Venetian Monopoly, with the expensive property along the GC, cheaper lots near the Via Garibaldi and on Murano, and cards for "Take a ride on Vaporetto #5," "Collect 50 euros," "Go directly to the Leads" and "Do not pass Avanti."

Drinking Select in place of Campari.

Picking up on famous Venetian family names that happen to be used in other contexts as if the person mentioned in history or as the citizen of another country were a long-lost relative.

Separating where you hang your Venetian pictures according to Venetian neighborhoods.

Checking Venice webcams and upcoming exhibitions and concerts instead of playing solitaire when you need a break from work.

Saying "Salve" to gondoliers as you leave a traghetto, "boh," to anyone who asks you an unanswerable question, and "magari" for no particular reason.

Listing Venice, Venetian, and Venezia as your Favorite Searches on eBay.

Refusing to make day-trips to the Veneto to see Venetian paintings or other treasures because it would be time away from Venice; or, conversely, traveling for hours just to see a Venetian painting that has landed in some obscure town.

Reading the classified advertisements in the *New York Review of Books* for a thrill—not the advertisements placed by married professors looking for discreet afternoon fun, but the ones under the heading "Foreign Rentals."

Recognizing the distinct sound of La Marangona, the one surviving ancient bell in the campanile of San Marco.

Finding tears of homesickness welling up as your waterbus pulls away from Venice proper to take you to the Lido for a dinner date, and freaking out when you step off and see automobiles.

Using a Venetian-themed Advent calendar to count down the months, weeks, or days until your next trip to Venice.

Going Native

All this is as nothing compared with the serious time and study that advanced Venetophiles put into learning Venetian ways. Elementary assimilation only requires learning what any Venetian knows, such as Venetian history, which routes to avoid during high water, and how to play *scopa* (the card game in which the suits are hit-you-over-the-head-type clubs, rather than our tame clovers; full swords, instead of spades; gold coins, not diamonds; and in place of hearts, drinking cups). Advanced assimilation would be learning a Venetian skill that few Venetians have. Such as speaking Venetian.

Presumably, the Venetophile is already making an effort to speak Italian, at whatever level of skill. While it is true that many Venetians speak English, many others cannot go much beyond

the terms needed for dealing commercially with tourists, and to
make friends with Venetians, you need to be able to sustain real
conversation. Fortunately, they are among the Europeans who
are flattered, rather than pained and disdainful, when foreigners
stumble along in their language.

It is sometimes also necessary to make Venetian adjustments to
Italian—to knock the vowels from the ends of words, including
proper names, to smush two names together or to change them
entirely. A Ca' Corner would not be the house on the corner, for
example, but one associated with the family that produced Caterina
Cornaro. The church of Giovanni e Paolo is known as Zanipolo.
And the popular given name for boys, Alvise, is, in the rest of Italy,
Luigi. Venetian has a profusion of Xs and Js, so that the proverb
"Better little than nothing," which in Italian is "E meglio poco che
niente," becomes "Pitosto de ninte xe mejo pitosto."

It would be more impressive to learn to speak Venetian. This
would wow Venetians, whom it would also flummox. Venetian is
barely being kept alive by a few scholars, by old people who
speak it among themselves, and old families, including hereditary
patricians and hereditary gondoliers, who speak it to their children as a second language, with about as much success as proud
old Italian-Americans used to have in getting their children to
learn Italian.

Even more obscure languages to learn would be those of
numerology and alchemy. Doing so is a fine way to creep out
people who assume that you will be playing the violin to corpses
to resuscitate them and setting your house on fire trying to feed
your greed.

Useful as these arcane practices might be to predict high
water accurately and to acquire gold to spend in Venice, that
would have nothing to do with it. The idea would be to learn the
symbolism and thought processes employed by some of the

major Venetian artists and architects so as to have a deeper appreciation of their work. That goal, although it falls short of fortune in both senses of the word, should not be considered quite so anticlimactic when we remember that soaking in beauty is one of the prime reasons for being in Venice.

Laymen tend to assume that artists are guided purely by aesthetic considerations, although spurred by such conventional artistic motivations as self-expression, anger at bourgeois society, and desperation for money. Architects, being restricted by the laws of physics and the demands of clients, are presumed to chafe at additional interference with their creativity. Modern cynicism assumes that religious themes were chosen by secular artists only for their market value and for the fun of passing off a mistress as the Virgin.

Palladian buildings are casually admired for their proportions on the assumption that he simply made them up. Where geometric shapes in variously colored stones are used on facades, such as Ca' Dario's, and floors, such as in the Scuola of San Rocco, the results are regarded as successful precursors of abstract art. But Palladio was designing carefully laid-out memory houses according to the staggeringly complex rules of numerology, and such elements as porphyry were minefields, so to speak, of symbolic meaning.

One could argue that ignoring all this would be like supposing that Renaissance artists invented a stock character who would be standing around calmly even though his chest was full of arrows, or that they must have been affectionate fathers to depict so many mothers with babies. Just as they used the figures and iconography of Christianity, they used the vocabularies of numerology and alchemy, confident that others would recognize their meaning. In the absence of *Alchemy for Idiots* or *Numerology for Dummies,* few people, including Venetians, now do.

––––––––

Another approach would be to take up a historic Venetian occupation. Within reason. Courtesan is not a good idea. Nor is choirmaster specializing in teaching orphaned young girls. Shipbuilder is theoretically possible, but not what it used to be in the one-a-day era, and caulker and ropemaker have lost the prestige they once enjoyed.

Merchant of luxury goods would appear to be the best choice, but it has been so long since Venetians dominated the field that this no longer seems exceptional. True, Venice is as stuffed as ever with costly treats for sale. The ancient shopping street, the Merceria, is still bustling. Necessities may be scarce, but there is hardly anything that you don't need that you cannot find. However, many of these shops are foreign, which is to say Italian—branches or franchises of the same Italian luxury shops that line Madison Avenue and upscale malls throughout the world. And while a great number of visitors may be said to be merchants of luxury in one way or another, they fail to evoke the medieval spice merchant.

In between these establishments are the small shops that offer rare to trite examples of traditional yet extant Venetian crafts: glass, lace, bookbinding. Scooping up such purchases, which Venetophiles naturally do, is what sets Venetians complaining about tourism taking over the town. Being able to make such things, which naturally Venetians do, considering the market, is an entirely different matter.

Whereas Venice once jealously guarded her glassblowing secrets, she heralded the influx of foreign glassblowers led by Dale Chihuly, which culminated with his chandeliers swaying over canals and streets all over town. (Outdoor art exhibits are not limited to the Venice Biennale. Bronze is more usual for such displays, however. Suddenly, fat Boteros will be lounging in the campos.) That was a hit-and-run appearance, but a number of resident Venetophiles have taken up glassblowing seriously. This

would be the arty version, not the ubiquitous goldfish in cats'
tummies, miniature orchestras, grape bunch wine stoppers, and
wrapped glass candy, including a version sold in the Ghetto
marked "Kosher for Passover." The result is a sprinkling of shops
around town in which highly assimilated foreigners sell their
high-end glass sculptures and jewelry.

Lace making may be up for grabs. It does not seem to have
attracted an equal amount of enthusiasm, possibly because of
the stories of young Venetian women going blind at a young age
from poring over richer young women's wedding veils and tea-
cloths. The industry still exists, based on the Venetian island of
Burano, but many of the handkerchiefs sold in town made the
longer journey from China. Jesurum, the nineteenth-century
Venetian lace and linens business, has radically scaled back in
the last few years, going from an historic showroom near the
piazza, to small shops in the piazza and on the Merceria, to a
back-garden location so far away from the usual shopping districts that saleswomen greet their old customers with an astonished "How did you find us?" Still, you would think that with
people getting married more and more often and having full-
scale white weddings each successive time, lace and linens might
be a field for an enterprising Venetophile.

Handwork with leather and paper are Florentine specialties,
but they are also practiced in Venice. The comparatively liberal
Republic flourished as a publishing center when censorship
elsewhere was so meddlesome that it was the only place to buy
the full story. Now that the shocking is inescapable, or perhaps
because it is no longer shocking, Venice puts out blank books,
beautifully bound, along with its glass pens. Perhaps that specialty, too, is doomed, now that telephones and personal digital
assistants store telephone numbers, dates, and to-do lists, and
public blogs disseminate those private thoughts that used to
sneak quietly into secret journals.

Best of all would be to take a Venetian craft and so excel at it that your work would enhance Venice's reputation. Venice would return the favor by considering that your very excellence proves that you are truly Venetian. This was pulled off by the Spanish Venetophile Mariano Fortuny, who is memorialized as a "Venetian by election" or choice (see chapter four). Venice's silk industry had been around for a thousand years before him. The Greek designs on which he based his dresses had been around more than a thousand years before that. When the combination resulted in those languid but finely pleated dresses with tiny glass buttons still treasured a century later, Venice had a new master craftsman.

The attitude that comes with surviving Venetian artisanship would be just as valuable to study. The following are admittedly arbitrary instances, but I have never had a counterexample.

The young woman, a new mother, who creates that ultimate indulgence, handmade and therefore perfectly fitting shoes, is not satisfied with a routine, "Yes, yes, they feel fine." She keeps poking and adjusting until they bring forth an attempt to explain that not only am I no longer tempted to kick off my (her) shoes under the table or in a dark theater, but now I have to remember that I have them on so that I take them off before I go to bed. Then she glows.

Challenged to produce a hat for a luncheon four days hence, the milliner took out something soft and velvety and asked for a day to ponder how to make it both seasonal and dramatic. She came through brilliantly, but the day before the luncheon I stopped by to report that when I put it at the exact angle she insisted upon, it slips slightly, and perhaps a hatpin would help. Mortified at being unable to produce the right one, she ushered me out the door, locking up the shop although it was late afternoon, prime shopping time on her busy walkway. "Please just tell me where to buy a hatpin" went unheeded as she trotted me to a notions shop several bridges away. When I attempted to pay for the hatpin, she looked hurt and explained with dignity that no, this was her responsibility.

At a shop that sells whimsically artistic puzzles, I took out a violin puzzle bought four or five years previously and explained that somehow the tiny wooden chin rest had been lost. Perhaps they had one on hand? Well, no, because it isn't made exactly like that now, but if I would leave it and say what color I wanted it to be, the missing piece would be made. I explained that I had left this errand until the end of the trip and would soon be gone. The shopkeeper took the little violin from me, put it on the counter behind her, and said I could collect it whenever I returned. No receipt was offered. Four months later, I walked into the shop, and the completed puzzle was handed to me without my having said a word. An attempt to pay was dismissed with a smile and a wave of the hand.

Then there is the taciturn man who makes beautifully meticulous models of the various boats and structures of the lagoon. I had bought a small rendering of the bunched logs that mark the water channels. The channel markers are as dear to my heart as they are to the seabirds that perch on them because they are the first and last thing I see when leaving or arriving at the airport— my equivalent of Venetian merchants' and sailors' last and first glimpses of the golden statue of Fortune on the Customs House at the tip of the city. The difficulty that brought me back to the model's maker was that in transit home, my seagull had lost a tiny leg. I had torn the suitcase apart looking for it, to no avail. On the next trip to Venice I ran to the shop, which is always locked and bears a sign directing customers around the corner to the workshop, but instead there was a sign saying everything was closed for the holidays, after which I would be leaving.

So it was on the next trip after that one that I attempted to explain the problem, making sure to get in that I had no complaints—I loved the piece, knew it was complete when I got it, and realized that the loss was all my fault. Silence. Finally he asked, "Which leg?"

Which leg? Which leg?

I foresaw another trip, after another few months with the poor lame seagull using a toothpick for a crutch.

Let's think. It is on the cabinet across from my desk, so which way would it be facing? Left? And would the missing leg be on the side next to the books, rather than the one facing me? Yet it gets moved around every week for dusting, so I can't be sure. "I think," I ventured, "maybe, I'm not sure, but it could be, maybe the right leg."

We had been standing on the sidewalk, but at this, the man turned around and walked back into his workshop. I waited, still wrestling with the leg question. Being wrong would not only mean facing a lame seagull for another few months. It would mean framing a whole new round of apologies.

When the craftsman returned, he put a tiny wrapped package in my hand. "Makes no difference," he said. "They're both the same."

Going Off the Deep End

The most audacious Venetophile who took the crafts route to Venice's heart must be the American who showed up at gondola yards with a degree in Appalachian studies, speaking no Italian, let alone Venetian, and asked to apprentice at the hereditary skill of making gondolas. Persuading a master to let him work and actually making his first gondola was nothing, he has declared, to getting permission from the government to work for free, as there would be no taxes or insurance involved. But eventually he developed his own gondola yard and Web site.

As with other crafts, there are different local attitudes toward those who make and those who consume. To hire a gondola is a (Caution: big insult ahead) touristy thing to do. For a foreigner to make one is a miracle.

A less drastic approach is merely learning to row those things. "Merely" should not obscure the reality that this is a strenuous and delicate skill that is also passed down in families. A case could be made that gondoliers, like hereditary Kabuki actors, must begin their training in childhood.

This does not deter the determined Venetophile, who begins to resemble a teenager lusting after a car.* In that state, nothing seems a deterrent—not myopia, not lack of rowing experience, not ignorance of Venetian (or any) nautical terms, and not even less-than-Byronic skills for swimming the canals should that prove imperative.

The experience itself is more like learning to ride horseback: You envision yourself speeding through the landscape only to find that first priority is given to stable chores. You discover that the stirrups and saddle contain no safety features that might prevent you from falling off. You become aware of accident possibilities you never imagined. Your legs ache for days afterward.

Finding and joining a boat club among the many on the Giudecca, on Dorsoduro, and along the upper reaches of Cannaregio, is surprisingly easy and inexpensive. In our boat club in Cannaregio the fee is annual, and includes ten lessons that can be used whenever you are in town. And here is the immediately joyous part: It includes both a T-shirt and a winter

---

*Venetian children also dream of cars. When a fair comes to town, the bumper cars are immensely popular. You watch toddlers whose experience of riding in a car is rare to nil suddenly careening around, laughing hysterically as they deliberately smash into one another, and you wonder: Are they just Italian, after all, and is it in the blood?

sweatsuit in the club's colors with the name of the rowing club
and the city emblazoned in large white letters.

However, that is about it for instant gratification. The boats
are not generally kept in the water, so the first lesson is how to
get the boat off the racks and onto a trailer, and then how to use
the crane to get it into the water. And the boat in question is not
even a gondola. It is a sandolo, a flat-bottomed craft about
twenty-five feet long.

Although it is propelled in much the same way as a gondola,
the sandolo used for training requires two rowers, at least one of
whom must know what he is doing. That would be the oarsman
in the back, the pupa, who is responsible for steering the craft;
the front man is more of a mule, propelling the boat. Both of
them stand and row looking forward, each holding one sixteen-
foot oar, rhythmically dipping their oars into the water in theo-
retical unison. Any wincing on the part of the Venetian
instructor is thus fortunately hidden from the beginner.

The Venetian oarlock, the beautifully carved forcula that
Venetophiles have been known to buy as art, is not quite so
benign when you realize that it is all that holds the oar in place.
The activity is very much like striding forward while making a
circular motion with the oar, and the stride and the stroke must
be coordinated. When this is done correctly, all of the energy is
generated by the legs.

Initial lessons are held inside a small, protective jetty, safe
from the waves created by passing boats. Then, without warning,
the instructor steers out into the lagoon. Motorboats whiz by
above the posted speed limit, and the sandolo turns into their
wake; he is testing the student's sea legs. Passing is not having to
be fished out of the water. The next test is turning into the network of canals, down narrow waterways with boats moored on
each side. There, failure—overcompensating so as to avoid hitting anything, in which case the oar comes off the oarlock—has

serious consequences. Meanwhile, there is the thrill of gliding past walkways and churches previously seen only from the land, with the instructor now opening up enough to provide commentary on who lived where and other tidbits more or less from Venetian history. Gondoliers do this even for passengers who have hired them for a truncated hour, but in this case, it is chatter between—well, not equals, even if you manage to keep your footing and the oar—but between people who have a serious commitment to Venice.

An even greater reward comes with the discovery that pretty nearly all of your Venetian friends have boats they didn't previously mention. It would have been as superfluous as our announcing to visitors that we own cars and know how to drive. But when you have shown interest and enterprise, they generously summon enough confidence in your skills to propose excursions. Setting out in the early morning from behind the church of the Gesuiti, skimming across the tranquil lagoon with few other boats in sight and an occasional fish breaking the water in a silvery flash; listening to the bells of San Francesco della Vigna pealing and being answered by the distant but distinct bells from Murano; your friend pointing out the various types of birds flying past, and their relative age; passing the back of the Arsenal, and the private shipyards; navigating an area of turbulent water and reaching the sparsely inhabited island of Vignole about three miles away for a lemon soda at a small café—it doesn't get better than that.

Going for Broke

"Why don't you just move to Venice?" friends ask all the time, with motives that perhaps should not be probed. If you don't pick up your American telephone on the first ring, they give up, explaining later that oh, they assumed you must be in Venice. Colleagues have started to suggest that you really live over there and only vacation at home.

Conversely, when I asked an American friend when he had moved to Venice, he replied, "I never moved to Venice. I live in New York."

"But you have an apartment here in Venice. You're always here when we are."

"Oh," he said. "I just started coming more and more often and staying longer and longer."

Uh-oh. Much as we love our native land and have no intention of emigrating, we went from visiting Venice once a year to twice to, Whoops!, four times a year. We have Italian telephone numbers on mobile telephones used exclusively in Venice and Venetian bank accounts to hedge against dollar problems and to facilitate making deposits on apartments. We store so much stuff—boots, books, eggcup, dictionary, garlic press, street gazette, pasta strainer—with a Venetian friend that he refers to part of his property as "the American corner." We break for real-estate shopwindows, knowingly skipping the ground-floor apartments and the ones that are four flights up.

These are the warning signs of what Henry James called Palazzo-madness. He had a case of it himself, although he managed to fight it successfully, and he recognized it in others. In spite of having had his choice of sumptuous guest quarters in Venice, the Master spoke so often of acquiring his own small place that his friends there started looking around on his behalf and he had to deny that he had been serious. He sneered at Pen Browning's acquisition of Ca' Rezzonico, writing that it was "altogether royal and imperial—but 'Pen' isn't kingly and the *train de vie* remains to be seen. Gondoliers ushering in friends from pensions won't fill it out." As he put it, "There seems but one way to be sane in this queer world—but there are so many ways of being mad. And a Palazzo-madness is almost as alarming—or as convulsive—as an earthquake—which indeed it essentially resembles."

We are still haunted, as Henry James must have been, by knowing that his friends had acquired historic treasures at bargain prices even for their time. Others who could have bought then but didn't probably lived to hate themselves—or their grandchildren to hate them. Some of the most imposing buildings on the Grand Canal are forever associated with past American owners, and the longing to join that tradition comes before the realization of what it would now involve in the way of paperwork, much of it taking the form of money.

Insidious thoughts spring up of their own accord: Why pay rent when we could be making an investment that is bound to increase in value? We could come whenever we wish and not have to bring much luggage because we would have everything here. We could pay for it by subletting when we're not here. We could time-share with our friends.

Eventually, we bowed to Henry James's reasoning and faced the sensible responses to these musings: Venetian property is now phenomenally expensive and competition for it is intense. People tend to stay put; we know grandparents who live in the apartment in which the grandmother was born. Investment property owned by Venetians or outsiders may sit empty for years. There is no longer such a thing as an unfashionable area that might spring back, now that the Giudecca is being settled by movie stars.

And buying is just the beginning. In their battles with age and the elements, these places slurp up money. Facilities are often primitive and delicate. Glamorous apartments, which are on canals or in fifteenth-century buildings, are all the more likely to have electrical wiring that is not up to code, outdated plumbing, roofs in need of replacement, and water at the bottom of the

For Sale: Historic Property, Historic Curse Included.

stairwell. Moving in and gradually fixing things up yourself is not an option. Virtually all work needs to be done by a licensed contractor, but before you can approach one, you must apply for a permit, which involves a long wait, possibly only somewhat shortened by ingratiating yourself with authorities. It is not easy to locate someone licensed since the number of people doing this kind of labor has contracted over the past half century. So if you do find a plumber and he asks how long you have had your problem with water seepage and you say, "About nine hundred years," he will tell you that there are lots of people ahead of you.

If you bought historic property, and Venice doesn't have many other kinds, you would be subject to regulations, for the inside of your dwelling as well as the outside, that make New York City condo boards look like the Welcome Wagon. I have listened to

the wailing of a Venetian who was trying to build a case for needing a second bathroom in his apartment even though there had
not been even one there in the fourteenth century. A sensible
household budget should include contributing to the support of
a government-employed art historian whose job is to stop you
from doing anything to your house that you might propose to do
in the interests of modern comfort. If the property is important
enough, you could even be caught in a jurisdictional dispute
between Venice and Italy and put on hold forever.

Nor would you necessarily have a choice about what and
when you would renovate. Others in the building or officialdom
could make that decision. Or Nature could. Although Venetian
houses were cleverly built so that the pressures on the facade do
not affect the rest of the building, we have seen a facade fall into
the canal and that is not a problem a homeowner wants to have.

Then there was the matter of subletting. How likely were we
to find tenants who were willing to move whenever we wanted to
be in Venice? And how do we manage them when we are not in
Venice, and they call at night to say the toilet doesn't work and
by the way, you do know about the leak, don't you? You can't
ask local friends to run by and solve the problem, and a rental
agency charges a month's rent in addition to a regular fee.

And time-sharing. We could ask a million friends to put in ten
dollars each, which would give each of us a vacation house—for
how long, how many years apart? Besides, that would break up
the old boardinghouse, because we would never get to be there
at the same time.

And so we let go of the idea. And went house hunting.

What we had in mind was a little something with a history, a
canal view, antiques, frescoes, terrazzo floors, balconies . . . We'll
have what Milly Theale had, please.

This turned out to be a failure of imagination. Even more exotic possibilities came along. One morning at breakfast, someone noticed that two abandoned nearby lagoon islands, San Clemente and Sacca Sessola, were advertised for sale. Everyone in the household crowded around the possessor of our one copy of the *Corriere della Sera*.

Sacca Sessola was not of great interest to us, having no more historical claim than having been the site of a twentieth-century pneumonia clinic, long since out of business. But San Clemente had real history. Doges entertained guests there, hermits retreated there (into separate huts, of course), pilgrims were quarantined there, and feral cats were relocated there, presumably under false names because no one could locate them afterward. Napoleon built a gunpowder factory and a prison on San Clemente, and during the Austrian occupation a women's insane asylum was added.

An insane asylum! As in Shelley, where he and Byron, as Julian and Maddalo,

> Sailed to the island where the madhouse stands.
> We disembarked. The clap of tortured hands,
> Fierce yells and howlings and lamentings keen,
> And laughter where complaint had merrier been,
> Moans, shrieks, and curses, and blaspheming prayers
> Accosted us. We climbed the oozy stairs
> Into an old courtyard . . .

Actually, these gentlemen were visiting the madhouse at San Servolo, established exclusively for maniacs of noble birth. But never mind. Close enough. Boisterous San Clemente sounded perfect for us.

It also sounded as if it needed work, but what property in Venice does not? We were prepared for the fact that the price might be steep nonetheless. But in the first place, it was being auctioned, and you never know what might happen at an auction. In the second place, we had already figured on selling Sacca Sessola in order to make the payments on San Clemente. As we all owned our Stateside houses, we were real-estate experts.

Sure enough, there was only one bid when the auction was held, and that one was disqualified by the health department. Not on health grounds, but because the bidder, a French company, had misunderstood the rules and submitted the bid in English, and failed to make a deposit. The health department's involvement had to do with its expecting profits from the sale.

A floor bid of about twenty million dollars had been asked, so we were holding back. When the authorities realized that no one else was going to come forth, we would explain to them the American custom of selling dilapidated property for a single dollar on condition that the owners fix it up and stay there, thus raising the tone of the community. And we would do so in Italian, so as not to risk being disqualified.

Alas, it never came to that. The next thing we heard, San Clemente had been bought and was being turned into a super-luxury hotel, from which guests are now ferried to and from the historic center without having to stay there, in the manner of the Cipriani Hotel on the Giudecca.

In other words, the historic atmosphere of San Clemente was destroyed. Venice, as well as our party, had lost out.

Some years later, another advertisement caught our eyes. This, too, was not for your run-of-the-mill Grand Canal palace but, as proclaimed, "a unique location." Only this time there would be no commute by boat, or any other means. This apartment was located in the Piazza San Marco. Not "near" it, as every fleabite hotel claims (and several are). In it.

It was in the Procuratie Vecchie. In it.

This is the arcaded building on the left as you face the basilica, extending all the way across the piazza as far as the clock tower. It is a sixteenth-century building, replacing a twelfth-century one that burned down, but preserving some of its architectural elements, along with the Renaissance updating, in which superstar architects Mauro Coducci, Bartolomeo Bon, Guglielmo Bergamasco, and Jacopo Sansovino were successively involved.

Its purpose was to provide working space for the procurators who had charge of developing and overseeing Saint Mark's basilica and piazza—an office of huge prestige, not to mention expense to the officeholder—and, later, procurators who oversaw the city on the two separate sides of the canal. Sansovino, their advisor, was given an apartment in the Procuratie Vecchie. When the Procuratie Nuove was built on the other side of the piazza, it became the dormitory for the procurators, who, like all dormitory residents, complained that it was cramped and unpleasant. That became part of Napoleon's palace and now houses the Correr Museum.

To us, the Procuratie Vecchie sounded even better than the insane asylum. We all marched off to inspect it. As this was one of those "by appointment; price upon request" deals, and we did not care to have our backgrounds and finances investigated, we left the arrangements to a Venetian friend who was curious to see it himself.

"I have some important American clients who might be interested in the apartment," he told the agency. "In fact, they are so important that I cannot tell you their names."

This went over very well. It remained only to cast Mr. and Mrs. Disappointingly Unrecognizable but Apparently Big in the States and their entourage. My husband and I snagged the leading roles, thanks to our wardrobes. I had a conspicuously showy coat and he wore an unraveling sweater and ragged chinos, such as only a tycoon (or a scientist) would not be embarrassed to be

*"If we lived here, we'd be home now. And we'd have a better view
of the parade—or military takeover, or whatever it is."*

seen wearing in public. Others volunteered to come as my secre-
tary, my maid, and our local advisors. My trusty sidekick was our
own Bernard Berenson.

Between the piazza itself and a small canal there is a dark passageway the length of the building, heavily favored by pigeons
seeking respite from being relentlessly bribed and photographed.
There, through a central entrance from the piazza, was our front
door.

"You see, there is a private elevator; very convenient," said the
agent as she ushered us away from its gate to a small, tightly
curved staircase. "It can easily be fixed." We trudged up and
around for two flights before arriving at the apartment's front
door. The two floors below the apartment were occupied by the
Caffè Quadri, favored by Austrians and boycotted by Venetians

during the occupation. Still, they might offer a discount to neighbors.

The piano nobile had two large beautiful rooms with long windows opening on the piazza, and etched doors between them, like the ones at the Caffè Florian across the way. There was a small but graceful open mezzanine on the opposite side of the drawing room.

"You could put a little work area up there," said the agent.

"Or a string quartet," I replied.

The cook-tycoon thought he could make do with the nice-sized kitchen. A large bathroom had been updated as late as the 1930s with mirrored dressing table and built-in cabinets. Through that, on the side of the apartment and facing the small canal, was the master bedroom. Having a back canal meant not only a view but also the convenience of having our furniture hauled up over it and through our windows.

We were beginning to see how we important people could be made comfortable. But then there were all those other people we had brought. So on we went to the next floor. This had several small rooms and work areas, some of which could not be seen because of a problem with the electricity, plus a tiny bathroom with shower.

"This must be my room, Ma'am!" my self-appointed maid announced cheerily. "And here's where I can iron Madam's dresses." I resolved to watch my back.

There were still others in our entourage to consider. We went up another floor, where there was yet another bedroom, although its occupant would have to use the sole bathroom of the floor below. With two to a room and eight or ten to a bathroom, we figured we could manage without compromising the master suite. And the best was yet to come.

The third story of the apartment led to an outdoor terrace with a staircase to the roof. Up we all went. The upper terrace was large enough to accommodate a dining table, and secluded enough, except from above, to suggest lounging chairs. The view encompassed most of Venice—from the front, close-ups of the basilica, the bell tower, and the Doge's Palace out to the basin, the entire piazza below; and from the back, the rooftops of the rest of the island out to the lagoon. Only our neighbors, the bell tower and the clock tower, had a wider range.

We asked the usual questions:

"Would it be difficult to get permission to put in another bathroom or two?" No, no, no, easy.

"Would that be expensive?" Not at all.

"How much would it cost to get the elevator fixed?" Very little.

"Do the chandeliers come with the apartment?" That can be discussed.

"If the city decides that the Procuratie Vecchie need renovating, say if they wanted to do over the facade, would we be charged?" Only your fair share; there are other tenants—offices of international organizations.

We weighed the pros and cons.

Pro: Visiting friends would have no trouble finding us.

Con: The piazza attracts an awful lot of people.

Pro: That finest drawing room in Europe that people speak of would be our front yard.

Con: The piazza attracts an awful lot of pigeons.

Pro: If we gave a dance, we wouldn't have to hire a band because the Quadri's band plays right below our windows.

Con: The Quadri's band plays right below our windows.

Then there was the big con: In a million years, we couldn't afford to buy it, and if we did buy it, we couldn't afford to fix it up, and if we did fix it up, we couldn't afford to furnish it. And that would be before contributing our communal share, which, because our six-window expanse was greater than that of any other tenant, would be somewhat larger than the assessments required of our multinational corporate neighbors.

And a pro: We would save money on watches. Those big bronze figures living right next door in the clock tower would surely have the courtesy to march down here on the hour and hit us with their big bronze hammers.

In the end, we did not buy the apartment. A year later, our friend who had made the connection said the agency had called to say that someone else was interested and did we care to up our offer?

We had offered nothing, so we said we would double it. And forever after, we have been unable to enter the piazza without glancing up at those six windows (still shrouded, last we looked) and murmuring, "If we lived there, we'd be home now."

Even this was not the final foray into the adventure that is Venetian real estate. We heard about an apartment that really was a bargain, in that a few of us could possibly stretch our resources and afford it. Off we went, wearing our very own personas.

This apartment had managed to escape history. It had no possibility of being assessed for landmark preservation by any sane authority. Nor was it likely to turn up traces of frescoes that would have to be analyzed. There was no danger of high water because it was on the top floor.

We thought it had possibilities. The stairway could be lit if others in the building agreed and an electric permit could be obtained. The walls could be painted. The walled-in windows could be reopened. The attic dormer room could get some light if a skylight could be put in. The floors could be resurfaced. The kitchen could be disinfected. With patience, work, and money, it might be made to look somewhat less like the sort of apartment in which people commit suicide.

It also had a quiet little man sitting in the living room.

Oh, him, we were told. He's the tenant.

He appeared indifferent to having his home offered to strangers, so we trusted that it was not a shock to him that the apartment was being sold. He was a widower, we heard, and, as we found out for ourselves, not much of a housekeeper. Perhaps he was going to live with the grown-up children whose framed photographs and school memorabilia decorated the rooms. In the guise of sociability, we made delicate inquiries.

No, as it happened, he planned to stay right where he was. An Italian landlord cannot remove a renter, who may or may not have a lease, and who quite possibly could have rent control. He came with the apartment.

But not for long, we were assured. Look at him. He's old and he doesn't look well. He can't last long.

Oh. So we would have a suicidal-looking apartment with a built-in death wish directed at an innocent old man who merely wanted to finish out his blameless years in his own home. A dynastical death wish, as it happens. We learned later that many leases allow family members to move into the premises, enjoying the same security as the original tenants. When the entire family died out, we would have our apartment to ourselves.

Stepping Back from the Edge

The fact that most of us do eventually go home is therefore one of the attractions that Venetophiles have for Venetian land-lords. Renting has its charms, once you beat back the worst of Palazzo-madness. Alighting in different parts of town, you begin to feel related to lots of people, as befits those who are on inti-mate terms with one another's drying laundry and pastry shop weaknesses. There are new routes to be learned, and new faces along those routes become familiar.

When the bent-over old lady who pulled her shopping cart

over our nearest bridge every morning missed a day, we began to worry. Then she missed a second day. Could she have bought three days' supplies the day before? Impossible; that is not how things are done. Were her grandchildren visiting and she was staying at home with them? Unlikely; surely her daughters would not have defied tradition and married out of the neighborhood, and if her sons did, they at least brought their families on Sundays. Should we try to find her? Who would know where she lives? It must be nearby, and we could ask around. We can't be the only people who noticed her absence. She was too small to be eating all that food she hauled, so she must be feeding relatives and friends, people who ought to be caring for her. Is she sick? Did she fall? She can't be—oh, no, please not—dead. Not just after we have become attached to her, and anyway, there would have been a commotion in the neighborhood.

We were working ourselves into a third-day froth when someone at the window spotted her valiantly trudging across the campo with her cart. Whew. But then we left Venice and have not again stayed right there in her parish where we could keep an eye on her. We go out of our way to check the bridge anyway, but have not been fortunate enough to spot her.

In addition to the neighbors, whose proprietary interest in the area takes the form of being proud to have it admired, and neighborhood shopkeepers, who generously count proven customer loyalty from the third visit, each new location provides fresh (although dead) imaginary company. We wouldn't dream of renting an apartment without doing research. Rental agencies name the properties they handle after more famous buildings nearby or for some architectural feature, such as a terrace, not using the names by which the houses may be known to Venetians. The agencies are remarkably uninterested and uninformed about all but the broadest history. In discovering what lingering spirits of centuries past you might find in your rented bedroom, you are on your own.

Much as we love our imaginary friends, there is nothing like having real ones. We have made it a policy to decline invitations to stay with residents, knowing that we are there so often that we risk their becoming sick of us. It is not as easy to have houseguests as it was when you could stash them in your annex or second piano nobile and put a gondola and gondolier at their disposal. Besides, keeping house, including entertaining those very people who have kindly offered their apartments, is much of the fun.

But if they are not going to be there . . .

This is not to countenance Henry James's game of pretending that he owned Ca' Barbaro in the absence of his hostess. We only do that to landlords; in regard to friends, the very thought seems indecent. On the contrary, we were dismayed when a Venetian friend said she would be visiting our hometown the same week that we had planned a trip to Venice. We would be able neither to show her around, in return for the marvels she had revealed to us, nor to enjoy her company on our trip.

But wait. She and her husband lived in the apartment in which she was born. Perhaps her forebears lent it to the eighteenth-century view etcher Visentini, because next to the living-room windows was his print of the campo of the Gesuiti and out of those windows, in real life, was the same view. We knew there would be a good kitchen because of the succulent meals we had eaten there. We knew the bathroom because we had used it.

An apartment swap turned out to be an even trade: Both dwellings were amply stocked with books on Venice, films with Venice, prints of Venice, fresh olive oil, balsamic vinegar, neighborhood shopping tips, and flowers.

We were even well acquainted with the neighborhood bartender for reasons that can be explained—as everything can be in Venice—in terms of history. It seems that Venice, which was not docile about submitting to the authority of the pope, was wary of the Jesuits, who were not docile about submitting to the authority of Venice. Now and again, things got dicey between them, and when the Jesuits refused to join the boycott of the pope's interdict (see chapter three), they were thrown out of town. Their church on the Zattere, Santa Maria del Rosario, was taken over by Dominicans and rebuilt by Giorgio Massari, with a ceiling by Tiepolo. They forgot to renovate the name, however, and after four centuries, it is still known as the Gesuati. When the Jesuits were allowed back after fifty years of banishment and needed a home, Venice used the same ploy it had used when the cathedral was built—specifying a location that was as far out of the center of things as possible. In Venice, that can't be very far, but the church they rebuilt from an earlier one is on the then-underpopulated northern shore. The Jesuit response was to make their church, Santa Maria Assunta, called the Gesuiti (not to be confused with the aforementioned Gesuati, which is not easy) so voluptuously beautiful that everyone would come to them. And so they did. The interior appears to be draped in endless yards of green and white damask, which turn out to be made of marble.

So that is why we knew the bartender. That and the fact that the current order is not quite so much on edge as when people routinely shouted at Jesuits in the streets. They are as proud as ever of the church, and when I was in there alone one cold day, a beaming monk couldn't help gesturing around and telling me "Beautiful, beautiful!" with an irrepressible enthusiasm that people rarely have about their workplaces. However, they are not so punctilious about keeping up with businesslike practices. It was long after the European community had adopted a common currency that we put a euro into the device for focusing light on Titian's *Martyrdom of Saint Lawrence* and nothing happened. We tried another euro. Then the monk presiding over the postcard table rushed over and put in some defunct lire. "Titian doesn't take euros," we warned other tourists who were approaching as we left.

Oh, and the bartender. Well, the first time we went to see the Gesuiti, it was closed for restoration, and we stopped by the bar to ask when it would reopen. He shrugged, and we had a nice conversation about the impossibility of knowing when anything would happen. A year or so later it did reopen, and when we found it locked, we stopped by the bar, where the fact that the church opened late, closed for lunch, and closed for the day early led to another such discussion. Thereafter, when we would go during the posted visiting hours and find the church locked, we were grateful to have a place nearby where you could have, among other treats, a soothing conversation about the relative meaning of time.

The Ultimate Crossover

Some Venetophiles mean it literally when they declare that they want to stay there forever. Upon making the usual inquiries about people who had taken a trip to Venice, although they were not regulars, we heard a touching story.

They had gone on a mission to fulfill the final wish of a dear Venetophile friend of theirs. Having known that he was dying in the United States and that burial in Venice was subject to enormous restrictions, even for Venetians, their friend had asked to be cremated and to have his ashes scattered in the city he loved. So they packed him up in a box and off they went.

Somewhere along the way they were tipped off that even scattering human ashes was forbidden. But there they were, on their way to Venice with their boxed friend and their sacred promise.

We were beginning to tear up at the thought of their having to bring him home to an eternity other than the one he had expressly requested. Was it the family plot after all? Or did they scatter his ashes at his second-favorite place? Or did they do the Venetian thing and scatter them in Venice, California, or the mock Venice in Las Vegas, assuring themselves that that must have been what he meant all along?

"No, no, no," was the answer. "They did it. After all, they had

The Ultimate Crossover.

promised him. There was no problem. At customs, they just declared him as potpourri."

We recognized the emotions behind the wish, perhaps better than the potpourri's faithful friends. So did Elizabeth Barrett Browning when she wrote that "I longed to live and die there— never to go away" (although she went right back to Florence anyway). This is no mere longing to stay in a choice vacation spot. Heavy doses of charming illusion have to be involved. If I am here along with all those historical figures, among all those history-crazed Venetians and Venetophiles, surely someone might eventually dig me up—metaphorically speaking of course.

There is visible precedent for thinking so. Remains of the dead are an integral part of Venice's topography and interior decoration. If you have to step up to enter a campo, it is probably because it was an old urban burial ground, now paved over. The whole north side of the city has the cemetery island, San Michele, as the chief feature of a desirable lagoon view. The

Scuola of San Rocco had the walls of its staircase painted with horrific scenes of plague survivors handing over the quickly accumulating bodies of victims. Stolen saints in their dim glass caskets lie in their altars in churches that have similarly supine stone bodies stacked up on the walls—doges, heroes, and members of powerful families lending their forms to serve as lids for their own sarcophagi.

Yet the focus seems different from the morbidity that afflicts and attracts so many foreign writers. Theirs is not the kind of art that takes the view that death and comfort come from the same source. But in lively, sunny, cheerful Venice, the idea seems to be that we are all here together, and that the dead have just sort of drifted into fresco-land.

In corporeal reality, so to speak, nothing could be less true. Regulations affecting the dead are necessarily almost harsher than we can bear to imagine. Napoleon banned in-town burials, outsourcing funerals to San Michele and the Lido. It is nearby and picturesque enough, with its border of cypresses, but speaking to a family whose funeral was invaded by high water will break your heart. Those going to honor their dead in wintertime are likely to encounter scampering rats. Today San Michele, with many of its bodies piled up in what appear to be filing cabinets, identified with photographs as well as names, is overcrowded. It offers only temporary respite on the way to the ossuary. The eerily beautiful fourteenth-century Jewish cemetery on the Lido was forced to contract in the seventeenth century, and its headstones were moved to the reduced area. Closed for burials in the eighteenth century, it was in a state of tangled neglect until rescued by preservationists. Increasingly, Venetians are buried on the mainland.

The best hope of your remains being allowed to remain is to achieve another sort of immortality—or at least to appear to achieve it at the time of death. A handful of Venetophiles who managed that have secure graves on San Michele, among them Igor Stravinsky, Serge Diaghilev, Ezra Pound, and, more recently, Joseph Brodsky. Even crazy Frederick Rolfe (Baron Corvo), the despair of the turn-of-the-century expat community who borrowed money, made public scenes, and slept in gondolas (and with gondoliers, but more indiscreetly than his compatriots) made it, in tribute to his novel, *The Desire and Pursuit of the Whole.*

Others have taken the funeral procession, so much grander on water than in honking traffic, and gone home. Robert Browning and Richard Wagner each made that stately trip down the Grand Canal, black bunting rippling as they progressed and crowds watching from the shore, before they were buried, respectively, in the Poets' Corner of Westminster Abbey and the Wagnerite town of Bayreuth. And they seem to have as much or more of a presence in Venice than if they had taken the island option.

In the end, it may not be a matter of hoping to be remembered. It may only be that hearing death so commonly called Going to a Better Place, Venetophiles picture somewhere where they would have to bring boots and umbrellas, and would expect to be assigned quarters from which could be seen reflections of water playing on peeling frescoes.

CHAPTER EIGHT

Bridging the Sighs

Imagine all the money that you can save by not buying a house in Venice. In one of Europe's most expensive cities, the seasoned Venetophile vacations at a bargain rate. Rent and groceries cost a fraction of comparable—actually less charming and no more pretentious—room and board at Venetian hotels and restaurants. When the dollar was stronger, we figured that we lived, palace, prosecco, and all, on less than it would have cost to stay and eat in a chain hotel on an American highway. Now that the dollar is weaker, the cost may be about the same.

Figuring phantom money into the budget is, as everyone knows, a sure sign of extravagance. Like other great passions, Venetophilia leads to unexpected expenses. In addition to the outlay connected with visiting the beloved more and more frequently and wanting to give her presents, there are the costs of acquiring keepsakes and consoling yourself when you are apart.

Visits (Spring)

It is not that we come running every time Venice beckons. Festivals of one sort or another are held almost the whole year around, some for her own amusement and some to lure in the visitor. We don't necessarily want to hang around when she is busy entertaining crowds.

"I suppose you go for Carnival," people will say. But it is Venetians who go for Carnival—somewhere else, anywhere else, to get away from the merry throngs. "Only if you would like to have Eurotrash throwing up on your shoes" was one warning we received. But we sampled Carnival cautiously, by including only two or three days of it at the beginning or end of an otherwise quiet trip and taking care to live at some distance from the partying. We missed such folkloric treats as the boat-sized Cinzano bottle that drifted up the Grand Canal and the giant, piñata-like dove (euphemism for pigeon) that was supposed to fly across the piazza on a rope, but instead got soaked in the rain and brained onlookers by dropping feathered chunks on their heads. But we were able to derive amusement from such mild sport as watching mimes and other poseurs, and hiding so that we could spring out and kiss unsuspecting friends. All this was accomplished without insult to our shoes.

We draw the line at the film festival. Going to Venice and then spending all the time on the Lido would be torture enough, but to be shut up in a darkened theater with Venice sparkling in the sunshine (or drooping in the rain; who cares?) nearby would be unbearable.

Some of the festivals we ache to attend are no longer held. Such as the eight-day Festival of the Twelve Marys culminating on Candlemas, the liturgical celebration of the Purification of the Virgin. This was a lot jollier than its pious title suggests.

Although Venice considered that she had a special relationship with the Virgin Mary, her attitude toward any holiday was, in the spirit of our modern Christmas, "What's in it for me?" In this case, the Venetian angle was the anniversary of a legendary event in which cabinetmakers from the parish of Santa Maria Formosa in Castello whopped a gang of pirates from Trieste who

"After them, Venetians! They didn't just get our brides, they got the dowry boxes!"

tried to steal a bunch of Venetian brides. And not only the brides, but hey, the boxes of dowry money the brides were clutching and the borrowed jewelry they were wearing. This remarkable rescue was celebrated for more than two hundred years, beginning in the mid-twelfth century, but then it got so rowdy that the Republic had to squelch it. So we are several centuries too late.

But what an occasion it was. January 31 had long been set aside as the wedding day for twelve poor but deserving young women selected by state and communal authorities to receive welfare dowries that instantly increased their romantic appeal. Two days later, February 2, is the anniversary of the Venetian response to those unexpected wedding guests. In any other culture's legends, it would have been princes who set things right. In the lore of labor-respecting Venice, it was neighborhood woodworkers who boarded the pirate ship, skewered the pirates, tossed them overboard, and scooped up brides, boxes, and jewels, all of which they reported to be still intact.

In the years thereafter, two out of sixty parishes would be chosen by the city to stage the celebration. A week of regattas, religious services, processions, and parties honored both the artisan-heroes and, it being her day anyway, the Virgin Mary. Twelve life-sized wooden statues of the Virgin were commissioned by rich people from the two sponsoring parishes. They were sumptuously dressed and hung with jewels. At the time, it was counterintuitively considered that an expensive outfit symbolized the virginity of the lady inside.

First, the twelve figures were carried around in a parade led by a priest who was cross-dressed as the Virgin and another priest who was fetchingly done up as the Angel Gabriel. Upon arriving at the church of Santa Maria Formosa (formosa means buxom), the two priests would reenact the Annunciation. Then the Twelve Marys were turned over to the young men of the winning parishes. This turned out to be a mistake. The boys thought it was a scream to spend the week rowing these virgins around town and mocking other parishes for not having been chosen. Nyah-nyah, the Madonna likes our parish better than yours, nyah-nyah. The results were predictable, and in 1339 the Republic passed a law making it illegal to throw turnips and apples at a statue of the Virgin.

The doge who was first asked to march in the Mary festivities drove a hard bargain. First he objected that it might rain on that day. Okay, was the answer; we'll give you a protective hat. Then he objected that he might get hungry or thirsty. All right, all right—we'll provide food and wine, he was told. But most doges were only too eager to parade around on both land and lagoon. By the end of the sixteenth century, there were sixteen annual ducal processions on the calendar, beginning with the Feast of the Annunciation. That was the day that opened the Venetian year, because Venice considered March 25, 421, to be her own birthday. There were liturgical and historical processions and regattas commemorating miracles, battles, and miraculously won battles.

On April 16, there was a procession to celebrate Doge Vitale Michiel II's having returned triumphantly home from the Crusades with the body of Saint Isadore and the three columns, of which two still grace the piazzetta and the third of which still graces the bottom of the lagoon. This holiday was later merged into a sort of Doges' Day, like our Presidents' Day, because April 15 marked the defeat of Marin Falier's attempt to overthrow himself (see chapter three). For Falier's procession, ducal regalia were excluded. Instead, members of the Scuole Grande emphasized the solemnity of subverting the state by marching around holding their candles upside down.

As a privilege of office, the doge got to play the role of Christ in Passion Week re-enactments. On the Thursday afternoon of Holy Week, a procession still enters the completely darkened interior of the basilica from both entrances to illuminate it with candles held aloft and flickering off the tiles of the mosaics.

In July and August, processions and regattas celebrated various anniversaries of fourteenth-century naval victories over the (boo!) Genoese, and on October 7, the Feast of Santa Giustina was celebrated as the victory at Lepanto in 1571, with the saint being credited for having helped to bring it about. On December 6, a procession to the Chapel of San Nicolò in the Doge's Palace celebrated old Doge Enrico Dandolo's detouring a crusade to attack Constantinople and beautifying Venice with the well-chosen loot (see chapter one).

When the Republic fell, these celebrations ceased. We have a few of the old holidays left, but in tamer form. Most poignant is the change in the Marriage of the Sea. It still takes place, but much has happened since the sea was first a bride. Then she married the splendidly dressed doge, who arrived on his magnificent golden state ship, accompanied by a flotilla of thousands of gondolas, galleys, and barges full of noblemen and Arsenal workers alike. Now she settles for the mayor who, even in morning dress with a decorated boat followed by gondolas, tour vessels, and waterbuses, looks like a second husband.

Determining the wedding date is more complicated than the doge's election, but it is the fortieth day after Easter Sunday (if it isn't the forty-third or the thirty-seventh—the moon has something to do with this), which is the Feast of the Ascension. The Venetian angle is that it marks a significant moment in the couple's courtship. It was on Ascension Day in the year 997, give or take a decade or two, that Doge Pietro Orseolo II went off to subdue Venice's annoying Dalmatian neighbor and thus to establish Venice's ascension over the Adriatic. It also marked the opening of the spring merchant shipping season and, in the less robust times that followed, the opening of the theater season.

From that victory on, annual blessings were said over Venice and the sea who, after all, had already been living together for centuries. It was at the nudging of Pope Alexander III that they made it legal. As part of his gratitude package to Venice for helping him out of his schism problem by giving him political asylum and delivering to him a penitent Frederick Barbarossa (see chapter three), he not only suggested, blessed, and gave permission for the marriage, but whipped out a gold ring for the ceremony before anyone could have second thoughts.

Every year, after a ceremony in San Marco, the doge and his groomsmen would sail to the Lido to pray at the church of San Nicolò of Bari, patron saint of sailors and fisherfolk. The wedding party would then reassemble on the ship of state and lead the rest of the flotilla to the channel where the lagoon meets the Adriatic. There would be a religious ceremony that ended in the doge's throwing the wedding ring into the sea and announcing that he was marrying and therefore—as if one naturally follows the other—dominating the bride. "I marry thee, O sea, as a sign of true and perpetual dominion." Just what every girl wants to hear. Especially since on all other occasions, Venice was referred to and pictured as a woman herself. Furthermore, it was rumored that the bridegroom had a literal string attached to the ring.

In the cynical eighteenth century, people used to say that the Sensa (Ascension) ceremony made no sensa. Still, the couple keeps having wedding re-enactments, and inviting everyone in town to witness them. We celebrate afterward by combing through the knickknacks, cast-offs, and occasional small treasures in a flea market behind the church.

Nothing could more thoroughly illustrate the difference between the rollicking old days and the modern sense of fun than the holiday that follows soon afterward: an exhaustive walkathon in which all survivors win.

However, this being Venice, it is charming, because the path is up and down the bridges. So it is hardly different from what we do for amusement every day, except for the length of the course and the fact that refreshments are offered at every checkpoint. This event is called Su e Zo, short for Up and Down the Bridges of Venice (Su e Zo i Ponti di Venezia).

Sponsored by the local diocese, the event attracts thousands of pilgrims from around and beyond the Veneto, who buy marathon tickets and solicit pledges for the distance walked. Everyone gathers at the Bridge of Straw at nine in the morning and ends up at the piazza for more refreshments, but there are two versions, a sixteen-kilometer route for stalwarts and a ten-kilometer one for wimps. If you make it through either, getting your ticket regularly punched to validate your claim, you are given a badge of honor in the form of a keychain depicting a Venetian site. As a different one is commissioned each year, there are veteran Venetophiles who take pride in earning a collection (and others who pick theirs up at flea markets).

While the rest of Italy is celebrating April 25 as the anniversary of the Liberation of the Peninsula in 1945, we are celebrating the feast day of our own Saint Mark. In the morning, an honor guard from the different services raises the flags in front of the basilica, and the mayor intones a few memorial remarks. The doge may have entertained regally afterward, but the mayor tends to dodge into the Quadri Caffè with his entourage for a quick espresso.

Three of the favorite forms of celebration in Venice, as elsewhere, are religion, shopping, and romance. So the patriarch presides over a special Mass in the basilica, to the chanting of priests who may be more devout than musical; there is a flea market in Cannaregio and a ceramics festival in front of the church of San Giovanni in Bragora; and little flower stands spring up everywhere, because men are expected to buy rosebuds for the women they love. Also traditional, as we have learned through rushing to the Molo in hopes of watching, is that a small, scheduled regatta either does or does not materialize in the basin of San Marco.

A more dependable time to see a water event is on the Sunday in early May when the Vogalonga is scheduled. Although it sounds like a Russian river, this has been, since 1975, a much-anticipated and beloved Venetian rowing marathon around the islands of the northern lagoon. It is not a competition, but a thirty-two-kilometer course ending in a grand sweep down the Grand Canal, and is intended to extol the virtues of rowing tradi-tional boats over merely motoring in those snazzy but wave-producing newfangled ones. As in Su e Zo, everyone who finishes gets a prize. When we say everyone in Venice who rows, we mean everyone. Men, women, octogenarians, and children are all out pushing oars in a variety of historically correct crafts that contain from two to twenty rowers. When the entire flotilla, which could be fifteen hundred boats, gathers at the Molo beside the Doge's Palace, you get an idea of what rush hour must have looked like in the sixteenth century.

Visits (Summer)

Heeding the mosquito alerts of Henry James, Théophile Gautier, and others, and aware that Venice does not share our belief in ubiquitous air-conditioning, we refrain from going in summer if we can help it. But there are persuasive reasons to brave it.

The Venice International Art Biennale is not one of them, at least for those not professionally connected to the art world. For more than a hundred years, this has been the place to check the direction of contemporary art, and on the second weekend in June of odd-numbered years, hordes of reporters, critics, artists, and dealers do go. The exhibitions, which have spread from the Public Gardens, where many countries have permanent pavilions, to the Arsenal and outposts all over the city, are hot and packed for four days, until they get out the word on the current state of art and go home. So we can learn the buzz immediately and yet wait to see for ourselves because the show is on until the first Sunday in November.

However, one of the most important Venetian holidays is held smack in the middle of mosquito-smacking summer, on the third weekend in July. This is the Feast of the Redentore, commemorating the cessation of the plague of 1575–77, which killed fifty thousand people, including Titian. To obtain relief, the doge had vowed to dedicate a church to the Redeemer. When relief finally came, he made good on this—quite good, because Andrea Palladio was commissioned to design it.

Getting to the church of the Redentore during the holiday is half the fun. Because it is located on the Giudecca, and because it would be unseemly to bundle pilgrims into a waterbus instead of letting them form a solemn procession to the commemorative Sunday Mass, a temporary pontoon bridge to the church is thrown across the wide canal from the Dorsoduro shore, the Zattere. This, in turn, prevents most through-traffic, so waterbus service on the canal is clogged and everybody walks.

Of necessity, the bridge is already in place on Saturday night, so private boats draw up around it for tailgating parties, arriving early to get a prized spot for a long day and night of eating, drinking, and merrymaking. The fireworks display put on after dark is so extensive and significant that the re-election prospects of the mayor are said to be contingent on its quality. In their glee at maneuvering into the center of the action, few stop to consider how prudent it would be to seek a modest site along a quay for all those hours of drinking.

Another plague anniversary is August 16, the Feast of San

Rocco, the plague-bearing and plague-administering saint who is always pictured showing off his bubo, the unappetizing sore on his leg. The procession to the Scuola Grande, followed by a special Mass in the saint's adjacent church, was captured several times by Canaletto. It still takes place, but without a doge leading it and without Canaletto. Anyway, he was not so much interested in the religious angle as he was in the corresponding outdoor art sale.

Visits (Autumn)

Kicking—or rather, paddling—off the fall regatta season is the grandest one of them all, the Regata Storica, held on the first Sunday in September. If you are fortunate enough to have Grand Canal windows, it is like having a costume party in your bathtub. Those who don't, crowd the waterbus stops like the infield at Churchill Downs on Derby Day.

This holiday marks the welcoming home of Queen Catherine, née Cornaro, after Venice had to pry her hands off the Cypriot throne. It was in 1489 that she was forced to trade her explosive but real kingdom for a toy one in Asolo. However, the regatta is done in eighteenth-century costume, which is not only more flattering but, because of its popularity for Carnival, easier to obtain. An historically festooned afternoon procession is followed by races of various kinds of boats, including women's and children's races, building up to a grand finale that heads up the canal from San Marco to the train station and back down to the traditional finish line by the university building of Ca' Foscari.

Two less-regal regattas are held in the following weeks. The Festival of Fish is celebrated on the third Sunday of September on the island of Burano. Menu: fish, polenta, and white wine. On the first Sunday in October, the Festival of Grape Pressing is cel-

ebrated on the island of Sant'Erasmo, which holds the only
regatta in which men and women compete together. Menu:
grilled chops and sausages and red wine.

Perhaps it was inevitable that Venice should seize on the
American version of Hallowe'en. Costumed revels in October
must seem to echo the substantial head start that eighteenth-
century Venice got on Carnival (see below). And the supplies are
ever at hand. Venetian mask shops operate the year around like
village Christmas stores. Mementoes of the dead, and indeed,
the dead themselves, in the forms of saintly corpses, are out in
the open. It is unnecessary to buy fake cobweb material to make
the houses look decrepit. Still, it is disconcerting to see Venetian
children wandering around in television-inspired costumes as if
bewildered about what they are expected to do next.

Another newcomer on the autumn calendar is the Venice
Marathon, run on the last Sunday in October unless it is run on
the first Sunday in November. The starting point is down the
road in Padua, and it continues along the Brenta Canal by the
grand summer villas that Venetians built, across the causeway
into Venice, through the maritime station, along the Giudecca
Canal to the Customs House, across a temporary pontoon
bridge to the quay near San Marco, along the Riva degli
Schiavoni, and ends by the public gardens in Castello. That last
lap includes bridges, which are fitted out with inclined boards for
the event. Now that high water is higher and more frequent, the
last lap may include a running-through-water segment.

Visits (Winter)

Kindly Saint Martin, the fourth-century bishop who cut off
half his cloak to give it to a beggar, is remembered on the

anniversary of his death, November 11, with cookies. And not just any cookies, but cookies big enough for him, his horse, the cloak, and the beggar, all frosted in pastels and dotted with tiny silver balls. One can fill an entire platter, until the picture of generosity and compassion is slowly decapitated and amputated. Saint Martin's Day is also when children, like American children at Hallowe'en, maraud around, trading their nuisance potential for treats. The differences are that Venetian children are canny enough to target shops, rather than residences (which are anyway controlled by entrance buzzing systems), and they merely make noise, rather than covering trees (of which there are few, mostly in locked gardens) with toilet paper.

On the Feast of the Presentation of the Virgin Mary, November 21, Venice celebrates the Feast of the Salute. In a way, it is a reprise of the Feast of the Redentore, based on a reprisal of the plague. The formula of vow, bridge, and church had brought more than half a century's respite, so when the plague reappeared in 1630, killing eighty thousand people, Venice proposed the same cure. This time, it was the Virgin Mary whose help was solicited, and Baldassare Longhena who was commissioned to design the church. Getting right to the point, it was named Saint Mary of Health, Santa Maria della Salute.

For its festival, the church is tarted up with red velvet covering its columns, and large candle holders are erected to enable pilgrims to buy, light, and place candles in the rotunda. Special Masses are said, concerts are held, and it gets its own Grand Canal bridge.

Old photographs show a temporary bridge made by resting planks across boats, so it was with some disappointment that we watched a huge steel structure, high enough for waterbuses to pass underneath, being floated into place. Nevertheless, it is eerie to be walking across the Grand Canal from the Campo Santa

Maria del Giglio to the Salute, even though we think nothing of crossing at the Accademia bridge not far away. It is as if we didn't belong there, but had conjured it up to walk across water. Venetians must feel this, too, because the bridge was crowded with local families, not just for the votive procession, but throughout the time it was in place.

Some of them may be using it for a shortcut to the food and balloon stands that surround the Salute for the occasion. At home, everyone is making castrated ram that is boiled down and served with cabbage and white beans. This castradina is the food that Venetians imported from the Dalmatian coast during the plague, when their neighbors on the mainland refused to supply them. Snacks to go, sold around the church, are nougat candies, caramelized nuts, mulled wine, ice cream, cotton candy, and a sort of fried doughnut with powdered sugar that is worth the delicious little burn to the hand and tongue.

For all the public carousing that Venice does for fun and profit, the holidays around Christmas seem quieter and warmer than elsewhere. With its mercantile history, Venice might be expected to cash in on the commercial bonanza, but the pull of family and friends is stronger. From Christmas Eve, through Saint Stephen's Day on December 26 and New Year's Eve and Day until after the Epiphany, many shops and restaurants simply close. One year we found a handwritten sign at our traghetto stop that read, MERRY CHRISTMAS. WALK.

Streets are thronged, but with people on their way to or from other people's homes, and from pedestrian bottlenecks created by the exchange of hugs with friends home for the holidays. Aside from a few narrow streets that string decorations from one side to the other for a tunnel effect, the only public spaces marking the holidays are the churches. In addition to the services, there are extra concerts and crèches that expand like the dioramas for model trains. Naples is the great center for those miniature scenes, but Venice has its share of ingenious little setups with special effects. The Frari's is the most elaborate, with music, lights that change to indicate the day's cycle from dawn to dusk to dawn, moving doors, windows and wells, and men and women performing their mundane tasks, all supplementing the birth scene. We were once dumbfounded to hear a cock crowing inside a Santa Croce church and were speculating about the source of the brothers' dinners when we noticed that a side altar had been turned into a tiny rural tableau, complete with soundtracked poultry.

New Year's Eve draws a crowd to the piazza to watch the great clock striking more or less midnight, but parties, ranging from the intimate to the elegant, are private. Even after the grandest of balls or the most sumptuous of dinner parties, we savor most sitting on the closed balcony, with the Grand Canal as still as glass, except when a motorboat roars through, taking home a reveler who lasted later than we did.

On New Year's Day, the local version of the Polar Bear Club charges out to the Lido for the first bath of the year, its organizing committee standing by with hot drinks and food. On Epiphany, there is the Regatta of the Befana, who is the sweet old lady who delivers presents down the chimneys. (Venetian children can hardly expect Saint Nicholas to appear from the North Pole when they know that his body, or at least one of them, lies buried out on the Lido.)

To end the year (we are using the old Venetian calendar, which begins in March), there is, finally, Carnival.

Carnival

There was rioting at the University of Padua when the faculty tried to abolish the students' Carnival-in-Venice break. What could those professors have been thinking? And that was in 1507, when the carnival season began after Christmas for a run of about two months. It has been expanding and contracting ever since. In the eighteenth century, carnival began on the first Sunday in October, took a break between Christmas and the feast of the Epiphany, and continued on until Lent, with a couple of weeks of carnival-like whoopee added on in April.

Clever students at either period could have made the argument that the Venetian carnival was an opportunity to study a peculiar sociological phenomenon. With the entire population, from the doge on down, privileged to run around wearing masks and hooded black cloaks, social class and individual identity were obscured for considerably more than pure holiday time, and intermittent leveling became a factor in everyday life.

One theory that might have been proposed to get out of class and go partying was that this had a democratizing influence. When the powerful are theoretically indistinguishable from the powerless, everyone feels free to vent. Venice, which had a history of laws aimed at narrowing the difference between the appearance of rich and poor, used this ruse inclusively. Gambling joints were nominally reserved for nobles, but anyone masked could play.

A less idealistic theory, widely circulated by those who did not want to go partying (or who did go, claiming sociological aims, but didn't have a good enough time to care about leaving open their options to return) was that the whole scheme was designed merely to protect libertines. This insult did nothing to discourage foreigners from attending.

In more sobering times, carnival withered, and in the 1930s Mussolini stamped it out altogether. It was revived in 1979, but only for the usual ten days before Ash Wednesday. Initially, Venetians were delighted to have back their jolly tradition, but their enthusiasm was dampened when they realized that the tradition of attracting international party animals had also been revived. So the traditional Venetian attitudes toward tourism kicked in, with some complaining and boycotting and others complaining and arranging masked balls for paying attendees.

There are people who spend the year working on their costumes, which range from commedia dell'arte characters to modern politicians. Eighteenth-century dress, complete with wigs, is the most popular choice for both ladies and gentlemen. This makes it a fine place for someone with a pile of naturally white hair to garner compliments. It is also a good place to have a melodic scream, such as a friend produced when a yapping white Venetian dog wearing a bow began running up her leg. It turned out to be a rectangular white mop whose bark came from the person at the other end of the handle. Victim and perpetrator exchanged compliments on their respective skills.

Venice's residential neighborhoods are fairly quiet during carnival, because the great numbers of gorgeously arrayed adults prefer to parade where they have splendid backdrops and the space to swerve toward cameras espied through the eyeholes of their masks. Only the small neighborhood children are costumed, in the conventional outfits we are used to seeing at Hallowe'en. In the mornings, sprinklings of damp confetti on the pavements mark the occasional detours of dedicated revelers.

All this, plus other boat races and flea markets, would keep us in Venice all year around, in which case we might as well move there. But then we would truly assimilate and leave town to escape all that fuss. So we would have to have a getaway. We might start fantasizing about villas in the Veneto, which is where the Venetians used to escape. We might even—this is frightening—succumb to the notion that a farmhouse in Tuscany would be restful.

Fortunately, we already have a good home to go to when we

are not in Venice. It is just that when we are there, we get a little homesick for Venice. So we have devised coping strategies to use between trips.

Venice Substitutes

If you can't get to the real Venice, you can always find another one. Such is the cachet of Venice, it has acquired numerous namesakes and nicknamesakes. To the north, we have Venise-en-Quebec. To the south, there is Venezuela, which means "little Venice," although it is bigger. To the east, there is London's Little Venice. The United States has Venices everywhere: Venice, California, with some houses set well back from the remaining scrawny waterways, vaingloriously imagining that it looks like the real thing; Venice, Florida; Venice, Illinois; Venice, Louisiana; Venice, Michigan; Venice, Ohio; Venice, New York; and Venice, Pennsylvania. Only bitterness can come of visiting any one of them and reflecting, "Well, here I am in Venice."

Then there are the cities that claim to be Venice, if only Venice had happened to be in their locations. In the United States, we have Fort Lauderdale, Florida, maintaining that it, not Venice, Florida, is the Venice of America, a title to which San Antonio, Texas, also lays claim. When Lowell, Massachusetts, opened its Pawtucket Canal in the 1790s, it marveled that its industrial town was now practically indistinguishable from the one on the Grand Canal. Dresden calls itself the Venice of the Elbe, Stockholm calls itself the Venice of the North, and Basra, Iraq, called itself the Venice of the Middle East. Amsterdam, Bangkok, Bruges, Hamburg, and St. Petersburg all famously think they are their countries' Venices, and the same claims are made in cities in China, Mali, Vietnam, Micronesia, and Brazil, among other places. They can't fool us. They can't console us, either.

———

Re-creations of Venice—well, sort of—also exist around the world. You can "discover the spirit and passion of Venice" at The Venetian hotel in Las Vegas, according to its advertisements. This takes place "under a ceiling that is painted and illuminated to simulate a gorgeous southern Italian sky." (Southern? We spotted some illuminating graffiti in Venice: "Why should the north pay taxes for the south?") Furthermore, it has conveniences that Venice lacks. Indoor gondola rides, for example. That crowded walk on the Merceria, to get from the piazza to the Rialto, is gone because the Rialto bridge is placed so that it connects the bell tower and the Doge's Palace.

But wait—the Merceria is Venice's big shopping street, as much now as it was during the Renaissance. Is Las Vegas, which made an effort to have its own Guggenheim museum, filled with respectable art, eschewing the Venetian mercantile heritage to focus only on the aesthetic? No. It moved the mall-type shops to the Grand Canal, possibly the only major avenue of any city that is not a shopping street. Except for a gallery or two and clusters of souvenir shops on either side of the Rialto bridge, the Grand Canal is residential. Or it was when the residents could afford to stay there; the residents are now mostly resident in hotels.

Shenzhen, China, has a Saint Mark's Piazza in its Window of the World theme park, alongside such other architectural excerpts as St. Peter's Basilica, the Egyptian Sphinx and pyramids, the Taj Mahal, Niagara Falls, the Eiffel Tower, the Sydney Opera House, Mount Rushmore, and the Kremlin. This made a mighty metaphor for a Chinese film about a young woman trapped in such a park and sealed off from real life. The Italian village in Nagoya, Japan, has a Campanile replica, along with a bridge and a giant gift mall. Günzburg, Germany, has not only the piazza but a campo, the Rialto market, a bridge, and a population of little tourists. The entire thing is made out of Legos.

Esch-sur-Alzette, Luxembourg, created a Potemkin Venice to rent to movie companies. Rimini, Italy, which is not all that far away from Venice for heaven's sake, has a small-scale Venice as part of its Italy in Miniature theme park.

Nearly every cruise ship has a lounge and food area called the Lido, but at least one, the *Costa Atlantica,* has a Caffè Florian, a replica (sort of) of the eighteenth-century café on the piazza. It also has Dante's Discotheque. That does not look a thing like the Arsenal.

You might think that Venetophiles would enjoy such places, which are tributes to Venetophilia as well as to Venice. They provide ample opportunity for showing off by pointing out the inaccuracies. Also, they are a scream. Not everyone gets the chance to go to Venice, and at least they can get the general idea.

But no. That tampering with scale, re-aligning buildings,* and sanitizing the water is disturbing. It is like seeing someone you love crudely caricatured. Or fixed in the public mind as the very thing she is not, the way Edith Wharton, who fought Victorian taste and manners, is now cited as the quintessential Victorian lady. Or treated as foolish in her decline by those who are unaware of her former magnificence. Suppose Venice does some day sink out of view. Will our descendents who know only these garish renditions think that is what we were making such a fuss about?

The only satisfactory semblances of Venice outside Venice are right outside Venice. Along the Brenta Canal, going west toward Padua, are Venetian villas, built for Venetians by a series of outstanding Venetian architects from the fifteenth through the eighteenth centuries. The closest major one is the Malcontenta, a villa designed by Palladio for the Foscari family in the 1550s. The

*We only let Canaletto do that.

finest is the eighteenth-century one in Stra, created for Doge Alvise Pisani and decorated by Giambattista Tiepolo. At Maser, there is Palladio's Villa Barbaro, decorated by Paolo Veronese. The nearby town of Treviso is legitimately reminiscent of Venice, complete with canals, a Titian Annunciation in its duomo and a gallery chock-full of Venetian paintings, including a series of Rosalba Carriera pastels.

But then, if you're that close to Venice, why can't you just experience Venice by going to Venice?

The Out-of-Venice Experience

It is not as though we miss eating in Venetian restaurants and riding in gondolas. When we are there and could do either any time, or at least until the budget breaks, we prefer to cook and walk. So why do our hearts leap when we find Venetian restaurants and gondolas in the United States?

It can't be the happiness of spotting something from home in a foreign land because, in fact, we are home. But it feels like that. There is a rush of warmth, only to be followed by the realization that were it in its proper place, we would have passed it right by. Under oath, we might have to admit that the Venetian cuisine, while pleasant, is not one of the great cuisines of the world, and the Italian is. But that's not the point when you crave home cooking.

America's Venetian restaurants often turn out not to be. They are only Italian, and the Venice name or mural is merely another use of that well-worn advertising device. One Washington restaurant that calls itself Venetian is decorated with neighborhood flags from Siena and sculptural reproductions of *David* from Florence and *Augustus* from Rome. And try asking for a sgropino in one of those places.

A what, signora? One time we were pleasantly astonished with the reply, "Sorry, I don't have any lemon sherbet." It really was a Venetian restaurant, after all. So we went back another time, handed over a box of lemon sherbet and received, in good time, a proper sgropino.

However, you can get a Venetian Bellini around the world. That smoothie of white peach puree and prosecco is a Venetian invention, and the descendents of the inventor, Giuseppe Cipriani, are doing wonders to remedy the geographical handicap of Venetian restaurants having been confined to Venice. In the 1930s, Harry's Bar became a huge success with an international reputation through the unlikely method of embracing tourist chic—a concept that everyone else still thinks of as an oxymoron. But it was named (as was Cipriani's son) for a tourist: Harry Pickering of Boston, a drinker whose family paid him to stay abroad and then cut him off. Cipriani, his bartender at the Hotel Europa, made him a generous loan that was belatedly repaid with a record-breaking tip that became seed money for the bar. It has attracted the richest tourists ever since, along with those who save up for a drink in their presence. After spreading out in Venice, with restaurants on Torcello and the Giudecca, where a lavish resort hotel also bears the Cipriani name, succeeding Cipriani generations built an international empire. There are Cipriani restaurants in London and Hong Kong as well as all around New York City. One of them so re-creates the Venice layout that a Venetophile does not have to ask where the upstairs bathroom is. The Rainbow Room at Rockefeller Center is now a Cipriani property, as are a Wall Street banquet hall and a Manhattan apartment building. For those who lack a neighborhood Cipriani, the Bellini now comes in a pink bottled version.

It seems that you can catch a gondola in any region of the United States—not only in New York's Central Park, the Boston

Commons, and in Las Vegas, but in Irving, Texas; Myrtle Beach, South Carolina; Moonachie, New Jersey; Seattle, Washington; Providence, Rhode Island; Orlando and Fort Lauderdale, Florida; and Newport Beach and Marina del Ray, California. The New Orleans gondola service is relocating after Hurricane Katrina, and there is one operating in Ottawa, Canada.

There are probably others; these are members of the Gondola Society of America, whose mission statement is:

To further promote the virtues, traditions, romance, and artistry of the number-one symbol of romance in the Western world. To provide a forum for gondola operators and enthusiasts' fellowship, collaboration, and the sharing of ideas and experiences. To never lose sight of the centuries of gondola heritage. To ensure the gondolas' safe passage through the twenty-first century and beyond. With reverence for the traditional and encouragement of the progressive.

They also sell rides.

You would think they would be embarrassed about the romance angle. Gondolas were notorious trysting places back when they had cabin tops complete with curtained windows. But apparently America's gondoliers have something more wholesome in mind. They offer roses, candy, strawberries, and inducements to use their boats for marriage proposals and weddings. (Boston Gondolas' advertisement: "Guys and girls, you will not find a more unique and special way to say, 'Will you marry me?' If you intend to propose on the gondola, please make sure you let us know beforehand!" Boston Gondolas also notes that "In the past five years we have never seen a single guest get sick!")

Except for the fiberglass imitations in Las Vegas, these boats are genuine Venetian gondolas that cost as much as luxury cars, plus shipping, because they do not fit in the overhead bin. The prices charged for rides and embarrassingly named "packages" ("Il Bacio," "Romanza," "Gondamore") are not out of line with Venetian rates. Accordion music is usually available, live ($89 extra, or is that $89 extra for a ride without accordion music?) or taped. Some mention warm blankets. One sells chocolate gondolas. The gondoliers wear striped shirts and straw hats and several claim to be the only American who participates in the Vogalonga. The chief difference seems to be that gondolas in Venice go around Venice.

Perhaps if they let passengers stand up in them, we could pretend we were in Venice taking a gondola traghetto. But there, as in America, one-oarsman gondolas are no longer used for mere transportation. So when we were finally able to close our eyes and evoke life on the Venetian waterways, it was accomplished by taking a rumbling old ferry around the Baltimore harbor, enjoying feeling the rattle of a Venetian waterbus.

As startling as seeing a gondola plying an innocent American lake is finding a Venetian building in a streamlined American city. Aside from the Palladian influence, which is everywhere, there are versions of Venetian Gothic structures on concrete avenues. These tend to date from Grand Tour days, when rich clients contracted Venetophilia on their youthful flings and architects contracted it from the American and English artists who were enthralled with the physical city. In the middle of Brownstone Brooklyn is the Montauk Club, which thinks it is the Ca' d'Oro. In Chicago, you can see two Venetian buildings just by taking a bus up Michigan Avenue and North Lake Shore Drive. Yale's Department of Music has Stoeckel Hall, an attempt to place Ca' Contarini-Fasan in New Haven. In Washington, D.C., the Inter-American Defense Board is housed in another Pink Palace, a Venetian building on Sixteenth Street.

Some are gone. The World Trade Center had arcading that was inspired by the Doge's Palace. The National Academy of Design in New York, which was supposed to be the Doge's Palace, was destroyed long ago—but by friendly fire, as it were.

The most audacious architectural souvenir still stands—Fenway Court, which houses Isabella Stewart Gardner's museum in Boston. She was not satisfied with the "inspired by" approach. For her home-away-from-Venice, Mrs. Gardner wanted the real thing. Others could copy the Ca' d'Oro; she bought one of its balconies, along with the facades of two other palaces and all the gothic windows and arches, marble columns, and stone carvings she could get her hands on. It was, she reported to her business manager, all so "grotesquely cheap."

It is not that Mrs. Gardner decided to carve up Venice before she left. She was the beneficiary of Venetians' doing this for reasons not uncommon elsewhere at the time—money, particular ideas about what needed preserving and what did not, and money. She bought from salvage dealers and was not above making offers to workmen in the act of demolishing property.

Mrs. Gardner must have had her own behavior in mind when she set a strict stipulation in her will forbidding anyone to mess with her place. I was listening to a museum docent explain that even moving a picture would mean that everything would go to the second-choice heir, Harvard University, when she looked up and was startled to see the Harvard deans, one of them my brother-in-law, who accompanied me. "Yeah, and we're watching," one said. So far only art thieves have dared to defy Mrs. Gardner. The biggest art theft in history took place there in 1990, and the museum has faithfully left the violated spots untouched ever since, as do Venetian churches.

That heist included three paintings by Rembrandt, five by Degas, a Vermeer, a Manet, a Napoleonic eagle, and a Chinese beaker, but—whew!—not Mrs. Gardner's Venetian paintings.

Looking at paintings by Venetians in major museums throughout the world is a solace for Venetophiles, as well as a source of
pride. "They're really ours," we think (although in Mrs. Gardner's
case, the possessive pronoun would be "mine"), as if we and the
pictures were fellow exiles. Hers included Titian's late *Rape of
Europa* and works by Giorgione, Gentile Bellini, Francesco
Guardi, and Giambattista Tiepolo. The museum also displays
Anders Zorn's portrait of Mrs. Gardner, appropriated (not
stolen) for the jacket of this book because it epitomizes the exal-
tation of the Venetophile on her rented balcony.

When a fifteenth-century Venetian government was pondering the question of where the Condottiere Bartolomeo Colleoni
wanted to have his equestrian statue (see chapter three), in the
hope of keeping it out of Saint Mark's Square, no one suggested
that he might like it to be in Newark, New Jersey. But it is there
all the same. A copy of Verrocchio's statue has a place of honor
in Newark's Clinton Park.

The other best places in America to visit Venetian national
treasures are Washington and New York. The National Gallery
of Art has Giorgione's *Adoration of the Shepherds,* Bellini's *Saint
Jerome Reading,* Titian's *Venus with a Mirror,* their unplanned col-
laborative effort of *The Feast of the Gods,* Tintoretto's *Christ at the
Sea of Galilee* and *Susanna,* Tiepolo's *Apollo Pursuing Daphne,*
Canaletto's *The Square of Saint Mark's,* a superb collection of
prints and drawings by Venetian artists from the early sixteenth
century to the end of the Republic, and—talk about one's
patrimony—a portrait, once attributed to Veronese, of our very
own Admiral Agostino Barbarigo. Periodically, it has blockbuster
shows of Venetian art, as does Washington's Corcoran Gallery,
including one of Whistler and His Circle in Venice, curated by
Eric Denker. (And I had the triumph of identifying the last

unnamed palace pictured, at midnight before the next day's opening.)

The Metropolitan Museum in New York has the most extensive Venetian painting collection in America. It is with culturally confused feelings that we are happy to be able to see such Venetian works as *The Meditation on the Passion* by Carpaccio, who is not well represented in American collections, an early Bellini *Madonna and Child,* Titian's early *Madonna and Child, Venus and Adonis,* and late *Venus and the Lute Player.* We can start there to see what may have been a set of four Veroneses, with *Mars and Venus United by Love;* hop over to the Frick Collection to see two of the others, *The Choice Between Virtue and Vice* and the allegory of *Wisdom and Strength,* and catch the fourth in Cambridge.

Yet we feel a twinge that Venetian paintings are not where they are supposed to be. *The Glorification of the Barbaro Family,* in the Metropolitan Museum's eighteenth-century rooms, which house the greatest collection of Tiepolo paintings in the country, belongs on the ceiling of Ca' Barbaro. Bellini's *Saint Francis in the Desert,* one of the great landscapes in the history of painting, is at the Frick, generally hanging near Titian's portrait of his friend, *Pietro Aretino,* the gadfly poet (see chapter four) and the *Man in a Red Cap,* which used to be attributed to Giorgione. But we know from the writer Marcantonio Michiel, who admired it in 1525, that it belonged in the Contarini collection in Venice. It may be unbecoming for Venice to join in the Italian outcry over its art-in-exile, considering the amount of foreign loot that significantly contributes to Venice's beauty. But this has never stopped Venetians before. Nevertheless, we are delighted to see Titian's *Penitent Magdalene* at the Getty in Santa Monica, and two more Veronese allegories nearby in the Los Angeles County Museum of Art. However, if you can't go careening around the United States, here is a budget tip: Wait for a seriously foggy day. You won't be able to see anything, so it is the same view you would have in Venice in winter.

"I don't know—it just spoke to me. Yes, all of it."

Making Your Own Venice

It is no longer feasible to collect big chunks of Venice to build yourself a souvenir house, the way Mrs. Gardner did. It would not be legal, right, or grotesquely cheap. It would not even be self-serving, because we like Venice to be intact when we get there.

But there is no need to worry, because the Venetophile's Stateside house gradually turns into a Venetian outpost. There

are books about Venice everywhere, held by winged-lion book-
ends, and Venetian scene pictures on the walls. A kitchen towel
has a map of Venice on it, and the refrigerator door is decorated
with Venetian-themed cartoons and a Venetian calendar held in
place by magnets with pictures of doges. In the dining room are
odd old plates, spoons, and serving dishes with the winged lion
or a painted scene of Venice. The bathroom soap has a raised
relief of the basilica cut into it and there is a bottle of Venezia
perfume on the shelf. The desk has an ink bottle with a winged
lion on it, a ballpoint pen with a floating gondola, an eraser
showing the Doge's Palace in color, and a ruler that is topped
with a cutout of San Giorgio Maggiore, and the pencil cup, letter
box, and covers of blank books all have reproductions of various
paintings of Venice. There is a brass lion knocker on the front
door, not unlike the brass lion doorstops inside, and a lion
medallion on the key chain.

All right, now you need to worry. Your house has turned into
a Venetian theme park.

And that is not even counting the things that are not decorated with a Venetian symbol or scene but are nevertheless obviously Venetian: the glass, the lace, the pleated silks, the mirrors,
the painted furniture.

. It is frighteningly easy for a Venetophile to slide into this without realizing until too late where it is going. Some of these things
are beautiful, some are amusing, and all are keepsakes of the
beloved. The farther you get away from Venice, the less you can
resist acquiring Venetobilia.

Before you know it, you have turned yourself into a Venetian
theme park. On two occasions, I bought skirts I didn't need:
once, in Portland, Maine, because a pattern that I thought surely
depicted the rigging of old whaling ships turned out to be
Venetian galleons; another time because a skirt with no apparent Venetian connection had a tag stating that the designer had

given it the name Venetia. Scarves and ties with Venetian motifs or maps make their appeal, as do lions on belt buckles and doges on cufflinks. I have resisted such favorite Venetian Renaissance items as the mega-platformed shoe and the wide-brimmed crownless hat (which they used for dyeing the hair), but I feel the pull.

Collecting Venetobilia begins innocently enough with buying a guidebook and a mystery or novel set in Venice for the trip. At the first sign of love, you will find that you need a history book and ones on the history of art and architecture. As you come across characters that interest you, you will want their biographies. If there is a peculiarly Venetian dish or drink you enjoy, you will need a cookbook. You may feel the need of a book to tell you more about Venetian glassblowing, or boats, or courtesans. If you pick up a dollar volume in a secondhand bookstore, you might find it entertaining to read the raptures of a tourist from two centuries ago.

The tipping point is when one from each genre is not enough; you need them all. One history book might have what another misses; one memoir will have a different point of view from another. It doesn't take long before you have to wade through stacks of books just to get to bed.

You start out by taking your own pictures of Venice and buying others as postcards or museum posters and prints. Then you begin to notice that there is no such thing, anywhere in the world, as an art fair or antiques show that lacks at least one original painting of Venice, complete with gondola and sunset. You see that auctions occasionally offer a genuine Canaletto or Bellini. It is when you find something that you like between the two—perhaps old etchings or the work of an unknown artist—that your walls get papered with Venice.

Our discovery of a relic of our ancestral saint, Gregorio Barbarigo (see chapter five) led to a collection that could form a household shrine. We found a coin from the reign of Doge Marco Barbarigo, an action figure of Admiral Agostino Barbarigo (fortunately showing him before the arrow lodged in his eye), and a photograph of the World War II (and thus enemy) ship named for him (before it sank).

Tourists of every era have wanted to bring home souvenirs, and perhaps you pick up glass earrings or cufflinks, a silk scarf or tie with a Venetian motif, a mask to wear at a costume ball or hang on the wall, a small Venetian flag, a paper lamp shade, or a deck of playing cards with a Venetian scene.

You may make larger commitments in the way of crystal or silk chandeliers, velvet jackets, and ten-thousand-piece puzzles of Venice. Things get more serious when this sparks an interest in the souvenirs of previous generations of Venetophiles: not only Canalettos and Guardis but micro-mosaic jewelry (the fine kind with Venetian scenes, or the coarser kind incorporating the word "Venezia"), beaded evening bags with Venetian scenes, Fortuny dresses, and the Republic's coins.

If you find kitsch funny, there goes your decor. There are endless amounts of it available everywhere: lamps, liqueur bottles, and tea candle trays in the shape of gondolas, snow globes of the piazza, Venetian screen savers, plush winged lions. The Delta pen company put out a special collection of rollerball and fountain pens with gold or silver overlays of a lion and gothic archways, priced from $600 to $1,010. Prada showed a line of clothing and accessories with Venetian scenes, including a sport purse for $960 and a skirt for $665. Neiman Marcus once offered, through its Christmas catalogue, an electric, aluminum, and fiberglass gondola compete with removable cassette player, built-in ice bucket, bilge pump, and emergency paddle, for $7,400. On the cover of a Hammacher Schlemmer catalogue there was a wed-

ding gondola with white lace seat covers for $60,000, not includ-
ing the two gondoliers needed to operate it.*

In defiance of good taste and good sense, all of this stuff, the
cheesy as well as the cheeky, speaks to the Venetophile. If you
came across your grandmother's old purse in a flea market, would
you just leave it there? The best way to resist Venetobilia is to ask
of trivial things, "Would I buy it if I saw it in Venice?" and of fine
things seen in Venice, "Would I buy it if I saw it at home?"

Supporting Venice

Not just to be nice, but to be more nearly Venetian,
Venetophiles involve themselves in restoration projects in
Venice. Beautifying the city, with no questions raised about the
provenance of the art contributed, was a tradition among citizens
of the Republic. Since we cannot continue that, the least we can
do is to help keep things looking good.

Thus it came about that I heard a strangulated voice on the
telephone from Venice, asking, with no preamble, "How much
does a pearl cost?"

In our little group, we are used to having to answer questions
before receiving explanations. So I pointed out that pearls can
cost anything from a pittance to a fortune, and was he talking
about glass, cultured, or natural?

"I don't know—a pearl! Two pearls! How much do they cost?"

The context was that several of us had taken a special interest
in the Scuola of San Rocco. We are not the first. Thanks to
Tintoretto, as Henry James ponted out, it is wall-to-wall genius.
(See chapter six.)

---

*The nineteenth-century painter Thomas Moran just shipped the one he had been
using home to East Hampton and—thinking canoe—hired a Mohawk Indian to row it.

Giving Back, One Pearl at a Time.

A member of the confraternity was kind enough to show us around, including taking us through a hidden door behind and under the great Tintoretto *Crucifixion,* which led to the treasury. This had been stuffed with the previous offerings from the membership over hundreds of years, which were then being sorted. For example, we were shown an exquisite crystal and gold reliquary and told that it enshrined the finger bone of a certain saint.

"No, it doesn't," said my husband.

"Perhaps not," conceded our friend. "But that is the tradition associated with it. We can't prove that it was this saint."

"I don't know anything about the saint," said my husband. "It's not a finger bone." He had learned that much at medical school.

We were also interested in the adjacent San Rocco church, and privileged to meet San Rocco himself. He was in his glass casket, on a shelf in the storeroom, waiting patiently while the altar was being restored. When we saw the crumbling limestone typanum that had been moved inside too late as protection from the weather, one couple was moved to offer to pay for its restoration. So the next one of us who went to Venice, some months later, took their check to the scuola one morning at eleven o'clock and found himself swept next door to the Scuola Bar to celebrate the occasion with three glasses of prosecco on an empty stomach. Careening back to the scuola, he asked about other projects and was shown a sixteenth-century portable gold altar encrusted with pearls, and two empty pearl settings.

It was some hours later that I received that telephone call. He was suddenly remembering that he had volunteered to replace those pearls.

My response was not reassuring, but he comforted himself with the thought that the way things worked in Italy, he would hear nothing about this for months. That lasted until the next morning, when he got a call from the scuola. The jeweler they used had offered to do the work and to pay for one of the pearls. So—maybe only half a fortune.

The good fortune we did have was that another of our group has a cousin in California who is also a generous jeweler. This time I got to be the dolt on the other end of the telephone, while the cousin asked minute questions about the size, shape, color, and luster of the pearls remaining in the little altar. "I don't know—they're old pearls. Sort of round, not perfectly round, some with squashed parts, and sort of white, but maybe more like off-white."

The happy ending is that he entrusted us with a variety of possibilities to take to Venice. With the altar before us, consulting with our benefactor by e-mail (thus astonishing the senior staff of the scuola, who had not yet learned how to use its newly installed first computer), we made the match. The Guardian Grande of the confraternity threw us a lovely luncheon party and made a flowery speech, and it wasn't the prosecco that made us glow—and ask to be involved in more little projects.

Many worthy organizations exist for foreigners who help restore Venice, and the groups belonging to the consortium of Private Committees for the Safeguarding of Venice have done major restoration projects all over the city. We few, who are not up to throwing masked balls in New York hotels and collecting the kind of money necessary to restore whole buildings and huge canvases, limit ourselves to the most modest needs that the scuole could find. Or in one case that found us: I was listening to a concert in San Rocco's ground floor when some plaster from one of the columns fell into my lap. It was not what you might call a subtle sign, so my husband and I sponsored the restoration of the columns. We think of it as our tax ducats at work.

Support Groups for Venetophiles

"You are not alone," is the comfort we are offered, now that American society classifies itself by afflictions. In the case of those of us suffering from Venetophilia, we know. Others may disdain The Tourists, as they call tourists other than themselves, but we love meeting other Venetophiles. It saves us from boring innocent people. In every possible gathering, we slip the word Venice into the conversation, and if anyone's eyes light up, we are off on our rhapsodies, while everyone else drifts away as quickly as decently possible.

Three Happy Venetophiles in Their Element.

This collaboration came about because many years ago, my
Italian teacher said, "I know someone who is as nuts on the subject as you." The next thing we knew, we were all traveling
together, sharing books, news, birthday cakes (iced as a map of
Venice, complete with a tiny wine bottle floating in the canal),
and friends to the point where we no longer remember whose

story is whose. (However, I am fairly certain that I am not the one who is taking gondola lessons.) And in the water taxi on the way to the airport, we think of the Venetians of old, leaving Venice on their merchant ships, and making the promise, "I'll be back when I have more money."

Credits

Page 21   Courtesy of Maidenform Corporation.

Page 26   *Doge Enrico Dandolo Leads the Crusade to Loot Constantinople* by Gustave Doré, illustration from *The History of the Crusades* by François Michaud, circa 1895, George Barrie, Philadelphia.

Page 40   *A Fête at Venice—the Rialto*, from *The Graphic*, November 5, 1870, p. 448. Private collection.

Page 48   Claude Monet (1840–1926) and his wife, Alice (1844–1911), St. Mark's Square, Venice, October 1908, French Photographer, (20th century) / Musée Marmottan, Paris, France, Giraudon, The Bridgeman Art Library.

Page 53   *The Finding of the Body of St. Mark* (panel), Tintoretto, Jacopo Robusti (1518–1594) / Pinacoteca di Brera, Milan, Italy / The Bridgeman Art Library.

Page 58   Jacopo de Barbari, *View of Venice*, 1500, woodcut. Rosenwald Collection, 1950.1.15. Courtesy of the Trustees of the National Gallery of Art, Washington, D. C.

Page 65   Photographs by Jacobina Martin and Jeffrey Meizlik.

Page 76   *Venetian Dogs* by Mark Leithauser, 2006, pen and ink drawing, courtesy of the artist.

Page 80   *Battle with Sticks on the Ponte Santa Fosca, Venice* (oil on canvas), Gabriele Bella (1730–1799) / Galleria Querini-Stampalia, Venice, Italy, Giraudon / The Bridgeman Art Library.

Page 82   *Festival of the Blessed Virgin Mary on the 2nd February at Santa Maria Formosa, Venice* (oil on canvas), Gabriele Bella (1730–1799) / Galleria Querini-Stampalia, Venice, Italy / The Bridgeman Art Library.

Page 87   *The Emperor Napoleon in his Study at Tuileries* by Jacques-Louis David, oil on canvas, 1812. Samuel H. Kress Collection, 1961.9.15. Courtesy of the Trustees of the National Gallery of Art, Washington, D. C.

Page 96   Photograph by Lorene Emerson.

Page 99   Photograph by Jacobina Martin.

Page 105 *The Miracle of the Cross on San Lorenzo Bridge*, 1500 (oil on canvas), Gentile Bellini (circa 1429–1507) / Galleria dell'Accademia, Venice, Italy, Giraudon / The Bridgeman Art Library.

Page 116 *Condottiere Bartolomeo Colleoni* statue by Andrea del Verrochio, 1480–1488, bronze, in San Giovanni e Paolo, by Joshia Wood Whymper (1813–1903) after a work by Harry Fenn, wood engraving. Private collection.

Page 132 Giovanni Antonio Canal, called Canaletto (Italian, 1697–1768) *Capriccio: The Rialto Bridge and the Church of San Giorgio Maggiore*, about 1750. Oil on canvas. Purchased with funds from the State of North Carolina, 52.9.

Page 135 *The Reception of Titian's Assumption*, drawing by Mark Leithauser, reproduced courtesy of the artist.

Page 138 Drawing by Mark Leithauser, reproduced courtesy of the artist.

Page 146 Portrait of John Ruskin (1819–1900), 1898–1899, Joseph Arthur Palliser Severn (1842–1931) / © Ruskin Museum, Coniston, Cumbria, UK / The Bridgeman Art Library / Gargoyle from campanile of the Santa Maria Formosa, Venice.

Page 160 From the Portfolio by Alfred Thompson in *Ididdlia—On*

The Grand Canal by J. M. *Whittler* [*sic*] from *The World*, Christmas #24, December 1879, private collection.

Page 182 Detail from Jacopo de Barbari, *View of Venice*, 1500, woodcut. Rosenwald Collection, 1950.1.15. Courtesy of the Trustees of the National Gallery of Art, Washington, D. C.

Page 194 Maiolica plate depicting Doge Agostino Barbarigo supervising the loading of money bags, tin-glazed earthenware, Venice, circa 1494–1495, © Fitzwilliam Museum, University of Cambridge, UK / The Bridgeman Art Library.

Page 196 *The Blessed Gregorio Barbarigo* by Gianmaria Morleiter, marble, Santa Maria del Giglio, Venice.

Page 201 *Caterina Sagredo Barbarigo as "Bernice,"* circa 1741 [the Egyptian queen who sacrificed her hair for her husband's safety] (pastel on paper mounted on canvas), Rosalba Giovanna Carriera (1675–1757) / © The Detroit Institute of Arts, USA, Gift of Mrs W. D. Vogel in memory of Mrs. Ralph Harman Booth / The Bridgeman Art Library.

Page 206 High water, or aqua alta, in Venice, Italy—Saint Mark's Square under water, published in the newspaper *La Domenica del Corriere*, 1906, Artist: BELTRAME, Achille, The Art Archive / Domenica del Corriere / Dagli Orti.

Page 231 *Summertime*, 1955, United Artists / The Kobal Collection.

Page 234 *The Comfort of Strangers*, 1990, Sovereign Pictures / Photofest.

Page 236 *A Little Romance*, 1979, Warner Brothers / Photofest.

Page 260 *Ca' Dario* by Jörg Schmeisser, etching, 2005. Private collection.

Page 265 Photograph of Procuratie Vecchie in Piazza San Marco by Jeffrey Meizlik.

Page 274   *Funeral Gondola Approaching San Michele in Isola, Venice,*
           b/w photo. Private collection / The Bridgeman Art
           Library.

Page 279   *The Brides of Venice* by J. R. Herbert (after H. Robinson),
           1845, wood engraving, J. Hogarth Company. Private
           collection.

Page 304   Photograph by Lorene Emerson.

Page 309   *Madonna and Child,* portable altar, beginning of the
           16th century, Scuola Grande di San Rocco, Legato
           Donà, Venice.

Page 312   *The American Girl in Italy,* Charles Scribner's Sons,
           New York. Private collection.

Index

Page numbers in *italics* refer to illustrations.